LEARNING ABOUT HUMAN NATURE AND ANALYTIC TECHNIQUE FROM MOTHERS AND BABIES

LEARNING ABOUT HUMAN NATURE AND ANALYTIC TECHNIQUE FROM MOTHERS AND BABIES

Nara Amália Caron and Rita Sobreira Lopes

Routledge
Taylor & Francis Group
LONDON AND NEW YORK

First published in Portuguese in 2014. Copyright © to Editora Dublinense
First published in Spanish in 2015. Copyright © to Ediciones Biebel

First published 2017 by Karnac Books Ltd.

Published 2018 by Routledge
2 Park Square, Milton Park, Abingdon, Oxon OX14 4RN
711 Third Avenue, New York, NY 10017, USA

Routledge is an imprint of the Taylor & Francis Group, an informa business

British Library Cataloguing in Publication Data

A C.I.P. for this book is available from the British Library

ISBN 9781782204848 (pbk)

Edited, designed and produced by The Studio Publishing Services Ltd
www.publishingservicesuk.co.uk
email: studio@publishingservicesuk.co.uk

CONTENTS

ABOUT THE AUTHORS

Nara Amália Caron is a medical doctor, child, adolescent, and adult psychoanalyst. She is a full member of the Porto Alegre Psychoanalytic Society (SPPA) – Brazil and a training analyst at the SPPA Institute. She was the director of the SPPA Infant and Adolescent Unit 2010–2011. She has been a seminar leader of infant observation groups according to Esther Bick's method for more than thirty years.

Rita Sobreira Lopes has a PhD in psychology from the University of London. She is a Full Professor in Developmental Psychology, with emphasis on emotional development. She is a senior researcher from CNPq and one of the co-ordinators of the Infant and Family Unit at the Institute of Psychology, Federal University of Rio Grande do Sul (UFRGS)– Brazil.

Nara and **Rita** have developed applications of the Bick method for intervention and research in the area of perinatality, such as pregnancy, delivery, and prematurity. They have written several joint national and international publications on infant observation and its applications. They are both members of the Latin American (ALOBB) and the International Association on Infant Observation according to Esther Bick's Method (AIDOBB)

"To our mothers, Ida and Rita"

PREFACE

Mrs Esther Bick would be surprised and delighted to read this book by Nara Amália Caron and Rita de Cássia Sobreira Lopes. Having conducted baby observation seminars for decades, the authors have discovered a method that shows indisputably the continuity between intrauterine and post-birth life of an infant. I can visualise Mrs Bick's amused smile, saying a warm "Really? Oh, my God . . . I should have known, shouldn't I?" In the authors' words, "Observing the interaction of the foetus with the intrauterine medium, we can verify that many features attributed to postnatal life are already present while in the uterus".

This discovery results from the use of ultrasonography to observe the development of the baby during the pregnancy. The authors describe and discuss the importance of the technician's expertise and capacity to engage in a fruitful dialogue with the professionals who will be following the development of that mother–baby pair for the following two or three years after birth. The authors also present us an unexpected feature: siblings were also included in the observations of the unborn babies. As these siblings were subsequently interviewed, their words and their drawings represent a fascinating view of such an early stage of the sibling relationships.

Caron and Sobreira Lopes focus on each participant individually and in groups, and present a rich and instructive description of impressions, explanations, discussions, and formulations that the various professionals put forward when observing the ultrasound images and, later, the mother and baby pair.

The book describes in detail several cases: a mother pregnant with bivitelin twins, another also carrying bivitelin twins, two other mothers who gave birth to single babies and an account of "Philomena", a young woman confined to an Irish convent, whose story became the subject of a film.

However impossible it is to have a *tabula rasa* to process our sensorial stimuli, it is still important not to approach each new case as no more than confirmation of our preconceptions. The book presents many quotes from Winnicott's works, but the authors succeed in describing and emphasising the importance of taking into account every detail of what is being observed. These findings have, indeed, to be considered in line with various theoretical formulations, but the discussions quoted in the book illustrate very clearly the need to have an open mind when processing the various data available.

Caron and Sobreira Lopes have broadened their research and they apply their findings to the training of psychoanalysts. They help trainees to sharpen their observation powers and proceed to teach them how their observations and formulations correlate to what happens in the analyst–patient encounter.

Such a deep and broad application of Mrs Bick's method is in sharp contrast to what we have in our British training institutions, where the observation of babies over their first one or two years of life is no more than an exercise in helping students to make contact with the characters that play such a fundamental role in the formulation of psychoanalytic theories.

I hope all students of psychodynamic therapies will read this book. Starting from Mrs Bick's theories and utilising many of Winnicott's views, it represents a rich piece of research that utilises modern techniques to show the validity of their formulations. The authors also demonstrate the importance of widening the field of work of our trainees.

A. H. Brafman
Psychoanalyst and author of
The Language of Distress: Understanding a Child's Behaviour

PART I

THEORETICAL AND METHODOLOGICAL FOUNDATIONS

CHAPTER ONE

A place where verbalisation has no meaning

> *Mephistopheles.* Not glad do I reveal a loftier mystery–
> Enthroned sublime in solitude are goddesses; Around them is no place, a time still less;
> To speak of them embarrasses.
> They are the Mothers!
> *Faust* [terrified]. Mothers!
> *Mephistopheles.* Do you fear?
> *Faust.* The Mothers! Mothers! Strange the word I hear
> *Mephistopheles.* Strange is it. Goddesses, to men unknown
> Whom we are loath to name or own.
> Deep must you dig to reach their dwelling ever;
> You are to blame that now we need their favour
> *Faust.* Whither the way?
> *Mephistopheles.* No way! To the Unexplorable
> Never to be explored; to the Unimplorable,
> Never to be implored. Are in the mood?
> There are no locks, no bars are to be riven;
> Through solitudes you will be whirled and driven
> Can you imagine wastes and solitude?
>
> (Goethe, 2007, *Faust* II, Act I: Dark Gallery)

> It will be observed that I am taking you to a place where verbalization has no meaning. What connection can there be, then, between all of this and psychoanalysis, which has been built on the process of verbal interpretations of verbalized thoughts and ideas? (Winnicott, 1988a, p. 92)

We intend to take you to this essentially feminine place where human beings begin their developmental journey and explore all the richness, vicissitudes, and demands of mothers who make themselves emotionally available for caring for their babies, there, where words have no meaning. Life starts in the maternal womb. It is our first home. Therefore, we invite you to enter this home, and we thank the mothers who generously opened this door for us.

When Winnicott[1] invited us to this "unknown" place, he already had outstanding clinical experience, including more than forty years of intensive clinical work, 60,000 treatments of adults, children, adolescents, and mother–infant duos. He was secure enough to confirm his discoveries and to declare that the inevitable had happened: psychoanalysts could no longer ignore the human being's dependence and primitive stages of development. He warned us about the psychoanalyst's own resistances to enter this space, and also how they would have to face external opposition. Both the internal and external resistances transformed the mother–infant relationship into a sacred, forbidden place:

> it is as if a work of art was being subjected to an analytic process. Can one be sure that the capacity to fully appreciate this work of art will not be destroyed by the search-light that is played upon the picture? It could indeed be well argued that these very early phenomena ought to be left alone, and I, who have found myself making a study of them, could not but insist that what we think we know about these intimacies is not useful reading material for artists, or for young mothers. The sort of thing that can be discussed when we look at these early phenomena cannot be taught. (Winnicott, 1989a, p. 251)

Winnicott gave a lot of careful thought to the study of early psychic phenomena. He was concerned not to interfere in them, and proceeded with caution, but he saw, in the subtleties of the mother–infant relationship, a great opportunity to learn about human nature:

> we shall be caught up in the immense needs of the dependent infant and, in the countertransference, with the massive responsive processes which show us, to some extent, what is happening to parents when they have a child. (Winnicott, 1989a, p. 252)

Through the contact with the baby and the mother, he also saw the opportunity to learn about psychotic pathology and about the technique with these patients:

> from schizoid patients, we can learn to observe mothers and infants, seeing more clearly what is found there. But *essentially*, however, it is *from* the mothers and the babies that we learn about the needs of psychotic patients or patients in psychotic phases. (Winnicott, 1988a, p. 101)

There are many challenges to anyone who decides to enter the "sacred area" of the mother–infant relationship, opening a field to important discoveries about human nature that can greatly contribute to the study of normal and pathological development, as well as to the analytic technique. First, you must have interest, curiosity, and courage to embark on the quest of the unknown and meet with the primitive, this place "inaccessible" by verbal language, memory, and other cognitive processes. We must also recognise the unknown and assume there is a lot to observe and learn.

It is worth remembering that it was in this spirit of curiosity about the depths of the soul that Freud, when working on the investigation of the unconscious, embarked on a fascinating and endless journey in search of the unknown in human beings. He emphasised that he had "learned the importance of observation as one of the best means to gratify his curiosity" (Freud, 1925d, p. 18). This great observer quality of psychic phenomena also developed thanks to Freud's contact in Salpêtrière with Charcot, his great teacher and role model for his journey into psychoanalytic observation, which requires, in the words of Borgogno (2004), "A long inner journey . . . based on direct, uninterrupted and unique experience, love and dedication to the object of study" and whose product is "a knowledge that comes through a relationship that is the result of a deep contact and intense personal involvement" (p. 18, translated for this edition).

Freud (1923a) had already emphasised that psychoanalysis was defined as a method of investigation of mental processes that are inaccessible by any other means. Only in a second stage of the theory, after having conducted many investigations, did he face the challenge of turning these findings into a treatment technique, emphasising again the empirical roots of this science. He also highlighted that psychoanalysis is not a clearly defined system of basic concepts.

> On the contrary, it keeps close to the facts in its field of study, seeks to solve the immediate problems of observation, gropes its way forward by the help of experience, is always incomplete and always ready to correct or modify its theories. (1923a, p. 253)

Freud's genius, with his innate curiosity and few limits to his observations of psychic life, allowed him to capture a wide range of human phenomena in an extraordinary way. However, due to the difficult challenge of developing a theory and a technique, he had to ignore many aspects in order to focus more on others. Thus, evidencing that psychoanalysis is not intended to answer questions in a saturated way, he left many potentialities open so that other researchers could continue to advance and deepen psychoanalytic theory, as he himself had done throughout the development of it.

The "sacred area" of the early mother–infant relationship is an example of a potentiality in psychoanalysis that had to wait for future developments. Borgogno (2004) describes Freud's special receptivity to the mother–infant relationship, its rhythms and primitive qualities, considered as a prototype of the hypnotist–hypnotised relationship. In 1892, at the beginning of his psychoanalytic career, Freud (1892–1893) describes a clinical treatment and an understanding of the vicissitudes of the mother–infant relationship for the first time. This is a case of a parturient with problems breastfeeding her baby, seen by him at home and written up as "A case of hypnotic healing". Perhaps understanding the specific context in which the patient developed hysterical post-partum symptoms, Freud diagnosed her as "histérique d'occasion". With this brief and early "descent to the realm of the mothers", an expression created by Goethe in Faust and later adopted by Breuer and Freud, he left "a legacy of great responsibility . . . from which he distanced himself thanks to his leading spirit of investigator and conqueror" (Borgogno, 2004, p. 39, translated for this edition).

We should also remember Freud's familiar proposition (1926d) that "there is much more continuity between intrauterine life and earliest infancy than the impressive caesura of the act of birth would have made us believe" (p. 137). Thus, the legacy left by Freud almost a century ago lay dormant for some time and was explored later, through the interest of some analysts in the earliest stages of human development, by means of psychotic pathology and, especially, through infant observation.

Esther Bick's method of infant observation

Winnicott's contemporary, Esther Bick[2] not only invited us to enter this "sacred place" but offered us a method to observe the phenomena found there. She also believed that we had a lot to learn from mothers and infants, but not much to teach them.

When she presented her doctoral thesis on the development of twins, in Vienna, 1936, she was asked to use a stopwatch to measure the interaction between twins, count the number of social responses produced by each twin, and then compare them. Not satisfied with that experience and concerned about the training of child psychotherapists, she concluded that, in order to understand the development of the human personality, not taking into account the prevailing theories and methods, she should study the baby's daily life in the family environment. Thus, she created the infant observation method which offers another way to delve deep into the human soul, have direct contact with the first infant experiences and interactions with his mother, and with the most primitive experiences in his natural environment[3]—the family—from birth up to two years of age.

We believe that the psychoanalytic method of infant observation created by Esther Bick in 1948 at the Tavistock Clinic in London (Bick, 1964) is a royal road to the primitive in human beings and a great opportunity for analysts—not only those specialising in child or adolescent analysis, but also adult analysts—to develop certain refined listening capacities necessary to establish contact with the psychic phenomena of early life . She stated that this experience was important for many reasons, but mainly so that students in this area could more clearly understand the infantile experience of their young patients. They could better understand the non-verbal behaviour of children in their play, as well as children who neither speak nor play. Finally, the method provides for each observer an excellent opportunity to observe the development of a baby from birth, in his home setting, and in his relationship with the family, discovering for himself[4] how such relationships originate and develop.

As far as professional training is concerned, Esther Bick also wished to provide the therapist with proper tools to better deal with the intense anxieties provoked by the work on primitive levels of emotional functioning.

Entering the depths of the Bick method, it is important to remember that it is divided into three stages: observation, written report, and seminar group supervision, in a series of challenges that we describe below.

First stage: observation[5]

During the first stage (the observation), with a pre-established internal and external setting for weekly visits at a specific time and place and a non-intrusive attitude, the observer begins her journey, which will be of two-year duration and in which she will observe the development of a baby inside his own home and with the family. Consistent with psychoanalytic listening based on evenly suspended attention, the observer—just as the analyst in the analytic session—does not take notes during the observation, or formulate hypotheses or *a priori* categories of facts to be observed.

Just as the analyst in the analytic process, the observer is invited, as much as possible, to step aside from her theories and merely observe, as proposed by Freud (1914d, p. 22): "I learned to control the speculative tendencies and follow my master's Charcot not forgotten advice; to look at the same things again and again until they start to speak for themselves".

In Bick's (1964) words, in order to observe,

> The observer must attain detachment from what is going on. Yet he must, *as in the basic method of psychoanalysis*, find a position from which to make his observations, a position that will introduce as little distortion as possible into what is going on in the family. He has to allow some things to happen and to resist others. Rather than actively establishing his own personality as a new addition to the family organization, he has to allow the parents, particularly the mother, to fit him

> into her household in her own way. But he must resist being drawn into roles involving intense infantile transference and therefore countertransference. (p. 559, *my italics*)

There can be many problems linked to intense transference which can be understood in the observer's supervision or analytic treatment.

It is important to remember that the opportunity to follow the patterns that unfold and the baby's emerging personality in interaction with his carers is anchored in a setting. This shows the close link with psychoanalysis; in other words, the same frequency and duration of sessions in the same place, attention to detail and to everything, the type of contract, continuous supervision, preferably with an experienced analyst, and understanding of conflicts and feelings with their dynamics.

The main difference between the observer–analyst in the infant observation setting and in the analytic setting is that in the former he is stripped of the interpretative tools usually used in the latter and becomes available to live an experience with the baby and the mother as a "participant observer" (Bick, 1964). This helps the observer to immerse himself in the emotional experience while strictly respecting the setting, and, at the same time, to be fully engaged in registering every event of life and indication of emotion.

One of the major challenges of this first stage—observation—is the intense internal activity caused by the live experience of the mother–infant dyad: the observer is thrown into a world of sensations, emotions, and primitive anxieties that have an impact in different ways and degrees, according to her personal makeup. Due to her non-interventionist attitude, she is in a privileged position to capture the mother–infant non-verbal communication through her own body and mind. The observer comes into contact with primitive states of helplessness and loneliness, usually experienced as strange-familiar or "uncanny", to use Freud's (1919h) expression.

The observer is in intense mental activity while listening; she is passive only in abstaining from action. This might help in understanding why Bick (1964) considered the observer as participant and, therefore, privileged. Thus, one could question the common criticism made that the observer "just looks" for two years. Listening involves all the senses. The presence of a baby stimulates regression to primitive states of mind and coenesthetic (bodily aware) communication, generating intense and wordless emotional experiences and physical sensations in the observer. She faces the challenge of living an experience together with the mother and the baby.

When Michel Haag went to London to do infant observation under Esther Bick's supervision, he mentioned that Bick always began supervision with the words "I know nothing . . . I want to see . . . What is fundamental to teach on observation is to not jump into any conclusion, to come as a *tabula rasa* . . . you do not know and that is all" (Haag & Haag, 1997, p. 3, translated for this edition). For Haag, this was "Bick's spirit", and rule number one for the observer. The second rule for the observer is the attitude of non-interference, which overlaps with Freud's abstinence rule and then of neutrality:

> . . . The observer should only be a receiver; never ask for a change, no matter what it is (or even ask a question), or interfere, because if you modify the situation you will no longer observe it just as it is. (Haag & Haag, 1997, p. 4, translated for this edition)

It is a great challenge to be in the position of not knowing anything, like a *tabula rasa,* to be only a receiver, without intervening. Stripped of her interpretative tools, the observer is in a similar situation to the mother, who suffers changes in her body, relaxing and expanding to gradually give way to the baby.

The observer is also at the mercy of intense and often unspoken feelings: he feels tired, hungry, is invaded by a variety of physical sensations, and might feel like leaving. It is interesting to note that the observer, when immersed in the first stage (observation), does not mind at all this lowering of defences. He accepts "wearing the clothes" the observation situation provides for him.

This attitude of the observer–analyst requires great attention. In effect, she is using her own zoom to choose what to focus on in different situations: to focus, approach, specifying the detail, while simultaneously distancing herself in order to capture the whole. It is an alternating micro- and macroscopic looking, focused and evenly suspended attention, in which the observer can turn her emotional kaleidoscope to capture the subtlety of the images that emerge. To develop this multiplicity of attention while maintaining continuity between the different situations and understand the emotional resonance within the viewer is a true experience of evenly suspended attention.

Without acting on previous theories and clinical practices, and not aiming at treatment, the method also offers the observer a unique opportunity to meet and engage with her own emotional experiences, favouring the development of the ability to receive the other inside herself. To understand the links between the resonance in the observer and her emotional state as part of the material of observation allows the consideration of countertransference as a valuable tool in the recognition and treatment of the primitive aspects of the psychic structure.

Relying on a certain kind of emptiness and availability, the observer assumes an eminently receptive condition through which he receives and accepts the baby's and the parents' positive and negative primitive communication and is deeply involved in the live dynamics of the observation. This creates a state very close to evenly suspended attention. Freud (1912e) used to advise that "... the doctor should turn his own unconscious as a receptive organ toward the patient's transmitting unconscious" (p. 116).

The Bick method favours the repeated look at the details, exchanges, gestures, sensations, and mother–infant mismatches. It promotes the discovery or rediscovery of non-verbal communication and regression in the observer. As far as non-verbal communication is concerned, Freud (1905e) wrote, in the case of Dora,

> When I set myself the task of bringing to light what human beings keep hidden within them, not by the compelling power of hypnosis, but by observing what they say and what they show, I thought the task was a harder one than it really is. He that has eyes to see and ears to hear may convince himself that no mortal can keep a secret. If his lips are silent, he chatters with his fingertips: betrayal oozes out of him at every pore. (p. 77)

Second stage: the written report

Following the intense inner emotional experience comes the challenge of the second stage of the observer's journey: the written report. This second stage in which dialogue gains fundamental importance is necessary so the observer can share the experience with the group. The method challenges the observer to put into words remnants of memories that contain fragments of the intense experiences described so far. Thus, the time has come to try to share what was experienced in a solitary way during the observation.

The observer uses simple words to try to report the details of the observation, without yet attributing meaning, as suggested by Bick (1964). She tries to find words that convey an experience that is still pre-verbal and is often experienced through bodily sensations, sounds, smells, and images.

Perhaps the biggest challenge of this second stage is communication itself: how to convey an experience that was lived in a predominantly sensory manner, without the support of logic and reason? Freud (1905e), when describing the challenges of reporting a clinical case, not being able to take notes in front of the patient, highlights the importance of writing as soon as one ends the session so that it is "a secure point of attachment for the chain of interpretation and recollections which proceeded from them" (p. 10).

In the observation reports, also without the possibility of taking notes, one seeks a certain common ground between the observation and the report, so that they are as close as possible. Through simple language, you can become connected to, and better convey, the experience. At times, there is a tendency to want to fix and brush up the text in order to present it to the seminar group, perhaps in an attempt to avoid exposing what the observer experiences in the observation. In doing so, the observer cannot rely on memory and the word lapses so precious when the object of study is the unconscious. The observer's freedom to convey the material in a more authentic way will depend both on her own characteristics and on the sensitivity of the observation and reporting, as well as on the seminar group's receptiveness.

However, this stage is not only characterised by the need to put into words and convey these experiences to the group: it also contains an important evacuating and creative quality for the observer. It is akin to a delivery experience. Producing a report brings relief, works as a discharge, and ends the anxiety of not knowing, of being in chaos forever. In this sense, the excessive detail that often accompanies the first writing is amazing, and perhaps reveals the need to get rid of the emotional overload. The excessive details of the report, necessary when it is being made, arouse a feeling that they could be reduced when re-read on later occasions. They can also provoke a sense of strangeness, a feeling that the contents are too raw, or that the observer was too open. Thus, the exposure experienced at the first stage—the observation—returns in this second stage, the written report. One must overcome the hurdle of being exposed to the group, like a game of hide-and-seek, in which "it is a joy to be hidden but a disaster not to be found" (Winnicott, 1988b, p. 186).

When writing the report, alone and in privacy, the observer provides himself with a new and different contact with the material itself. Now he is no longer the recipient of the projections coming from the observation, and can become their active agent. He releases them as a receptor of these experiences. This stage becomes important, and with good reason; it is vital for the observer to move on from the initial position of being filled up by the experience.

The written observation report slowly acquires some order, some elaboration, and resembles an account of a dream. It can, in a way, transform partial and fragmented memories into a relatively coherent discourse. In a similar way, one can see that the mother–infant relationship also acquires certain order and form as time goes by, as a natural evolution of the state or primary maternal preoccupation (Winnicott, 1987a).

Third stage: the seminar group supervision

The third stage—the seminar group supervision—is a revelation in which the private experience, previously described is given its first public appearance, and shows the solitary observer's hard work to a group of colleagues who have a common goal: broadening their knowledge of the early, primitive, mother–infant relationship. Between the initial impact of the observation experience and beginning to develop thinking about a report, the group, along with the observer, will undertake the sometimes hard task of searching for a deeper understanding of the material observed.

The report makes its impact on the seminar group, permeates, and resounds in, its participants, who take on different roles and functions and work towards an understanding of the text's primitive communications. The group acts as a necessary presence that enables the private experience to be transformed and reorganised. This movement helps the observer to emerge after being submerged in the depths of observation.

If the observer can remain in this to and fro movement without closing off anything new, she might gradually adjust the focus of the observation and develop the ability to observe, which is fundamental for the Bick method, for theory, as well as for psychoanalytic technique. Understanding the contents allows the observer to be free once again, "empty" and receptive, available to return to the field of observation.

Within this established setting, we can say that infant observation is an exercise in successive listening, on different levels, from the most regressive to the more elaborate, which gradually integrates the material. They are separate parts of a single process.

Bick (1964) emphasised the importance of consecutive observation and of not precipitating oneself in search of conclusions. It is possible to see an emerging pattern, which will only be able to be confirmed in subsequent observations. We can observe not only patterns, but also changes in the patterns. In Bick's (1964) words,

> He can see changes in the couple's mutual adaptation and the impressive capacity for growth and development in their relationship, i.e. the flexibility and capacity for using each other and developing which goes on in a satisfactory mother–infant relationship. The excitement in the seminar has been just as much in searching backward as in looking forward. (p. 250)

An important aspect in relation to the patterns is that, due to the couple's emotional proximity, it is difficult to tell whether the choice of certain preferred modes of communication originate with the mother's or the baby's preference.

It should be emphasised that there seems to be no doubt about the richness of the learning experience and the improvement of clinical skills the method provides for those who allow themselves to participate in this experience. What we now discuss is the progress that the experience in this primitive area can bring to psychoanalytic theory and technique, taking into account especially the contributions from Esther Bick and Winnicott.

Bick and Winnicott in this "place where verbalisation has no meaning": main discoveries

By distinct, personal, and unique pathways, but both guided by the analytic technique and with great interest and respect for infants and their mothers, Bick and Winnicott came to very similar findings in relation to early psychic phenomena. Both helped to illuminate the subtleties and delicacies of the mother–infant couple, which adapts to the baby's initial conditions of unintegration and dependence.

Esther Bick's journey and her discoveries

Esther Bick left few written works—only four. After long experience of infant observation and analysis with psychotic children, she described her theory of the early development which precedes when the baby starts to feel mentally sustained enough by the mother who can understand his helplessness. In her first theoretical paper, "The experience of the skin in early object relations", Bick (1968) introduced her main points quite succinctly—in contrast to her usual interest and dedication to detail, the core of infant observation—and enunciates her thesis on early development:

> In its most primitive form, the personality parts are felt to have no binding force amongst them and must therefore be held together in a way that is experienced by them passively, by the skin functioning as a boundary. But this internal function of containing the parts of the self is dependent initially on the introjection of an external object, experienced as capable of fulfilling this function. Later, identification with this function of the object supersedes the non-integration state and gives rise to the fantasy of internal and external spaces. (Bick, 1968, p. 114)

With the observation of infants and children's analytic material, Bick (1968) illustrates the fluctuations in the infant's primal state to show the difference between non-integration as a passive experience of total helplessness, with catastrophic anxieties[6]—falling through space, liquefying, the dead end, life spilling out—and disintegration, through the processes of splitting, as an active defensive operation in the service of development, accompanied by persecutory and depressive anxieties.

Bick (1968) highlights that, in the unintegrated state, the baby searches desperately for a containing object—a light, a voice, a smell, or other sensual object—which he can hold, momentarily at least, in maintaining the personality parts together. She reminds us that "the ideal object is the nipple in the mouth, together with the mother's holding, her speech and the familiar smell" (p. 115). This function would be of primary skin. Pathological development can come from defects in the adequacy of the real object or from fantasy attacks on it, which impair introjection. According to Bick, this would lead to a "second-skin formation,[7] through which dependence on the object[8] is replaced by a pseudo-independence . . . for the purpose of creating a substitute for his skin container function" (p. 115).

This second-skin phenomenon that replaces integration by the first skin produces a general fragility in later integration and organisation. It "manifests itself as either partial or total type of muscular shell or a corresponding verbal muscularity" (Bick, 1968, p. 118). In her view, the psychoanalytic treatment of this type of phenomenon in analysis requires the elaboration of primal dependence on the maternal object, the setting being fundamental in this situation: "the containing aspect of the analytic situation resides especially in the setting and is therefore an area where firmness of technique is crucial" (p. 118).

In this first theoretical paper, Bick highlights that her aim was to open up this topic for detailed discussion in a later paper. Curiously enough, this paper was published almost twenty years later. In this paper, published after her death, Bick (1986) declared that she wanted to extend and investigate her findings in greater depth, integrating infant observation and clinical material from child and adult analysis. The paper was entitled "Further considerations on the function of the skin in early object relations" (Bick, 1986).

For Bick (1986), at birth, the baby is like ". . . an astronaut in space without a spacesuit" (Bick, 1986, p. 296). In this condition, he is subject to catastrophic anxieties already described. For Bick, the mother also loses her spacesuit at moments. She is subject to the same catastrophic anxieties. In Bick's (1986) words,

> The mother feels that she has lost her identity as a capable adult in control of her time and activities. Instead she is assailed from all sides by overwhelming demands; the demand to be a perfect mother, to have nothing for herself, not even sleep. These feelings have their roots in her own infantile complaints about the inadequacy of her own mother. (p. 295)

Bick shows the importance of the baby's orientation towards the mother's body in order to grasp and explore objects. For her, "this capacity is founded on the primal relation to the grasping, clinging adhesive contact with the mother" (p. 298). In this second stage of her theorisations, Bick (1986) extends and develops her ideas on the mother–infant primitive relationship and introduces the concept of "adhesive identification", more primitive than "projective identification".

In this paper, she reaffirms her idea that if not held by the mother,

> The baby would focus on a continuous sensory stimulus as for example a light or a continuous sound like that of a washing machine. Feeling protected, be it with the eyes or with the ears as with the touch, these organs would function as suction pads like a mouth holding on to the nipple. At this early stage there does not seem to be any differentiation of the separate functions; they all work as suction pads for adhesion. The need to cling applies in a similar way to the mother. (Bick, 1986, p. 297)

Therefore, one can conclude that the baby sucks not only through the mouth but also through the eyes and ears, which have the same function of adhesion or of clinging to the mother.

At this moment, Bick deepens her discussion on the technical difficulties associated with patients with failures in the early mother–infant relationship and concludes that the problems of ego strength, two-dimensionality, adhesive identification, and second-skin formation are rooted in the unconscious and have their origins early in the preverbal period and, restating her previously presented ideas, Bick (1986, p. 298) reaffirms that "They are not available for analytic research *in the transference*, unless the setting and the technique are extremely firm" (p. 298).

Winnicott's journey and his discoveries

The owner of a profoundly perceptive clinical understanding of early psychic phenomena and great sensitivity for working with babies, children, and their mothers, Winnicott also conceived the baby's initial state of unintegration, in which the mother's presence is fundamental for his integration. He dedicated himself to the essence of motherhood and to the investigation of mother–infant relationships. He tried to transmit his discoveries, derived from extensive and consistent clinical experience, through a variety of psychoanalytic papers. He shed light on the initial stages of the mother–infant relationship, showing the fundamental human needs, the necessary conditions for meeting them, and, simultaneously, the aetiology of psychosis and psychotic mechanisms.

Expanding psychoanalytic theory, he introduced an initial phase of unintegration in which the baby emerges from a state of essential loneliness where nothing has yet been separated from the non-being: there is no self, no mother, no external object to the self. In 1942, at a meeting of the British Psychoanalytic Society, Winnicott, still young, in the heat of the period of the famous "Controversial Discussions" (King & Steiner, 1991, p. 240), enunciated his fundamental thesis about the baby: "There's no such thing as a baby . . . One sees a nursing couple".[9] In a paper written ten years later, he described how surprised he was at the time by what we believe to have been a sudden insight: "I said with much enthusiasm and heat . . . I was shocked to hear me say those words" (Winnicott, 1987b, p. 99). Probably unaware of the profound implications of what he had said, Winnicott was penetrating an area hitherto little explored in psychoanalysis, the early mother–infant relationship, prior to the capacity for object relations which would bring important contributions to our understanding of primitive emotional development and analytic technique.

For Winnicott, human nature is almost everything we own and is essentially an innate tendency for integration into a unit throughout maturation: "The only passport the baby brings to the customs barrier is the sum of the inherited features and inborn tendencies toward growth and development which may never happen despite the good tendencies" (Winnicott, 1989a, p. 256).

Joining the pieces is not natural and, from the beginning, there is a fundamental need to be and to continue being. That is why it is necessary for someone to keep the baby integrated into a unit, otherwise he falls to pieces. When a mother is able to hold the baby in a natural way,

> A baby does not have to know about being made up of a collection of parts. The baby is a belly joined on to a chest and has loose limbs and particularly a loose head: all these parts are gathered together by the mother who is holding the child, and in her hands they add up to one. (Winnicott, 1989b, p. 568)

Revealing deep understanding of mothers and babies, Winnicott illuminated the primitive stages of human development, including pregnancy and childbirth. In his paper, "The ordinary devoted mother", he wrote in an original and empathic way about mothers: "One day they find they have become hostess to a new human being who has decided to lodge in them" (Winnicott, 1988c, p. 5). Pregnant women adapt fully to the development of the foetus: they undergo transformations in their bodies, become fragile and regressed. The foetus takes possession of the space, makes changes in the mother's body, mood, and emotions, leaving her more passive, expectant, and dependent. Winnicott (1987a) designated the special condition that mothers develop during pregnancy "primary maternal preoccupation". It is a disposition that mothers develop which increases during late pregnancy and continues for a few weeks after birth. It is fundamental for mothers to empathise with, and care for, their babies. This period is not easily remembered, as it tends to be repressed. If a woman was not pregnant and had such a condition, she would be ill. The mother depends on the baby both to enter this state and to get out of it. Thus, the new mother–infant duo is constantly permeated, in this period, by an absolute and profound relationship of maximum dependence of both the infant on the mother and the mother on the infant. The intrauterine environment could collapse at any time and the mother or the baby might not survive.

In his text on birth experience, Winnicott (1987d) gives us a clue to thinking about the mother's experience in labour, which we find helpful: "There comes a state in labour in which, in health, a mother has to be able to resign herself to a process almost exactly comparable to the infant's experience at the same time" (p. 184).

It is quite demanding for the mother to connect with that primitive level of psychic functioning, just as Winnicott said it would be demanding for the analyst to work with regressive, psychotic patients. He even said that he could only see one or two patients at a time in such a state. He commented on the treatment of one of his patients:

> . . . the treatment and managing of this case has called on everything that I possess as a human being, as a psychoanalyst and as a paediatrician. I have had to make a personal growth in the course of this treatment which was painful and which I would gladly have avoided. In particular I have had to learn to examine my own technique

> whenever difficulties arose, and it has always turned out, in the dozen or so resistance phases, that the cause was in a countertransference phenomenon which necessitated further self-analysis in the analyst. (Winnicott, 1987c, p. 280)

We can say that, although the duration of delivery is short, it is an intense experience and it has the potential for a disruptive emotional overload and for being able to interrupt, at least momentarily, the labouring women's sense of going on being. In a previous paper on the observation of women in labour, helplessness was perceived in many women entering into a strange, frightening space, defying death and madness. To experience the physical and emotional regression that occurs at birth is really a challenge, for most women, to their limits and to their flexibility in moving through different levels of their psychic structure.

To abandon oneself to this regressive state of "normal madness" is healthy and necessary. In his paper entitled "This feminism", Winnicott (1986) comments on the risk of the childbirth experience for women: "It is no good pretending that childbirth carries no risk . . . there is a danger inherent in woman's natural function". And he goes on to say that it is not easy, not only to go through childbirth, but also "the whole confinement and the terribly restricting responsibilities of infant care" (p. 193).

Therefore, it is not difficult to understand why many women are unable to achieve this disposition, this identification with the baby, experiencing it as a foreign body whose expulsion she waits in order to be relieved and to quickly return to her previous living conditions. These women go through the whole process without living it, a situation that complicates the possibility of mother and baby immersing themselves in an experience of mutuality and for both to emerge transformed by that experience. The infant's self emerges, necessarily, from within that mother–infant unit.

The mother needs to be healthy enough to contact her helplessness, to accept it. The maternal regression to the state of helplessness that characterises human beings from the beginning to the end of life is inevitable and necessary for mothers to meet with their baby's helplessness at an "exact" moment to identify with him.

> Certainly there is something that happens to people when they are confronted with the helplessness that is supposed to characterize a

> baby ... We could almost say that those who are in the position of caring for a baby are as helpless in relation to the baby's helplessness as the baby can be said to be. Perhaps there can be a battle of helplessness. (Winnicott, 1988a, p. 102)

These findings led Winnicott to highlight the fact of the real and absolute dependence in early life and to value the study of the environment. There is a very subtle kind of need that only human contact can satisfy. The baby might need to be involved through the mother's breathing rhythm, or even by hearing and feeling the heartbeat of an adult. He might need to smell the mother or father, or hear sounds that convey his vivacity and the life of the environment, or colours and movements in a way that he is not left alone with his own resources, while he is still too small and immature to assume full responsibility for life. In this beginning, the baby is an immature being who lives in a state of extreme, real dependence and, therefore, is subjected to the most terrible anxieties, always on the edge of experiencing an unthinkable anxiety:

> If left for too long (hours, minutes) without familiar and human contact, [babies] have experiences which we can only describe by such words as: going to pieces, falling for ever, dying and dying and dying, losing all vestige of hope of the renewal of contacts. It will be appreciated that with good enough care these awful feelings become good experiences, adding up to a total confidence in people and in the world. For instance, going to pieces becomes relaxation and restfulness if a baby is in good hands; falling for ever fall becomes the joy in being carried, and the excitement and pleasure that belong to being moved; dying and dying and dying becomes a delicious awareness of being alive. (Winnicott, 1988d, p. 86)

Winnicott repeatedly highlighted the qualities of the mother as a subjective object for her baby, constantly adapting to his needs: for her to be real, empathic, devoted, ordinary, monotonous, good enough, constant, predictable, and preoccupied with him. These attitudes favour the individual's going on being, integration, the formation of a psychosomatic unit, the transformation of unthinkable anxieties, and the condition for the true self to begin to form. For Winnicott (1987e),

> An infant who has had no one person to gather his bits together starts with a handicap in his own self-integrating task, and perhaps he cannot succeed, or at any rate cannot maintain integration with confidence. (p. 150)

Gradually, if the mother is good enough, her adaptation to the baby's needs decreases proportionally to the baby's development and separation. They both progress to a stage of relative dependence and then towards an independence that will never be total. This passage from illusion to disillusion is essential for both mother and infant and helps in the development and integration of the newborn. Existing as a unit, he acquires more stability and consistency, but these will never be safe, permanent achievements. After reaching unitary identity, the child is able to truly experience the oedipal anxieties and reach neurosis. If all went well in this first stage, although it will not be registered in the child's ego, the fact of being an essentially good enough mother will prevent the development of psychotic disturbances in the baby.

CHAPTER TWO

A research journey to this place where verbalisation has no meaning

Our hope is to illustrate for you the "sacred place" of the mother–infant relationship, and we invite you to come along as we try to translate into words the experiences of observing six babies, two singles and two pairs of twins, in their first three years of life.

Our extended and stimulating contact with the primitive side of humans in clinical psychoanalytic work with adults, adolescents, and children exposed a need for attaining more knowledge about babies and their world, using research that is focused more on first-hand experiences in the first stages of life, and to acquire more appropriate tools for therapeutic approaches in this area. It was in this context that Nara Caron and Ruth Maltz discovered the Bick method in the early 1980s in Rio de Janeiro, in the works of psychoanalysts Joaquim Couto Rosa and Geni Talberg. The method's potential for understanding the depths and mysteries that surround the mother–infant relationship was clear. We were excited to apply this new approach and confident that we had found the right course of action. We began the training (adapted for distance learning) some time later, despite the inherent difficulties of pioneering the work in Porto Alegre and being supervised in Rio de Janeiro.

The wealth of experience, technique, and learning we found in the Bick observation method surprised and impressed us, further stimulating our curiosity and interest. Thus, since 1987, we have co-ordinated standard infant observation groups and developed applications of the method.

Years of practising infant observation and of supervising observation groups have demonstrated that spending two years in a baby's home is a deep emotional experience that produces important changes in the observers: it develops intuition, stimulates emotions, exercises imagination and personal skills development, and heightens sensitivity to non-verbal aspects of communication, thus resulting in the observer's being able to listen more accurately by using their emotions and their own bodies. Working through such powerful experiences can lead to changes in their clinical work, better connection with their own psychic reality and that of their patients, and greater reflection before formulating interpretations. The method acts as a catalyst by adding new questions and creating new challenges to research. Some observers experienced personal growth and were able to create new projects and clinical applications that expanded the objectives of the method. The experience rekindled interest in the origin of psychic life—of looking psychoanalytically at increasingly primitive stages of development. The effects that infant observation had on us were fascinating and brought us face to face with the mysteries of life and death, transformations, birth, and human development, and our persistent desire to unravel them.

The Bick method has been highly productive in psychoanalytic investigations of early stages of development and has been generating scientific discoveries ever since it was created by Esther Bick (1968, 1986). The method allows us to truly experience the baby's first two years of life and enhances our psychoanalytic listening to primitive psychic phenomena.

This book is the result of both our professional and personal experiences. Nara Caron is an analyst that treats infants, children, adolescents, and adults and is a supervisor of the Bick method of infant observation. Rita Lopes is a researcher in the area of emotional development. We are both interested in using the Bick method as a tool to research what is most primitive in human nature.

By the late 1980s, after co-ordinating supervision groups using the standard Bick method and observing several mother–infant pairs during their first two years of life, Ruth Maltz and Nara Caron had gathered numerous ideas and questions about the initial human relationships, which fostered a desire and curiosity to understand these issues in the prenatal stage as well. Those of us in the supervision groups often wondered about this period and how it connected with the postnatal stage. At that time, we had the opportunity to work alongside the obstetrician Jose Antonio Magalhães at the Alpha Clinic in Porto Alegre in caring for pregnant women who had just received an ultrasound diagnosis that their babies had some kind of congenital malformation. All these women accepted our intervention proposal (Caron & Maltz, 1994). The intensity of delving into the female experience of motherhood had a transforming impact on us due to the ethical, social, and religious issues involved in this acute and serious conflict of having to decide whether to interrupt a pregnancy once the diagnosis was confirmed. This was especially intense for the pregnant women, but also for everyone involved, including the medical staff. In Brazil, this kind of situation is additionally complicated because our legislation does not permit abortion, except in cases of rape or when the mother's life is at risk. In fact, ten out of the twelve babies did not survive.

Our technique evolved spontaneously from our own professional experience as psychoanalysts and as co-ordinators of infant observation groups. Later, we extended the technique to our therapeutic approach for children between the ages of zero and three. The work was exciting, dynamic, and especially motivating for us as analysts in being able to deal with psychic phenomena in real time as it happened in the womb and the infant's first relationships at the very moment they occurred, all of which differs greatly from treating older children who already speak or play, or adults reporting facts about their children's lives. The opportunity to follow these situations is always remarkable and challenging to the analyst's previously established knowledge, experiences, and techniques, in spite of the whole arsenal of basic theoretic resources at their disposal. Working with these mother–baby pairs allowed us to observe and participate in this history-in-the-making because we were present at the time and place of the events.

The combination of using this technique in clinical practice along with co-ordinating observation groups offered us another option for delving deep into the human soul and being directly connected to the baby's first experiences and interactions with his mother and with the most primitive experiences in his environment. These experiences were a considerable challenge to everything we already knew, and prepared us to leave our comfort zones and deal with primitive situations that required enormous receptivity and empathy from the analyst (Caron, 2000b). These strong and unforgettable learning experiences identified a need for more knowledge and studies regarding even more primitive stages of development, such as pregnancy, delivery, and prematurity.

Extending the standard Bick method to this primitive world brought greater challenges to the observer–analyst. These initial stages further expose the fragility and helplessness of tiny human beings who need other human beings in order to continue existing. We hope to show how this "descent towards the realm of the mothers", that place where words lose their meaning, represents a significant opportunity to learn not only about psychic phenomena at the beginning of life, but also about the basic principles of therapeutic work, which, according to Winnicott (1999a), can be learnt from the mother–baby pair.

Visiting caves

The desire to know what is most secret and to decipher the enigmas from the hidden side of what is known has always fascinated mankind and has prompted the search for, and achievement of, important advances in scientific technology. Obstetric ultrasound emerged from this environment. The ability to enter the "sacred place" of the womb, disclose its mysterious content, and find answers seems to be one of contemporary man's fascinations.

Being able to make contact with the world of the foetus and its mother provides the training ground for understanding and approaching this area, which, in turn, produces the proper tools for entering this primitive world. With this in mind, we proposed using the Bick method to observe the ultrasound examinations of pregnant women in the same clinic where we had conducted our previous work, where we then remained for five years (Caron et al., 2000). Our goal was to observe a large number of women in different stages of pregnancy in order to train the listening skills of the parents and staff.

At the same time, we needed to become familiar with the signs, movements, and gestures that are revealed by the foetus's images and which triggered intense feelings and emotions in everyone present, including the observer.

To do this kind of work, the observer must be experienced in the standard method. The driving force for applying the method is in the observer's function and the transformations she undergoes throughout the experience, specifically in refining her ability to listen to primitive psychic phenomena and to participate subtly and gently in investigating this "sacred" place at such a decisive moment (Caron, 1995). Also crucial is the sonographer, who must have good experience in conducting the examinations and be able to understand the special concerns of the parents, as well as to be curious, interested, and to take pleasure in the work. We worked with the same sonographer during all the years we dedicated to this study. We noticed repeatedly how everyone present in the examination attributes to her a "divine" power of seeing and, thus, she was considered able to decipher secrets, explain the morphology of the foetus and its dynamics and growth, and diagnose anomalies. They also give the sonographer implicit permission to transgress, meaning she is free to explore the mother's inside, thus opening the door for everyone else present. As the sonographer presents the foetus, she explains what is being seen and answers the parents' questions, thus establishing the facts, alleviating primitive anxieties, and accommodating impressions about the baby. This helps parents to digest and neutralise those feelings and make them less toxic. Without using moral criticisms and quick answers, the sonographer plays a containing function that relieves anxieties. Her way of using clear, accurate, empathetic language in order to identify with the pregnant woman certainly facilitates the process of becoming a mother. Each parents–foetus–sonographer relationship is different and unique, and is dependent on a complex network that is interactive, challenging, and unknown.

Although scientific knowledge is fundamental, it is not enough to handle the full range of psychological challenges produced by the emotional weight of confronting the foetal image. We verified that parents see predominantly what their unconscious mind sees, rather than what is shown to them objectively. The parents often determine temperaments and characteristics of their unborn child based on their movements and gestures. Certain statements are repeated in consecutive tests, such as aggressive, agitated, sweet, peaceful, masculine, feminine, looks like so and so. For example, at one obstetric ultrasound, a couple was sure their baby was a boy and just wanted confirmation, which was not given. They insisted it had to be a boy! This led to the couple having a heated argument about the future growth of the foetus's penis, the sonographer's incompetence for not locating their son's penis, and affirmations that they would return to prove the doctor wrong.

The surprise reaction of all those present when the images are revealed is a moment of emotional impact concerning the strange–familiar (Freud, 1919h), constituting a manifestation with significant unconscious expressions. Childhood experiences are suddenly brought to mind, especially anxieties and primitive beliefs from which human beings are never completely free. Hence, an image seems to shorten the path to the unconscious and affect it more intensely. That is precisely how the ultrasound examination works at a time when the parents are highly motivated and the mother is regressed by her pregnancy (Caron, 2000a).

Pregnancy is an exclusively female experience. Despite all the current technical advances and knowledge that surmounts numerous infertility problems, a pregnancy carried inside the uterus continues to be truly essential and irreplaceable in terms of creating a new human being. There is still no uterus substitute that is capable of containing a pregnancy.

It is no simple task to hold another being that has its own life, rhythm, movement, gender, and independent features inside your body. The foetus is separate yet non-differentiated. Although the foetus's circulation is independent, the mother's respiratory, digestive, and excretory systems work for both.

The expectant mother experiences a specific and unique situation that clearly reveals details of the female specificity. Pregnancy is a hormonal, physical, and psychological earthquake that carries with it the greatest challenges, secrets, and uncertainties faced by human beings. The expectant mother experiences transformations in her body as it relaxes, expands, and grows to make room for the foetus, which develops vigorously and extraordinarily fast, beyond the mother's control, yet sustained by her in this dynamic environment until delivery.

Women tend to regress and become fragile, they allow their defensive structure to relax, and their unconscious and mind–body exchanges become more permeable. For example, at one ultrasound scan, the mother's appearance is simple and spontaneous. She is forty years old and forty weeks pregnant. She seems disconnected and a little "spaced out". She gives the impression that she did not pay attention to how she dressed or combed her hair. The only thing that seems to connect her to the outside world is her huge belly, which is impossible not to notice. She seems to be floating on a substance that is not the air from planet Earth; she is waiting, biding her time. She says she has a ten-year-old son who says she has only got half a neuron working.

The helplessness women often experience during pregnancy is noticeable when their bodies become a stage for exhibiting transformations that shelter the sometimes unexpected life of another being, or their unexpected death.

Everything is prepared for the parents who come to record the growth of their baby, but, in the first image, they see that it is dead. The opposite can also happen, as in the case of a woman who went for a regular check-up after chemotherapy and found out she was pregnant with twins.

Although often accompanied, women face these changes alone, in their own bodies. The mother is the one who experiences maximum dependency. She both inhabits and is inhabited by her baby in a relationship of mutual dependence. She gradually abandons her personal interests, giving more space to her baby. She progressively identifies with the baby, who is initially completely dependent on the mother's regressive state which continues until delivery and the following first few months. The report below of an expectant mother's dream three days before her delivery illustrates how she is attuned to her baby:

> She could see her baby through the transparent skin of her belly: size, features, various details, and a lot of light brown hair. She recalled that babies born in both her and her husband's families were bald.

When the baby was born, the mother was surprised because she was exactly like she had been in her dream! Identical! She recognised her right away, including the brown hair.

The participants' greater psychic permeability is facilitated by the regression provoked by the ultrasound setting itself. The examination room is relatively dark, silent, a cosy size, with closed doors and windows—as if it is a separate reality from the outside world. The silence, the image, the non-verbal atmosphere very quickly touches the participants deeply. It is something difficult to translate, to put into words, and sometimes expresses itself through the body or through bizarre ideas or attitudes. The ultrasound examination allows quick access and entry to the intrauterine space, which is facilitated by a setting, described above, that is similar to the analytic setting. The pregnant mother is lying down with more than her abdomen showing, her belly covered in a sticky gel.

Everyone is looking inside. No one leaves, circulates, or moves. The anxieties that arise remain; they are not dissipated by any distraction or by escaping to another activity. The observer has the least space in the room, while the baby appears independent, loose, and spontaneous, moving without obeying any external order.

In accordance with the principles of the standard Bick method, the observer is invited to participate in the experience. The sonographer uses the transducer to illuminate the inside of the womb, and the impact of light and dark immediately compels us to enter this "small–large" cave, as one of the observers called it in an effort to express what she felt as she looked at the image.

Caves are fascinating. Inside are mixed images of silence and darkness and a fear of the unknown. None the less, there is a strong desire to visit caves and unveil their mysteries:

> Caves cannot be visited without feeling their effect. There, everything is different, beautiful, and new . . . These worlds of silence and darkness have no seasons, there is no superior vegetation because there is no sunlight and time itself seems to fossilise. It is a place of a silence so great that our brains, with their restless neurons, can be heard as if they were factories producing dreams . . . Its dark cavities, age-old silence, and ample underground spaces are beautifully and bizarrely ornamented; caverns and chasms freed our imagination and most certainly contributed to creating our own concepts about the unknown, the infinite, the secret, and the supernatural (Lino, 2001, p. 11, translated for this edition)

Observations of obstetric ultrasounds are similarly fascinating. Viewing an ultrasound image is never neutral. It shows the unusual, the primitive, the foetus. Images are the first resources of words. Freud, in *The Interpretation of Dreams* (1900a), pointed out that because dreams consist mostly of images, they more authentically depict unconscious contents. The impact is also due to the immense amount of information contained in these images that assail our senses all at once. It is as if a dream is suddenly made real and condensed into a single image, which echoes true primitive psychic content in each person. It discloses what is felt, not what is said.

> A woman did the exam on a Friday, which confirmed that the foetus was a boy. This seemed to make her very happy and she said she felt fulfilled. The following Monday, she cried and confessed to the sonographer that she was sad. She said that she lost her baby. The doctor was surprised and asked what had happened. The mother said she cried a lot because they—she and her husband—would not have the girl they had imagined. Just a boy!

Little by little we discover the contours that shape and outline a baby's tiny body. As we observe the foetus interacting with its intra-uterine environment, we find that many postnatal characteristics are already present in foetal life. The foetus is no longer a stranger. On the contrary, it exposes a large part of itself, and, in the process, also exhibits the inside of the mother's womb. A five-year-old boy looking at his sister's ultrasound image said very spontaneously, "Oh, it's already born?!" In another study where we asked children to draw pictures of their little brother or sister after the ultrasound examination, we found that they often drew them as children already born and bigger; for example, wearing slippers or drinking from a bottle (Caron & Fonseca, 2011). For this reason, we suggest that the ultrasound is "an anticipated birth and the sonographer is the midwife" (Caron et al., 2000, p. 182).

We can think from the perspective of how visiting the womb-cave is a challenging and intense experience for all who visit it, especially for the mothers, who offer their inner space to these "visitors" so they can relive going back to where they had already been, to where they always want to return and be reborn. It is an inexhaustible, universal dream.

There are numerous births happening simultaneously. The transition from one phase to another—from son to father, daughter to mother, mother to grandmother, child to sibling—produces changes in the psychic structure of each one. New identities must be created and new roles acquired. Bick (1986) had already drawn attention to the impact of a baby's presence on each member of the family, especially regarding varying degrees of identity changes.

Each person, mother, father, sibling, grandmother, and great-grandmother, is affected by the image according to each one's stage of evolution, coloured by regression. Although primitive experiences rise more easily to consciousness during the prenatal period, making them a privileged space for resurfacing, reviewing, and redrafting the past, they are a challenge to the psychic structure. Pregnancy is a period of reorganisation that includes the mother, father, siblings, grandparents, and great-grandparents that occurs at the same time as the foetus takes its place and role in the family and intergenerational dynamics.

We observed that the father is more present during pregnancy and ultrasound exams, sometimes describing himself as being pregnant and going through a phase of biological and psychological reorganisation:

> During an examination, the father seemed very proud of his role and talked about his achievement. He was happy the baby was a girl. To facilitate the examination, the doctor asked the mother to walk and move about a little so the foetus would change positions. Several manoeuvres were tried with no results. The father, who had been quietly watching, stood up and said, "Leave it to me!" He approached the mother's belly and said in a honeyed tone, "Where is Daddy's little princess?" And the baby started turning . . . and the atmosphere in the exam room turned as well. He was thrilled with the result.

In some cases, the father clearly identified with the expectant mother and/or the foetus:

> In one exam, the father felt sick and short of breath, saying he felt anxious about seeing the baby all "closed up" in the womb. Another said he felt like he had a foetus inside his stomach.

At times, the fathers, as well as other family members, clearly demonstrated they could not be in the exam room. They reacted with extreme ambivalence, lost control, or behaved in completely unexpected ways. When frustrated, especially after discovering the sex of the baby was not what they had wanted, we saw strong and violent enactments of unconscious conflicts, rude words and attitudes, forceful exits from the room, and doors slammed, with no return to the examination room.

We often observed grandmothers entering into conflicts or competing with the mothers during the examination. The daughter's pregnancy forces the future grandmother to face her own successes, failures, and expectations and to accept a supporting role, which was sometimes a difficult task. Playing a secondary role is not only related to the grandparents' phase of evolution. It is part of the specific context of pregnancy: everyone except the mother–infant couple is relegated to second place.

Beginning in the late 1990s, we observed a growing presence of siblings in the prenatal ultrasound examinations, with brings new questions for further research. The siblings are on the verge of stepping on to the stage and enacting their personal conflicts related to their mother and this new being, as well as those related to their own primitive experiences. Therefore, we decided to conduct a study focused on parents–foetus(es)–sibling(s), also using the Bick method but, in this case, complemented by the analysis of children's drawings after the exams (Caron & Fonseca, 2011). Given that the birth of a sibling corresponds to a cross-section in a child's life curve, we believed their participation in the ultrasound exam was a rich opportunity to learn from their experiences. This privileged setting helps children to express the inner world of their emotions, their most vivid and most secret desires, their search for satisfaction, their dreams, frustrations, and conflicts, especially those connected to this new transition phase of becoming siblings and experiencing fraternal issues.

For this study, observers trained in the Bick method observed seventy-five children that participated in their mother's ultrasound examinations during a span of six months. Their unique and intense verbal, behavioural, and graphic manifestations were surprising in that they demonstrated the level to which the ultrasound environment allows psychic regression, which affects both the adults and the siblings. The reactions we observed were very individual, but always intense: deep sleep, agitation, anxiety, escape, hostility, and contempt. Both the observation reports and the drawings translated deep psychic content especially related to the fraternal complex.

The intense internal mobilisation caused by the foetal images and the created setting provokes an emotional impact that favours regression in all the participants in the ultrasound examination, making everyone more permeable and transparent, and able to express their feelings of helplessness, loneliness, vulnerability, ambivalence, and idealisations. There is a narcissistic investment in the baby, who is seen as an indiscriminate part of each one. Frequently and quickly, the participants defend themselves from disillusion, renouncement, and disintegration, using the foetus's image and the doctor as a multi-faceted mirror that reflects the omnipotence, power, and authority of the various majesties who take part in the examination. It is not His Majesty, the Baby; the baby itself disappears sometimes. It is of fundamental importance how the special features, and sometimes the wounds, of this initial phase of development appear at this moment, demonstrating the family members' level of maturity or immaturity (Caron et al., 2008).

We believe that in order to have a deeper understanding of the cave, it is necessary to go all the way to where it ends, to be able to come and go, to enter and exit so that its interior is seen more clearly every time. The observer must be able to offer internal availability and be highly receptive in order to maintain an empathetic listening attitude towards everything that is communicated verbally and, especially, non-verbally. The observer functions as a special sensitive receiver who is used by the expectant mother to share her emotions, fears, and anxieties, as well as experiences that were hidden, unknown, or even prohibited. The mother can reveal doubts about her ability to gestate and maintain the pregnancy, about having enough physical and emotional space to contain the baby, and about the internal and external changes to her body image caused by this unique experience of two bodies in one.

We verified how the feeling of perfect unity is recreated in this womb-cave that offers the qualities that are necessary for creating an environment for foetal development, such as space, protection, rhythm, repetition, and monotony. This feeling counterbalances the intense turmoil and transformations the foetus experiences for forty weeks. Another being effectively inhabits the old familiar body of the mother, creating single system that is highly organised, refined, and differentiated. In the prenatal period, followed by the first months after birth, the dependence between them is so absolute that theirs is not a relationship of two, but, rather, a peculiar two-in-one. During pregnancy, this mother–infant fusion suffers small breaks in continuity that prepare the foetus for delivery and the pair for their endless process of separation.

The delivery experience

In order to give continuity to our observations of the most primitive stages of human development, we extended our observations to delivery, where the female interior continues being the stage for intense emotional events. Applying the observation method to childbirth is a more recent effort that was made possible because of the interest of an observer, Tagma Schneider Donelli, who observed women in labour followed by their delivery during a period of nineteen months (Caron et al., 2013; Donelli, 2008).

At the point of childbirth, mother and infant have already gone through an important developmental stage, pregnancy, but they are still faced with life and death challenges and the helplessness and mutual dependence that characterised the previous period. In addition, both mother and baby have to experience the enormous discontinuity that occurs at birth: the baby moves from the uterine environment to the world outside the mother's womb. He will now need to be held in his mother's arms and will have to negotiate separateness. Discontinuities such as this will be present in other developmental stages, but never with such a degree of intensity as at childbirth.

It is frightening, even terrifying, to recognise that the baby is totally dependent on the mother, who simultaneously experiences states of helplessness herself. However, it is precisely this condition of physical and emotional regression, which Winnicott (1987a) called primary maternal preoccupation, that makes women able to identify and empathise with the baby and, thus, be able to welcome him and take care of him. One might say that childbirth is a paradoxical moment of mutual and utmost helplessness for both mother and infant.

In the first contact with the obstetric centre, the observer described it as intimidating, frightening, and embarrassing.

> I managed to cross the room, but at the insistence of the nurse, who wanted to show me where the delivery rooms were. I was half-embarrassed, thinking that I should be wearing different, hospital clothing, or perhaps that I should stay still so as not to feel I might be disturbing something.

It seemed to be inevitable that the observer would allow herself to feel taken over by feelings of insecurity, confusion, or lack of preparation. Everything seemed very different from what is usually expected. The corridors had many turns, without clear signposts to tell people where they were, or directions to tell them where to go.

The reports made it clear that it was not an easy task to keep looking; at times, there were dramatic events and the possibility of death. There were times of despair in the face of physical and emotional pain and of the imminent event of birth, as well as the experience of enormous demand for emotional care. There was rawness, an overexposure to all of this that disarmed the observer. The obstetric centre seemed like a place where people came closer to something they were trying to cover up, something that revealed more than they would have liked, something that went beyond intimacy to soul-baring, highlighting primitive fears and anxieties. The contradiction of it all, the mixed messages, disarmed and depressed everyone.

After the first observation, the observer could see how the emotional climate, generated by the chaotic and unwelcoming environment, would require quite a commitment as well as emotional investment in order to carry out the work:

> I started coming back, coming the opposite way, trying to get back to the examination room and to the newborn admissions, but always staying close to the nurse, because I could not imagine myself there alone. Where would I be in the next observations? Would I be able to sit down? Which way could I look?

Issues related to the female body were described in practically all observation reports, and they surpass all the emotion that is also present. Words and symbols gave way to concrete expressions of pain, disgust, anxiety, and shame, and all are shared by the observer. The proximity to the primitive is frightening, and even something familiar to everyone, like defecation, vomiting, and bleeding, seems to provoke the need to ignore them or to hide them away.

Despite being natural, these human bodily experiences are constantly denied and hidden in social life. But there, the smells and colours would mix to form a screen full of details that could never have been seen in this way in any other environment.

The physiological aspects of childbirth, such as the pace of contraction and the progression of the dilation of the cervix, evoke feelings of losing a piece of oneself with a fear of surrendering to the process and losing one's reference points. These experiences resemble the infant's unthinkable anxieties, still not integrated and with no environment that contains him and them. Such experiences might be responsible for attempts by the women in labour to exert some control over the process of the baby's birth, or of using other means or mechanisms, mental or physical, to protect themselves from the invasion of extremely powerful feelings.

This need for control seems to be experienced by women in an intensive way, spanning the entire labour and delivery itself. The lack of control over the whole process of the baby's birth seems to cause great anxiety in patients.

Labour and delivery carry the risk of transforming into a traumatic situation for women, since they are forced to deal with feelings of loss and separation from the baby in the womb. It is possible to witness women's expressions about the "missing" belly soon after birth, like a concrete loss of a part of herself.

Women show from the stretch marks on their bellies the numerous marks that a pregnancy and childbirth can leave. It must be made clear that, here, we are not only concerned with the physical stretch marks on the body, but the marks left on the mind and soul of these women. The marks left on a woman's life by the birth of a child are undeniable, but to witness those left on the body leads, undeniably and in a more dramatic way, to thinking about the emotional impact.

Another common aspect of the women in the maternity ward was described in the reports as alienation. This appeared to us to be a kind of altered state of consciousness that would make the women feel foreign to their surroundings, so they would interact only minimally with the environment, they would speak little, and would even sleep during the process of labour. This state, in our view, can be an indicator of women's deep regression and of their predominant attunement, during labour, with their inner emotional experience, which is required in order to identify and empathise with the baby.

> There were four patients there, all very quiet, as if they were asleep. . . . they were very shy, all with their eyes closed, and I didn't want to bother them. . . . Julia remained facing the wall, lying down almost the entire time. I could see her face for just one moment when she sat up to turn sideways. She had beautiful features, but her face was a mystery;

> she had the face of a woman, but at the same time she looked like a young girl. She saw me standing there, and smiled before lying down again and disappearing. She made me think of the sea, and how these women seem to dive into an endless ocean, surfacing for a few moments, perhaps to show that they are still there. In fact, we know they are there, but we do not really know where they go.

Labour pain was another common experience observed. Like any other pain, it has biological, social, and physiological elements, and it is also subjectively a unique experience. The way each woman expresses her pain seems to have a close relationship with her personal character, with her subjective need for care, with her level of confidence, and in her own capacity to endure pain and her capacity to experience becoming a mother. Numerous expressions of pain were observed during the study. Most of them were linked to the evolution of labour, to the increased intensity of the contractions and the decreasing interval between them, and also to the reality of not knowing for how long they would have to endure the pain, confirming their belief that that suffering would be endless and intolerable. This experience could be perceived as a threat to the integrity of the woman and to her own life; it would be like being stuck in a dead end without the ability to manage the situation.

There were also observations of the women's reactions to feelings of fear, helplessness, suffering, and exhaustion during and after labour, and the observer was the witness, strongly in identification with the woman (or the baby) observed.

> The hours dragged and I was getting tired. There was no place to sit and I started walking from one side to the other, trying to be as discreet as possible. This time, I realised even more clearly how narrow the prepartum room was. You could hear all the noises from the hallway as well as from the street and the hospital car park entrance. People came in and out and the three of us in there were in a world completely apart. Even time seemed different.

Many of the women in labour seemed to communicate their loneliness and helplessness to the observer—through verbal, but mainly non-verbal communication—not just for establishing connection with someone, but as a way, it seemed, of communicating fears and anxieties. This makes one think about how women are really alone as they confront the birth of a child. Although they are in a hospital, surrounded by professionals, equipment, technology, and materials, the whole process of birth is experienced in mother's own body, in a solitary and private way.

Undertaking weekly observations in an obstetric centre for a period of nineteen months was a unique experience. On many occasions, the observer wondered what made her carry on with experiences that mobilised such anxiety, tension, and discomfort as observing childbirth. Carrying out observation in an obstetric centre provides the opportunity for the observer to connect with, and experience, something exciting, moving, but also something nameless which is so primitive that it cannot yet be expressed verbally or have meaning. Moreover, it was very gratifying to let oneself be used by the mothers, to develop an empathic capacity and an identification with the women. One is also able to go beyond physical holding and care to offer a kind of emotional holding similar to the maternal function.

To be together, to listen, to welcome, and to share, uncritically, the unconscious experiences of a woman in labour are aspects of the observation which, in our view, are themselves therapeutic and mostly welcomed at this challenging moment in a woman's life. Both the women and the observer profited by the experience, which felt increasingly meaningful as the weeks passed. It is clear to us how much an observer can modify and enrich herself with such an experience.

Through the observer, we can understand Winnicott's suggestion, in his paper entitled "Environmental health in infancy", that ". . . the main things that a mother does with the baby cannot be done through words" (Winnicott, 1988e, p. 61). The intense, silent, psychic activity required by the mother during early development should not be trivialised. There is a parallel, we believe, in the observer's silent mental activity. In Bick's method of observation, and in parallel with psychoanalytic technique with regressed patients, as Winnicott suggested (1987c), the setting becomes more important than interpretation (see also Caron & Lopes, 2015).

We can conclude that, although the duration of labour and delivery is short, it is an intense experience and has the potential for emotional overload and for being able to disrupt, usually only temporarily, the women's sense, during labour, of going on being.

The beginning of life in an essentially female place

After many years of continuous work with the method and its applications, a desire emerged to join loose pieces of our experiences to our curiosity for investigating the continuity between prenatal and postnatal life. We began fulfilling this dream in 2000, when we organised a longitudinal research project using the Bick observation method to follow the development of the baby and the mother–infant relationship beginning at the twelfth week of gestation and ending when the child was three years old. We were truly passionate about this herculean project that required intense personal participation and being deeply connected, and we were sure it could satisfy at least some of our curiosity.

Our wealth of experience in conducting numerous studies on the primitive stages of life—that essentially feminine place where human beings begin their development, along with our expertise in analytic treatment of babies, children, adolescents, and adults, placed us in a position of being able to integrate and more deeply develop the findings of our research on the first three years of life, including pregnancy and delivery, which we will now describe.

We faced many challenges in this long journey, similar to those experienced by psychoanalytic researchers who launch into the unknown in search of the primitive in human beings.

Our project was inspired by the pioneering work of Alessandra Piontelli (1995), who conducted in Italy the first longitudinal psychoanalytic study of its kind that included the prenatal period. She conducted monthly observations of eleven foetuses (three single babies and four sets of twins) using ultrasound images starting at the sixteenth week of pregnancy. After birth, she used the mother–infant observation method developed by Esther Bick to conduct weekly home visits until the child was two years old. After the child's second birthday, the observations occurred three times a year until the child turned four. Piontelli (1995) combined aspects of the foetus' behavioural development, ethology, and psychoanalysis.

Although inspired by Piontelli's (1995) work, we sought to counteract some of the methodological limitations we observed in her study. Piontelli had conducted all the stages of the study herself, personally observing all the foetuses without any participation from other observers and without any group discussions of the written reports, which are one of the pillars of the method. In some cases, she even conducted the obstetric ultrasound herself.

We believe the three phases of the Bick method of observation, written report, and group supervision, as described in detail in Chapter One, support the structure, purpose, and philosophy of this kind of infant observation. Maintaining the setting and the function of the observer is what allows observation to take place and opens the door to discovering specific information about each unique mother–infant--observer relationship.

Thus, in order to maintain the fundamental principles of the Bick method, especially Bick's rule number 1 that states, "come as a *tabula rasa* . . . you know nothing and that is everything", we formed two independent teams, each one made up of observers and supervisors. One team worked with the first stage from pregnancy to childbirth, and a second team used the standard method in the second stage of post-birth. The teams did not exchange information until the end of the study. This was done because first stage observers and supervisors were deeply involved with the ultrasound reports, raising ideas, creating assumptions, and fostering desires about the parent–infant relationship, which, in our opinion, would make it very difficult for them to do post-birth observations without any preconceived ideas or prior hypotheses, as recommended by the standard method. In other words, it would be difficult for them to eliminate the assumptions made in the supervisory group during pregnancy, and approach the post-birth baby with no expectations. This would risk jeopardising three years of arduous, sensitive, and demanding work in a baby's home and family.

In the data collection phase during the pregnancy period, six babies were observed (two single and two sets of twins) at an ultrasound clinic in Porto Alegre, Brazil. The mothers of the babies were all married to, and living with, the fathers of the babies, presented no gynaecological malformations, and no history of chronic physical diseases, severe psychological disorders, or infertility. Neither did the fathers of babies present any history of chronic physical diseases or serious psychological disorders. The first contact with the expectant mothers was through the obstetricians. To begin the research, the parents signed an informed consent regarding their participation in the study and any future publication of material collected during observations. The observations of the babies, mothers, and mother–

infant relationships were conducted in three phases and in different observation contexts, as listed below:

1. Pregnancy: obstetric ultrasound setting. Some features of the observation setting in the traditional Bick method were used as a model for this research. The observations were carried out every month by observers experienced in the method for a pre-defined period of twenty minutes, always at the same time and day of the week, and with the same sonographer, a specialist in the technique. Written reports of the observations were read and discussed at the weekly meetings of the supervision group that comprised four observers and a psychoanalyst supervisor who was a project co-ordinator experienced in the Bick method and in this type of application. The images of the tests were videotaped and then watched by the supervision group. For a more detailed analysis of the videotaped foetal movements, we formed two other teams that had no prior knowledge of the cases.
2. Delivery and immediate post-birth: hospital setting. The observation of the labour and delivery in the hospital was conducted by the same observers who observed the ultrasounds. The observer reported her observations of the delivery and descriptions of the first contact between the mother and the baby(ies) in writing, which was subsequently read and discussed by the same first phase supervision group. In addition to these procedures, we filmed the birth and the first few minutes of mother–infant interaction. Furthermore, a mother–infant relationship observation was conducted approximately twenty-four hours after the birth, while the mother and baby(ies) were still in the hospital. A written report of this hospital room observation was also submitted to the supervision group.
3. Post-birth: home setting. An independent group of four observers and two psychoanalyst supervisors was formed for this stage of the research. Each home observer in this group made an initial contact with the expectant mother at the penultimate ultrasound session. The procedure adopted for this stage was the Bick standard observation method. The observations were conducted on a weekly basis for the first six months of the baby's life, and the observer's written reports were read and discussed by the supervision group. Changes were made to the frequency of

observation sessions after the first six months: from six to twelve months of life the sessions were conducted twice a week, from twelve to twenty-four months they were monthly, and from twenty-four to thirty-six months they were quarterly. Another modification was that every six months the mother–infant pair was filmed by someone other than the case observer.[10]

Writing challenges in a fourth phase of the Bick method: publication

Once the observations were concluded in the baby's third year of life, we were confronted with the same challenges faced by analysts intending to write about their clinical experience. Making this experience public is, and always will be, a challenge, as evidenced by the small number of psychoanalytic clinical cases that are published. Its creative nature brings unconscious material to life. There is an aspect to it of giving birth, remembering that no one is born on his or her own. On the other hand, writing also brings suffering, since the raw material that analysts work with is the unconscious, which provokes internal and external resistance. Clinical work deals with memory fragments that register intense emotional experiences that are difficult to translate into words, much less publish. It is at this point that the challenge of exposure grows exponentially.

After several years of work and not always successful attempts to transmit our lived experiences with mothers and babies, we wrote an article about the challenge of writing for observers using the Bick method (Caron et al., 2012).[11]

In this article, we proposed an optional fourth phase where the observation material is published, to be added to the original three phases described in Chapter One—observation, written report, and supervision. Reaching this fourth phase means the material, which was initially for the observer's private use and purposes, should be translated into a language understandable to a larger, unknown audience.

As in the second stage, once again, the observer is faced with the challenge of writing and communicating an experience. Faced with this challenge, she tends to use the figures of speech commonly used in literary writing, for example, those that seek to touch the reader with the words, in order also to provide an emotional experience. We believe that the contents originating from these experiences can be passed on to the reader, and enable him or her to experience them at an obviously more integrated level of listening to listening. Ogden (2002) notes that this is the literary style of Winnicott, who seeks to convey his deep knowledge of primitive emotional development using language to create experiences in the readers, given that the literary style and the content of the text are inseparable. Thus, Winnicott, with his seemingly simple and straightforward writing style, touches the readers through the impact generated by way of not only his words, but also of the emotional tone that governs his writing.

In this new transformation of the material, the author finds him or herself with the task of having to highlight certain more expressive aspects that emerge from the material and give them theoretical contours. There begins another journey, in which, through writing, the observer tries to allow the reader to experience some of his or her own experiences while also sharing some theoretical and practical conclusions. While some aspects are explored and examined in depth, others, just as rich, become inevitably overshadowed, as it would be impossible to cover all aspects in an in-depth manner. Through this personal or theoretical construction, the author leaves his or her own mark on the text, with its potential and its limitations, which may be challenged by other readers. Moreover, she shows aspects of herself and of the whole process which she could be uncomfortable with or afraid to expose. Freud (1905e), in the preliminary notes to his description of the case of Dora, pointed out his discomfort about publishing such intimate notes of a case, anticipating possible criticism by his peers.

Therefore, this fourth stage requires courage and motivation to expose oneself and exchange ideas with colleagues. Although there is this great challenge, which causes many excellent projects not to reach this stage and to end in being shelved, we emphasise its importance for the advancement of psychoanalytic theory and technique. What direction would psychoanalysis have taken if some theoretical publications, now classic, had not been published? Perhaps today we would not be writing this book if Esther Bick had not published the articles that revealed her brilliant discovery of the infant observation method (Bick, 1964), as well as the theoretical articles derived from it (Bick, 1968).

Maybe, at this stage, it is important to emphasise the potential contribution of workgroups. The different components of the same group provide the observer with different views on the same fact (as in the third stage of the Bick method). Writing can also benefit a great deal from being constructed with colleagues. The group, when composed of members who work together creatively, produces a fertile ground where ideas/seeds have a place to germinate, when fertile, or remain in a dormant state when sterile. This flow of ideas between different members of the group allows the initially partial views of each to obtain a place in the minds of the others, who, in turn, complete, enhance, and modify. Thus, the group carries on, spiralling upward, sharing and constructing new ideas. Thus, it might be that, through these workgroups, we could come closer to the truth. The group lets itself be touched by the live mother–infant–observer experience. When this process, which is supported by the group, continues, new meanings emerge as well as the unexpected possibility of sharing access to newly emerging psychological truths.

In our research experience with the Bick method, we have made use of a kind of group discussion which we believe to be of great use in the fourth stage, Through this method, it is possible to establish a deep and intimate exchange of ideas, in the context of a welcoming and facilitating environment, in which each group member can rely on one another, and which results in a joint construction based on openness and reliability. This way, ideas can be freely expressed, and then be supported or refuted, always with the aim of creating a dialogue that is rich and creative, never saturated. This stage is in line with the ideal of remaining as open as possible to the others' experience, always allowing each member to be affected by, and to affect others with, her ideas and perceptions. It is amazing how the observer goes on reliving the experience with every opportunity he has to return to the material, and repeatedly allows himself to be affected by the experience, which is at the core of research in psychoanalysis.

Here lies the great challenge of writing material for publication, where a balance needs to be found. On the one hand, one risks giving in to academic requirements and being overly conclusive and objective, narrowing the material too much, and, thus, eliminating its wealth and its great potential to generate new questions. On the other hand, if one goes to the other extreme, one risks giving in to the temptation of revealing every intense experience provided by this type of research in too much detail, of overly expanding the material and making it so subjective that research could become endless and, above all, incomprehensible to the larger audience.

It should be noted that the challenge of writing is present throughout the observer's journey through the Bick method. It is especially challenging when such writing involves an element of translation of an intimate experience, which must be both recognised as personal and validated as communicable, while helping in the formulation of new ideas and new theoretical constructs.

In the following chapters, we present the clinical reports generated by the group discussions of the observations conducted in the first and second stages of our research. These reports were based on readings of the raw material and produced by us in collaboration with experienced infant observation work groups that had had no direct contact with the observed cases. Observers of the first and second stage did not exchange information among themselves, during or after completion of the observations.

PART II

MOTHERS' AND BABIES' JOURNEYS IN THE FIRST THREE YEARS OF LIFE

Observers and supervisors who accompanied the trajectory of the infants were: first group: observations of ultrasounds (in the ultrasound room) and deliveries (in the delivery room): Josênia Heck Munhoz, Vera Lúcia Teixeira, Vanya Elizabeth Dalcin, Aline Grill Gomes, Nara Amalia Caron (supervisor), Rita Sobreira Lopes (supervisor).

Second group: standard observation (at home, up to three years): Tatiana Ruffoni, Cátia Correa, Lisiane Oliveira-Menegotto, Paula Esteves Daubt Sarmento Leite, Beatriz Chwartzmann, Ivanosca I. Martini (supervisor), Angela Wirth Fleck (supervisor).

Other groups that collaborated at different points throughout the research: ultrasound images group: Lisandre Matte, Rodrigo Mendonça Valmor Boettcher, Carolina Chem, Vanessa Heck, Monica Echeverria de Oliveira.

Foetal movements group: Daniela Levandowski, Daniela Schwengber, Clarissa Corrêa Menezes, Giana Frizzo.

First discussion group for the observation cases: Aline Groff Vivian, Clarissa Corrêa Menezes, Gabriela Schumann Bichinho Anton, Gabriela Filipouski, Maria Cristina Bressani, Nara Amalia Caron, Rita Sobreira Lopes.

Second discussion group for the observation cases: Margared Steigler, Denise Steibel, Lea Lubianca Thormann, Marlete Diesel, Nara Amalia Caron, Rita Sobreira Lopes.

CHAPTER THREE

Maiara and her twins, Raoni and Anahi: one womb to gestate two, each in its own time

Pregnancy

We accompanied Anahi and Raoni's life story from their eleventh week of gestation until they were three years old by observing eight ultrasounds, the delivery, and by conducting forty-nine home observations. They are fraternal twins.

The observer's first impression when she was introduced to the parents was a welcoming sense of peacefulness that continued throughout the rest of the pregnancy and after.

> When I entered the ultrasound examination room, I had a good feeling, a mixture of tranquillity and receptivity. The room was darkened and there was an air of quietude. The doctor introduced me to the couple and they both smiled and greeted me. I went to the corner of the room where the father was, with a sense of walking into a special sacred place.

The mother, whose name appears to indicate that she is of indigenous origin, is thirty-nine years old, of medium height and large-boned, with a broad face, and wide hips and shoulders. She has short wavy black hair, big brown almond-shaped eyes, and the dark complexion of a native Brazilian. She seems nice as she smiles and expresses herself, and she speaks slowly and infrequently.

> My attention was immediately drawn to the mother's belly, which was large and broad. My first thought was, what a coincidence, she has room for two.

This image of her, pregnant, with ample hips to contain the growth of foetuses, remained throughout the ultrasound observations, and later that image of safe containment expanded to include her four-year-old son, her husband, the doctor, and the observer. Although the mother is silent during most of the examination, she pays close attention to the images on the monitor. It is an active silence. She is very observant and tries to tell the babies apart, for example, their little arms and legs. She says: "Look at their little feet." She looks for individual characteristics and differences between them.

The father is a thirty-eight-year-old white man of small stature with brown eyes and a bald head. He also seems nice. He is interested in the pregnancy and happy that they are twins. He collaborates and pays attention to the images of the babies. Husband and wife seem to fit; they complement each other in an attuned relationship that has room for movement. The mother is satisfied with being closely followed: "I was happy to learn I would have a psychologist with me, because I already have a son who is four years old and I'm worried about his reaction to the arrival of the babies . . . especially because they are twins."

From the beginning, each baby has its own space, as described in the eleventh week examination. The observer says,

> When looking at the first images of the babies on the monitor, I was struck by how each baby seemed to be in a small dark cave separated by a thin wall, allowing each its own space. Physically, the two were fully formed. The babies were still, and the sonographer said they were sleeping. They had their heads positioned in opposite directions and one was above the other in a complementary position.

The observer describes feeling as if she were entering the mother's belly and going inside the cave to accompany the lives developing there.

Thus, from the beginning, the observer and the rest of the team are invited to enter this sacred space, the womb. As we will see, this invitation speaks volumes about Maiara's rare ability to accommodate unusual situations such as a twin pregnancy in a very natural and ordinary manner. This receptive environment affects everyone, including the sonographer, who realises that the mother has the capacity to discriminate, which she values in the examinations.

The sense of welcome emanating from this womb is such that it affects how we write about this case. Not surprisingly, almost half of this chapter is dedicated to the gestation period. Maiara offers us a unique opportunity to learn about what it means to have the internal intrauterine space to safeguard, gestate, and give birth at the right time. We were delighted with the opportunity to watch these two lives blossom in a wealth of unique details that only a mother like Maiara could provide.

At the first ultrasound examination, the father asks, "Is there any connection between when the mother sleeps and the babies sleep?" The sonographer says there is not, because normally babies establish their own separate rhythm. The mother pays close attention to the monitor, her eyes wide and eyebrows raised. Her mouth is slightly open as she cranes her neck to see her babies better, giving the impression that she is trying to capture them from every angle possible and get to know even their smallest details. Her glance is an internal search that involves her body, too: she sees with her mouth, her eyebrows, and her muscles that strain to reach something. This remarkable image is seen repeatedly as the examinations progress: as the mother gazes at her babies, her body seems to acquire eyes. There is a combination of being doubly happy about the pregnancy, and of being apprehensive and awed at the task of sustaining these lives. Will a twin pregnancy require double the effort?

The babies begin to move. The baby on the bottom moves first, in waves, like a dolphin diving in and out of the water. It moves its head up and down, belly side up. While this one is very active and agile, the other one at the top remains quiet and still, belly side down.

The sonographer checks their measurements: the one on top measures 4.6 mm and the one below, 4.4 mm. The father says that the babies have grown, remembering the first ultrasound measurements. His comments show how, from the beginning, he is in tune with the pregnancy and in contact with the babies.

The baby on top wakes up, giving the observer the impression that the other had awakened it. The father asks the sonographer: "Is one kicking the other already?" The sonographer replies, "Not yet. Right now they are only slightly aware of not being alone. Later, however, they will start touching each other and then they won't stop kicking!" Everyone laughed.

The observer was impressed by the father's comments that seemed to express what she was seeing in the babies' movements, which was a fluidity moving from the inside to the outside and *vice versa*. A harmonious communication begins to develop in the ultrasound environment. The observer's sensitive and subtle reporting expresses her growing involvement and empathy towards the couple and the babies: she wants to see. In the second examination, the observer describes the feeling of "beginning to be able to see more" when the mother's pubic hair shows. Could this be a circular or empathetic network of communication?

The two babies move faster, diving in opposite directions, doing a kind of swinging ballet: one above the other, both lying face up.

The mother asks the doctor if it is possible to see the babies' arms and legs a little better. At that moment, the baby on the bottom turns sideways and kicks, as if it had heard the mother and was trying to show her what it could do best. Once again, the communication in this environment is finely tuned and harmonious. Maiara's womb is special in that it stimulates a desire to be inside its pleasant and welcoming space.

When the observer meets the couple for the twelfth week ultrasound, she describes being eager to see them and find out about the babies, and once again feels welcomed.

> I'm excited to see both parents, which I associate to this being a pregnancy with two babies, which requires greater care in the form of, say, a bigger belly, more space, two parents, more people getting involved with the babies, or a mother with a very good holding capacity. When the ultrasound begins, my attention is drawn to how the father positions himself next to his wife and the monitor so he can see the monitor better. He seems to want to see what is really happening and how the babies are doing.

When the sonographer asks about how far along the pregnancy is, the mother answers confidently and accurately what the babies' weights and positions had been at the last ultrasound. She says, "I am twelve weeks along. Today they are facing the same way. Last time, they were facing in opposite directions." She once again pays close attention, is perceptive, and connected to both babies, and is able to discriminate better between the babies: what they do and what she thinks they are, or will be, like. The observer focuses on the image of each baby in its own small cave, separated by a thin wall.

The sonographer announces that she will start the procedure of measuring the babies. A silence settles over the room and both babies and parents are still. The father says it must be difficult to identify which baby is which. The sonographer measures them both: the one on top is 62 mm and the one on the bottom is 59 mm. The father comments that they have grown almost one centimetre since the last scan, showing that he is attentive and connected to the babies. The sonographer confirms the measurements remembered by the father and asks if they want to know the sex of the babies, warning them that there is an error margin of ten per cent. They immediately agree and the images confirm that one is a boy and the other is almost certainly a girl. The mother happily exclaims, "A couple!" She smiles at the observer, who smiles back, and grips the father's arm.

Later on in the examination the doctor mentions another woman who is pregnant with quadruplets and Maiara asks about their sexes. The sonographer answers that three are boys and one is a girl. Maiara says, "A girl! That's good; at least there is one girl!" The sonographer then performs a nuchal translucency scan, and the results are normal. The babies' strong, vibrant heartbeats make the observer think she is in the drumming section of a samba school. The father says that one of the babies' heartbeats "is beating a million miles an hour: dum, dum, dum . . ." The parents' comments express their happiness about the sex of the babies and the nuchal translucency results. The mother immediately thinks of their elder son, saying he is going to love the idea of having a little sister. She cries, saying it is a "relief to know that everything is normal with the babies".

At that moment, the girl wakes up and starts moving and creating waves, giving the impression that she is hitting her brother again. The boy wakes up and joins the rhythmic wave motions of his sister. The father asks, "Did one just hit the other?" He again verbalises what the observer's thoughts and perceptions are. It seems that these intrauterine rhythmic movements come from inside the mother's belly and affect the external environment. Coincidentally, a similar harmonious network of communication and perception is also circulating in the external environment.

The babies continue to move in waves. The girl turns face down and shows her little foot, evoking comments from the mother. One of them shows its face. Then the two are visible at the same time, causing the observer to feel as if they want to be together but to be seen as two. They seem to have an unspoken intrauterine agreement occupying this space—a space made up of two for two. It is as if they are saying, "If we help each other there will be space for both of us." The mother is impressed at how much they move. She says, "Good Lord! They're so active!" The mother's comments indicate her satisfaction at both babies having survived until now.

The next examination took place at the seventeenth week of pregnancy. The parents continue to be friendly, receptive, and seemingly relaxed. The mother's belly has grown visibly, her uterus expanding to accommodate what it carries. She knows exactly how far along her pregnancy is and remains attentive to everything related to her pregnancy and her babies. Today, she wants to know if she can see the babies together on the monitor. The sonographer said it might be difficult, since the further along the pregnancy and the more they grow, the harder it will be to see them together. However, the babies contradict the sonographer and her explanation, appearing together on the monitor. They have grown, and seem to fill almost the entire intrauterine space. The cave impression has now been replaced by one of *place*.

The babies are positioned facing the same side, one above the other. The sonographer shows the parents the girl first, and then the boy. She measures their size and asks the parents if they know which baby is in which position and place in the womb. Looking at the monitor, the father replies that the girl is above and the boy is below, which the sonographer confirms. The mother observes her belly and points out the babies' positions with her finger, saying, "This is the boy and this is the girl." She seems to externally demarcate each baby's place, as if drawing a map of a country and its territories, thus creating external representations to support her internal and psychic representations of the babies. She seems to wonder: who are these babies? What are they like? Where are they? What do they do? What do they like? What are their personalities like?

The next sequence of scans shows how the babies' physical space has developed, which helps to build the mother's psychic space regarding the babies, which will, in turn, help to build the babies' identities.

The sonographer registers the weight of both babies as 190 grams, and gives a number to each one—the boy is number one and the girl is number two—which is recorded on the video scan. In this manner, she non-verbally records the intrauterine birth of the babies. It is as if the sonographer senses the mother's need to register each child and, therefore, provides a solution. The girl is facing forward and waves. The mother smiles and waves back at her daughter. Their communication is defining itself.

The babies begin to communicate formally by making gestures, moving their bodies, and touching. They seem aware of each other. The girl faces her brother, as if looking at him. She moves down a little, and he runs his hand over her head. The father notices and says, "Did one just hit the other?" The girl bends her head forward, giving the impression she is leaning her forehead against her brother's belly. It is a beautiful scene that shows the intense relationship the twins seem to share.

The twins' older brother, Jandir, is getting used to the idea of becoming a brother. Initially, he watches the taped scans at home, alternating between watching his siblings' taped scans and his own taped scans, which he takes to school. Then he comes to the twenty-second week examination and wants attention. He tells the sonographer, "Take the little brothers out of there; I want to see them. Can you open up her belly? I'm dying to see them. . . . I wish they would come out of mummy's belly so I could wrestle with them." Everyone laughed. The sonographer says the babies have to stay "quiet inside mummy's belly, because they need to grow some more before they are born; let's have a look at them in there." This examination forecasts the coming birth.

The mother is relaxed and everything is happening in its own time. Typical of a child, Jandir wants everything immediately, yet his parents handle him calmly in a way that acknowledges his needs. Maiara tells her son to quiet down and the father reinforces this by holding him, "so we can see your little brothers". He speaks affectionately with his son, trying to calm him down. Jandir is contained by his father, who once again proves to be strong, assertive, and able to establish limits to contain environments of distress such as this one with the restless boy.

During the examination, Jandir tries to monopolise the sonographer's attention. He asks for the tube of gel, wants to leave the room, insists that his mother look at him and not at the babies, and demands to see his little sister several times, especially her genitals. In this preview of the sibling rivalry that is to come, the father takes charge and explains what is happening to his child, demonstrating he has the ability to carry out the paternal function in this pregnancy.

The babies' genitalia is clearly visible, first the boy's and then the girl's. Jandir says he wants a girl and appears to have calmed down a bit, perhaps because of having to face only one rival of the same sex in the future. The babies' faces are visible and for the first time the observer can identify the differences in their facial features: the girl has a smaller feminine face and chubby cheeks. The boy has a bigger and thinner boyish face. They are calm and quiet as they look out from the monitor.

The sonographer examines the babies' organs and weighs them: the boy weighs 526 grams and the girl weighs 540. They have doubled in size and the mother says she is not surprised, because "my belly has grown from one minute to the next", showing with her hands how much her belly had become bigger. She is a sensitive and very aware mother and says she thinks the babies are "all right in there since there's still enough space, right?" The mother can sense that the babies still need to stay inside, and she has the time and space to wait. The sonographer agrees with the mother. She then asks if the babies have names, to which the mother replies quite naturally and calmly that they are still thinking about it. The brother mentions some names and says that the babies do not cheer for the mother's favourite football team, but that they cheer for the same one he and his father support. The mother disagrees, saying that as long as the babies are inside her, they cheer for her football team. Jandir says, "Mummy is going to the rubbish." She says, "Heavens, child! Don't talk like that." Jandir says that after the babies are born they will cheer for Grêmio,[12] to which the father says, "Obviously!" Jandir whispers, "I'll take mum out of the rubbish", and then asks the observer for sweets and lollipops. In the end, the father leaves the room with his son before the end of the examination. The husband and wife have a good relationship, each with their own function and space that allows differences to be expressed within the family, which now includes the observer, who provides a consistent emotional presence.

The babies lie face-to-face, giving the impression that they are looking at each other, talking and touching in a way that creates a sense of intimacy and relationship. It is evident at this ultrasound exam that the maternal and paternal function being played out facilitates the babies' development in the intrauterine space.

The mother complains of discomfort for the first time during the examination in the twenty-sixth week. She says, "My belly is bigger and sometimes it is difficult to move." She asks the sonographer to examine "a burning sensation on the left side of my belly, just under my ribs . . . it's as if a piece of muscle is coming off my ribs; it burns."

The observer is reminded of the biblical legend of how God created Eve from Adam's rib. Maiara is halfway through her second trimester and approaching the last one before childbirth. Could this "muscle coming off" be her expression of a fantasy of the birth of the babies? Or could it be her concern about childbirth?

The sonographer examines the babies. Initially, they move a lot and their faces cannot be seen as sharply as in previous scans. They have grown and almost doubled their weight—the girl is 924 grams and the boy is 886. The mother remarks how the girl is still bigger than the boy. As always, she remembers the babies' previous measurements, showing that she is still attentive to the changes in their details and growth. The doctor finds no physical explanation for the burning sensation the mother complains about. She says that her cervix is excellent, and could even hold four, and says that the pain might be linked to the babies' growth, as they fill out the spaces inside her belly.

Just as the mother has a cervix that could hold four, she also has the psychic space to hold her anxieties while she prepares for delivery, and devotes herself to her son, whose birthday is at the weekend. The father says they will not take the ultrasound tape to watch at home, because it is Jandir's birthday and they want him to have all the attention.

In previous examinations, the girl had moved more than the boy. In this one, the boy is much more active than usual, although the girl still moves more. She shows her face, genitals, and little hands more times. The mother says, "You should see them! They make such big bumps on my belly! They pop up all over the place." The sonographer says the girl is "a little imp; she doesn't stop moving for a second. She is having a party in there." The parents smile and show their satisfaction when the doctor says the babies continue to develop normally.

After the ultrasound, when they were scheduling their next appointment, the mother expresses her anxiety about the twin pregnancy in a rare moment of showing her frustration that will only be seen again when the babies are three months old. She says her "belly is very big; I don't know much more I can take", mentioning that her belly is almost as big as it was at the end of her last pregnancy. She also says that the obstetrician gave her some medicine "to help the babies' lungs mature" and that she thought the delivery would be "two months from now". The father says he believes she will be able to carry the pregnancy to full term. The mother seems reassured by his comment. This conversation with the parents after the examination shows how the burning sensation the mother felt was related to her anxiety about childbirth and of a possible premature delivery, and also shows how the father anchors and supports the mother, who is experiencing not only a different pregnancy but perhaps a more intense one because of carrying twins: things are duplicated.

Before the examination in the thirty-first week, the second observer, who will accompany the family after the babies are born, is introduced. It is interesting that the mother barely looks at her, does not speak much, and gives only brief answers to her questions. The father gives her their home address and they say goodbye. The mother wants to wait for the examination in the waiting room because "It is too hot in here."

What heated the environment upon the arrival of the new observer seems to have once again been the prospect of the approaching birth and the presence of the new—still unfamiliar, but already known. It is an announcement of change: from the first observer to a new observer, from the time of now to later, from the time of the babies inside her belly to the time of the babies being outside. The new is circulating the environment, bringing changes and separations. The mother wants to leave the hot room, as if she is asking to cool it. It sounds like a request to cool the heat of the emotions, as if she needs additional time to gestate her feelings and ideas regarding the approaching new experiences. The mother's ability to continue gestating is equivalent to the abilities necessary for analytic skills.

At the beginning of the examination, the father says the observer's name for the first time, asking her about how the delivery will be recorded. She is thrilled to hear her name, as if this registers their bond and the parents' ability to discriminate and separate. The observer's surprise expresses the pleasure one has when something experienced internally becomes reality, and the father made this happen.

The sonographer locates the babies, and, to everyone's surprise, they are positioned upside down, as if ready to be born; the girl a bit higher in the womb and the boy further down. The father asks the doctor if this is their final position. She says no, that there is still enough amniotic fluid and space for them to move. The mother says, "That's good!" The boy, weighing 1,876 grams, appears on the monitor and begins to move, seemingly having heard his mother's request for him to show signs of life. The girl weighs 1,742 grams, and the mother says, "Wow, she's so big; she's doubled in size. She was 900 plus grams the last time." The subtle details of each baby are visible and noted:

> The little girl's hair, the movement of her eyelashes . . . the boy's testicles are visible and the father smiles . . . he has his father's nose and his mother's full lips . . .

The rich details and peculiarities are delightful. The babies move peacefully and everyone in the room can see their details. There is a sense of harmony and communication between the babies. They expose themselves and their particularities. Their differences, such as their noses, mouths, cheeks, and different movements and rhythms can be seen more clearly. The girl seems to be always seeking out physical contact with her brother, usually taking the initiative to find him. Her higher level of activity has been evident in the scans from the very beginning. The observer describes her curiosity to see what these two will be like after birth and her intense desire to accompany their delivery.

The seventh examination takes place in Maiara's thirty-fifth week of pregnancy. Her belly is beautiful to look at, well rounded like a balloon. Despite the size of her belly, the mother appears to be physically fine, and as always, she is sure about the time, space, weight, and location of the babies. She is now more sensitive and complains about feeling discomfort and pressure during the examination. The sonographer examines her and brings up the ultrasound image: their two little heads can be seen, and then one turns its face to the side, showing its profile and swallowing. She says that at this point in the pregnancy it is uncommon to be able to see the babies together like this. "This is good! We can see them." The parents are focused on the image, smiling.

Once again the two little heads and their hair is visible. The babies are right side up, lying next to each other. The boy is positioned on the right side of the womb. His genitals, his little head, and his back are visible, and his feet point toward the left. The girl is on the mother's left side. You can see her ribs, and the sonographer says, "Her bottom is against her brother's legs, she's anchored to him." They are beginning to fit together.

The mother says, "What a little rascal! She's on his lap!" She holds her husband's hand, and the observer thinks Maiara is identifying with the baby girl, in the sense that she is also in need of a lap at this point in her pregnancy, which might be more difficult for physical reasons such as the size of her stomach, having to carry babies now that they are larger and heavier, and perhaps also for emotional reasons due to the forthcoming delivery.

The mother asks, "What is that?" She moans and scrunches up her face, pressing her belly in what seems to be expressions of pain and discomfort. The sonographer says it is the boy's foot. She shows her the boy's foot, and says, "He must be kicking a lot in there." The mother smiles. The image of the boy's foot reminds the observer of the expression "to hit the road". The babies are "hitting the road" of life, ready to come into the world that is outside their mother's belly. There is a sense that the babies' movements represent a series of changes, not only to the relationships within the family, but also to external relationships, for example, between the family and the observer.

The observer suddenly realises that this is the last observation with this family, which makes her become emotional. She thinks of the mother's discomfort and knows it will be difficult to separate herself from these parents and their babies. On the other hand, the harmony and positive circulation between them and their babies in this environment is delightful. Seeing the baby's little foot triggers a series of associations and comments from the people in the examination room. The subject now revolves around the delivery, birth, changes, and separations.

The mother asks if the babies' heads are really pointing up, and if they might still turn their heads down. The sonographer explains that at this stage of the pregnancy, babies do not change positions any more. She questions the mother's concern, and she explains that the obstetrician had told her that if the babies were in the birthing position, "it would be easier to get the babies out. He said he would only use his hand like this, and pull." She motions with a twist of her hand. "But with their heads up here, he said he would need to do something else that I didn't quite understand. I just know he said it will be more work during the delivery."

The sonographer tells the mother not to not worry because the obstetrician is used to babies giving him trouble, and that "Babies are supposed to be a lot of work; they mess things up a bit." The father adds, "Imagine, him not wanting any trouble! He'll have to work hard, believe me!" Everyone laughed. The mother smiles and her face relaxes, seeming relieved to be able to share her fears about any problems that might occur with the twin births. It is clear that although they want the babies to be born healthy and safe, they are concerned about the delivery—a delicate moment of life and death anxieties.

The babies have gained 600 grams since the last examination. The weight difference between the two is insignificant, with the boy weighing 2,455 grams and the girl 2,630. The mother exclaims, "She passed him again! Wow!" The babies' little heads can be seen side by side, and the membrane that both separates and unites them seems very thin.

The eighth ultrasound at thirty-seven weeks had not been planned. Five days earlier, Maiara had called saying that the obstetrician had asked for another ultrasound closer to the delivery day. She asks if the observer could come, and she agrees.

As usual, at the examination the mother seems calm, physically healthy, and beautiful. Her body shape has not changed except for her belly, which is much bigger. She and her husband smile at the observer. The observer describes her as a woman–mother that maintains her own shape, despite having a balloon belly. Maiara and Moacir have eyes that smile; they are the very picture of a host couple for the babies. As usual, the parents' orientation, their perception of details, and their ability to discriminate with regard to their babies is impressive. These characteristics have been present in all the observations, from the first one until this last one.

The sonographer begins the examination and says she does not know whose head appears on the monitor. The mother says it is the boy's head, since "the boy is on the right side of her belly and the girl on the left ... the two of them had their little heads up here the last time." The mother's attentiveness is impressive; she is always looking to differentiate and discriminate between what belongs to each baby.

The mother asks if the babies have turned. The sonographer replies that it is impossible for them to turn at this point in the pregnancy, especially because they are twins. The examination continues with the sonographer describing as she tracks the images with the transducer probe: the boy is lying right side up on the right side and the girl should be right side up on the left side. Then, to the sonographer's surprise, where she expected to find the baby's head she finds its legs and umbilical cord. She says in amazement, "Can you believe it? She turned! That's incredible! What a little rascal!" Her head is leaning against her brother's belly so that they fit together.

The mother says, "Oh! How sweet! She's leaning her head against him! I'm so glad she turned! Thank God!" She recalls that she had told the obstetrician she had a feeling the girl had turned because "last week she was making all kinds of bumps here on the left side of my belly. Then I felt a sharp pain and saw a bump here, and then I felt an empty space up here where the girl's head had been." The obstetrician had repeated that it would be good if one of the babies turned down to facilitate the birth, even in the case of a caesarean. In reporting this, the mother shows her ability to connect with her inner self and to realise what is happening with the lives developing inside her. She has the insight and discrimination to determine what belongs to her and what belongs to the babies. This fact leads us to believe that this facilitating environment will be most likely to foster good development for the babies. Both the parents and the babies have uncommon space and mobility in this context.

The sonographer jokingly says, "Now, here are her feet. What a rascal! This girl is going to give you a lot of work." She says that in all her years of doing ultrasounds, she had never seen twins turn this late in the pregnancy. The parents smile.

It is truly a lovely image! You can see the baby boy's eyes, nose, and mouth perfectly when he presses his face against the sac, which gives the impression of being a clear, soft, plastic curtain. Its transparency is inviting and allows those watching to enter. The observer describes:

> It is as if I were entering her belly and those small caves that I had seen earlier when I was introduced to the family.

The sonographer says the boy looks like the mother; they have same mouth and nose. The transparency is such that it allows the babies to be identified and differentiated, to begin existing with well-defined identities.

The sonographer then focuses on the girl's face, saying that her mouth and nose are similar to the father's. Everyone agrees. The boy weighs 2,636 grams and the girl, 2,889. As in previous exams, the mother says she feels bad that he always gains less weight, "Oh, poor thing! . . . It's because she was pressing against his belly with her head and wouldn't let him eat right, so he couldn't gain weight . . ." She laughs and glances at the observer. The father also looks at her, asking and asserting at the same time, "They are ready to be born, right?"

The sonographer emphasises the need to look carefully, since it is difficult to see the images clearly at the end of the pregnancy, especially in the case of twins. The boy's face, mouth, and nose are broad, and the girl's smaller, more rounded, and delicate—she really looks like a girl. The sonographer freezes the image, commenting how beautiful it is. Then she announces that this is the last time we will see the babies in the womb, because tomorrow we will see them on the outside. The observer's report is as follows.

> The room goes silent and we all stand motionless for a while, watching the babies. It is a very beautiful moment. On the one hand, it is a joy watching these babies, but on the other, I am saying goodbye to this stage of their lives. It has been a privilege to share in the intimacies and the development of the babies in the hope of better understanding the birth and emergence of human life that transforms itself into a physical, psychic body.

Delivery

The observer is excited as she begins this report, and cannot seem to find the words to describe this very intense moment.

> I'm afraid I won't be able to remember everything and make a good observation report.

The father calls about the time scheduled for the delivery. The observer meets the parents in the hospital lobby. The mother is quiet and serious, but alert and looking from one side to the other, walking fast—too fast, considering her large belly. The observer thinks she might be apprehensive, and remembers that when they first met she was even more reserved. The father is smiling and greets the observer with a kiss on the cheek, something unusual for him. The mother says that their eldest son is also there, but that he is sleeping, "which is a shame because he won't see his brother and sister." As always, the father calms his wife saying, "There's still plenty of time, he'll be awake by the time they come." Maiara's sister and Jandir's godmother, Ana, who is living with the family, is with him and says they are all set up for the arrival of the babies, which the father confirms.

The relatives begin to arrive: the paternal grandmother, the maternal grandparents, and aunts and uncles. The maternal grandmother is nervous and asks several questions that the observer answers, reassuring her that everything is fine. Maiara feels somewhat abandoned in the obstetric ward as she is being prepared for the delivery, and the obstetrician and anaesthestist are late. She says, "I can't find a comfortable position any more . . . I had to sleep on the living room sofa, because if I lay down I wouldn't be able to breathe." The husband comes over and helps her get more comfortable on the bed.

The observer asks about the babies' names and the mother says they will be called Anahi and Raoni. They are indigenous names and she explains their meaning. The names are beautiful and strong and refer to nature, specifically water and forest. It is interesting that the names for the babies have only come up now. It is another example of Maiara's ability to allow things to happen in their own time, from the inside out. This case shows us that the lack of a name does not necessarily mean there is no representation of the babies in the parents' psyches, which, conversely, means that the mere existence of a name does not mean that there is representation. The babies had a very clear place in Maiara's physical and psychic space from the beginning of her pregnancy.

An assistant leads Maiara to the delivery room, and the observer waits in the corridor with the father. She leans against the wall and watches the hospital traffic. There are many births that night, and parents, babies, and doctors come and go. The obstetric clinic is filled with the cries of newborn babies as if it were music. The father comes over and says he is "starting to get nervous". He talks about their house and how he wished they could have moved into a larger place before the babies were born. He is concerned because they have only two bedrooms. But then again, they are more organised now than they had been when their eldest was born, rushing to get things done. He says he will have to see about the house. The father quite clearly takes on the function of being concerned about the space outside the belly, the external reality, which, unlike the psyche, has limits. He talks about how two babies, in the external reality, take up more space than one baby. He is worried, wondering how to provide more external space for the babies to grow in, a concern that will mark his participation in the first three years of the twins' lives.

The obstetrician calls them. The father goes to stand next to his wife and the observer positions herself behind him. The mother looks at her and smiles. She asks about the paediatrician, and the anaesthestist says he will be right there. She says she is not feeling well, that she feels lightheaded. She asks again for the paediatrician. The doctor assisting the obstetrician says, "The babies will not be born without the paediatrician." The obstetrician confirms this and the mother relaxes. She shows her concern for the babies, which are heard and respected by the medical team.

> The paediatrician enters the room accompanied by a colleague. They get into position to receive the babies. I follow them and stand next to the paediatrician. The obstetrician says the babies are coming and wants to see who will be first. He breaks the sac and eases out the bottom baby first; it is the boy. The doctor suctions him quickly and firmly. He cries weakly and sounds as if he is choking. His skin is whitish purple and he seems to have breathed in some liquid. They give him oxygen and his colour improves slightly, but he still seems weak as he lies with his legs and arms flopped apart. He keeps his eyes closed. The paediatrician wraps the baby in a cloth, wipes his face, and takes him to his mother. She kisses him, saying, "Oh, poor little thing! Quick, take care of him, quick." He says everything is fine, and leaves immediately with the boy.

The obstetrician breaks the second sac saying, "Now the girl. She has a lot of hair! Here she comes!" He eases her out, head first. She comes out crying loudly, and her colour is pinker than the boy's. Her birth seems to have gone smoother and she looks fine. The paediatrician takes the girl gently and cleans her face and little head then takes her to her mother. The baby stops crying when she is near her mother and her eyes are open. The mother says, "She's so sweet", crying and kissing her daughter. The paediatrician says that the girl is doing well, and that he'll bring her right back.

Just as in the ultrasound examinations, the mother pays close attention to everything. Now she asks about the babies' differences in colour and reactions, which the paediatrician explains, and she relaxes. He asks the father to accompany him. The observer congratulates the mother, who smiles, closes her eyes, and sighs, perhaps in relief or joy.

In the examination room, the boy is being given oxygen and the paediatrician suctions large amounts of secretion from him. He explains that because the boy was breech he had inhaled liquid, but that he would be fine. The observer remembers the mother's concern about the babies' positions. Even if the birth had been by caesarean, it would have been important for them to be positioned with their heads down to make their delivery easier. The paediatrician asks the father to come close to his daughter and help weigh her. The female pediatrician uses her index fingers to hold the girl in a standing position, and the baby grips tightly to the paediatrician's fingers. Her strong movements are a delight and reminiscent of her intrauterine movements of always being the one to initiate movements and trying to get close to her brother. She truly is very active, moving a lot and keeping her eyes open the entire time, without crying. She weighs 2,335 grams, measures 46 cm, and has an Apgar score of 8/9.

While she measures the girl, she asks the male paediatrician to turn the boy on his side so he could expel fluids better. His colour improves slightly, but he still lies limp with his legs and arms apart. They give him more oxygen. The paediatrician inserts a tube into the boy's nose to suction out any lung secretions. He cries, but starts breathing better and his colour improves. They take his measurements and he weighs 2,445 grams, is 47 cm long, and has an Apgar score of 7/9. His eyes are still closed. The father asks if his son is "really OK". The paediatrician says he is, his glucose is just a little low, but that is not a problem, he is going to be fine.

The babies are dressed and taken to their mother. One baby is placed on either side of her, and she kisses each one. The girl's eyes are open and she is very alert, as if she wants to see what is going on around her. The boy's eyes are closed and he whimpers a little. The mother kisses him saying, "Oh, poor little thing." She says she has an "itchy nose", to which the paediatrician says, "Poor thing", and scratches her nose for her. She says the babies are fine and that she will help the father take them out for the family to see. But the father is able to hold them both, one in each arm.

The observer says goodbye to the mother, saying she did very well and that her babies are very beautiful and healthy. Maiara smiles and thanks her "for everything". The observer is very moved and says she will call the next day to see how things are going. She also says goodbye to the paediatricians and the family.

The next day, the observer phones Maiara and learns that she and Anahi had stayed up all night watching Raoni in recovery, but that he is fine. Maiara hands the phone over to the father, who gives her more details. Last of all, the observer says goodbye to the father.

Accompanying this family until the birth of the twins and the end of this stage of observation was a positive and exciting experience for the observer, who felt close to the parents after participating in this very intimate and private time in their lives. The delivery had taken the same pace as the pregnancy, meaning there was a sense of calm, tranquillity, security, and concern for the babies that emanated from both the mother and father. Their relationship with the staff was empathetic and of mutual help. The father was close to the observer, and was always attentive and made sure she felt included in the family.

The observer found it interesting that when she first saw the babies, she felt she had already known them for a long time. Their little faces and expressions were exactly what they had been in the womb. The boy had a broader face and fuller lips, and the girl had more delicate features and fuller cheeks. The boy was more like his mother and the girl was more like her father. Their body movements and facial expressions at birth continued in the same ways. What they were seeing outside the mother's belly mirrored what they had seen in the womb. The girl was active and alert, kept her eyes open, and had firm muscles. The boy was more passive, kept his eyes closed as if he were sleeping, whimpered occasionally, and had less active muscle tone.

The observer left the hospital with the sense of mission accomplished.

The first three years of life

When the babies are three days old, the new observer visits them in the hospital. It was difficult to move around and "they were a bit disorganised and the room was a mess". Could this scene be an enactment of the impact these babies were having on the life of this family? The parents are radiant about their children and want to show them off. While the father goes to get some photos the mother starts pointing out the differences between the twins to the new observer: "The girl is the bigger eater, even though she was smaller when she was born, and she has learnt to breastfeed; Raoni is calmer, takes longer to do things, and has to take supplements." Thus, just as in the ultrasound exams, each baby has its own unique characteristics, and both are allowed to establish themselves authentically.

The home observations begin when the babies are twenty-two days old. Their place is found easily, which corroborates the open communication channels observed in this family. An environment that fosters growth, development, and observation is a facilitating one.

> Although simple, it is a new, well-organised structure with a lovely garden in front that is full of flowers and shrubs.

The front door is decorated with the announcement of the babies that had been on the hospital room door: "We're here!" The observer feels welcome and reports that Ana, Maiara's sister, looks a lot like Maiara and that she seemed to have been waiting for her. Everything communicates continuity from the intrauterine environment to delivery and post-birth.

The flat is relatively small for the size of the family. The mother sleeps in her own room and Anahi and Raoni begin their lives sleeping in their brother's room, which is described as follows:

> The room is small, all white, and has a single bed. The two prams, which are similar but not identical, are set up between the bed and the closet. I realised that this was the older son's room since it had his toys, a computer, and school materials . . ."

The observer has trouble finding a place to sit and feels a little cramped, thinking the house must have become smaller since the arrival of the twins. The babies are very different from each other and it is easy to distinguish them by their facial features.

> The boy has a thinner face, and more, spikier hair; the girl is chubbier, has rounded cheeks, and less hair. Raoni sleeps on green and white sheets, and Anahi on pink and white ones.

The discrimination between the babies is clear. Raoni moves a lot, whimpers, and stretches his legs, while Anahi sleeps peacefully. "The babies are quiet and only require attention to be fed," says the aunt, Maiara's sister. Maiara alternates breastfeeding both every three hours—day and night—and changes their nappies, which is quite tiring. The babies seem to respond well to this peaceful environment.

At twenty-seven days, the observer is received by a blond woman who looks about seventy years old. She says the mother and babies are asleep. On her way to the babies' room, the observer sees Maiara sound asleep in her room. The babies are also asleep on their brother's bed with pillows tucked around them, and a hotdog-type pillow between them. Although they are together, something separates them, which again conveys continuity from the intrauterine to the post-birth environment.

The observer notices that the babies are bigger and is surprised at how much they have developed in a week. She feels the room is less cramped and that the babies occupy "more space". The babies show they are interconnected in their behaviour as well, one watching and responding to the sounds and movements of the other:

> When Raoni moves and makes a louder noise, Anahi takes a deep and loud breath, like a sigh.

Anahi is aware of her brother's more agitated movements, and gives the impression that she is communicating with him: "I'm here, calm down". There is a wonderful harmony between the babies as they continue to communicate through breathing, sounds, and movements.

Until the babies are two months old, Maiara is somewhat withdrawn and sleeps through most observations. She takes advantage of Jandir being at school to rest after the babies are breastfed and in the care of their paternal grandmother. Maiara's reserved personality and ability to maintain her own rhythm are in continuity with the pregnancy period. She welcomes the care offered by her mother in-law, her sister, her mother, her husband, and, later, the nanny, who are all in such harmony in their care for the babies that they become a kind of extension of her belly. An example of this was a time when the father, who was taking care of Raoni, put the boy in the pram and he started crying. Maiara, in the other room changing Anahi, suggested, "Rock him and put his head a little lower, he must be sleepy." The father followed her suggestion and Raoni settled down quickly and almost fell asleep.

Gradually, they form an empathetic, respectful, and large "family-belly" that takes satisfaction in participating in the care of the babies and the mother. Maiara's relationship with her mother in-law is very sensitive, respectful, and reliable. When the mother in-law does something with the babies, she always asks Maiara how she would like her to do it; there is no competition between the two. During this period, the aunt and grandmothers are included into this new family nucleus, and represent its sensitive and non-invasive way of doing things.

The paternal grandmother says, "If we don't help Maiara, she won't be able to handle it. This is her time to rest because later on it's all on her . . ." Anahi continues sleeping calmly, and Raoni moves, mumbles, and seems uncomfortable. The grandmother picks him up and talks to him, smiling slightly. He strains upwards and looks firmly at his grandmother. She puts him back in the pram and caresses his belly until he goes back to sleep.

Maiara clearly develops the state of primary maternal preoccupation and becomes attuned to the pair she must relate to. She accepts and meets the needs of the babies well, and speaks calmly about how difficult it is to take care of two: "I'm fine, but tired . . . I tell you, it's a lot of work! But thank God they are doing really well! Just breastfeeding would be one thing, but it's changing nappies, breastfeeding, winding them, and when they fall asleep, the whole thing starts all over again. They nurse every three hours or so, meaning I don't get much sleep at night. But that will pass soon enough. Jandir started sleeping through most of the night by his third month. It's like this only when they're tiny!" (one month and eleven days).

Maiara is also present and has her own pace when taking care of her firstborn: "And then there's Jandir, we have to take care of him, too. Whenever he calls me I go, so he doesn't think that now I only take care of the babies . . . He says that when he calls me I have to go because he is number one and got here first. Sometimes I just get started nursing one of them and he calls, so I joke saying that number one was late and forfeited his turn to number two . . ."

Raoni and Anahi's characteristics and differences continue being noticed and mentioned by family members and the observer. The mother says, "The only thing that makes them twins is that they were born from the same belly together, because they are so different physically and in their personalities, ever since they were very small." At another observation, Maiara reports the breastfeeding schedule and comments, "He's like an alarm clock, any delays in his feeding schedule and he screams. Anahi is the opposite, I have to wake her to nurse, otherwise she'll sleep right through feeding time; she is much more relaxed about it. He can't stand waiting at all" (one month and eleven days). Another time, the grandmother says, "I think she will cheer for Colorado[13] like her mother and he will cheer for Grêmio. Moacir and Jandir are diehard *Gremistas* and Maiara is a *Colorada* . . . now I think she's looking for a partner" (one month and four days).

Male and female peculiarities that characterise this family begin to be noticed. At one point, the paternal grandmother says, "Look how quiet she is, but it's always that way. Raoni takes longer to quiet down; he's more restless and agitated. But then of course, he's a little boy. But she is always totally calm." Later, when referring to Anahi, she says, "She's a little doll, so calm and sweet."

When the babies are about two months old, some changes are noticed: the babies are moved out of the bedroom in their prams and into the living room, the mother leaves her room and participates more in the observations, toys are placed in the prams so the babies can see them, the "We're here" sign disappears, and Raoni is diagnosed with reflux.

Reality is introduced to the babies in this delicate and respectful rhythm. They gradually get to know the limits and possibilities of this family's interaction, which becomes the benchmark of their development. Over time, they are presented with new aspects of reality, and even their toys are added gradually to their daily lives. New toys and new play possibilities are offered a little at a time.

In this period, Maiara says she would like to spend time alone with her children and husband at the weekends, because she can count on Moacir's help and believes such moments are important. Her mother-in-law comments, "It's so wonderful; I like spending time with the children . . .. At the weekends Maiara wants to have more time alone with Moacir. He helps her and so no one has been coming. But during the week she wants help" (two months).

When the twins are two months and fourteen days, Maiara has been out of the house for the first time. She comes in happy and smiling, wearing her hair pulled back, lipstick, jeans, and a loose blouse. She is no longer wearing a nightgown and she looks healthy. The babies sleep in their prams: Anahi is covered with a white sheet and Raoni with a green one. Maiara naturally goes to her room, darkens it, and lies down. Everyone sleeps and the observer has to wake up the grandmother, who was taking a nap, to let her out.

The mother transmits her capacity for rebirth by occupying other spaces, by being able to come out of the regressive puerperal state along with the babies. Just as she did not indicate much need of the observer in the first two months of the babies' lives and allowed herself to sleep during observations, she also used the same attitude to protect herself at other times, such as when she was getting ready to go back to work, or when she was moving to another house, or when she decided to take an extended holiday. She interrupted the observations during those periods to take care of her own needs in a very direct and authentic way. It is worth noting her ability to take care of herself while, at the same time, being discretely able to pay close attention and be connected to the babies, thus respecting her needs as well as theirs. For example, when the babies are two months old, the observer writes,

> Maiara was quietly watching television, when she turns and says: "Look, he's trying to reach for the toys in the pram . . ." I don't know how she saw his gesture, since she had her eyes firmly on the television.

At two months and twenty-one days, Maiara is holding Raoni; he has reflux, and she slowly and patiently tries to soothe her son: "There is nothing I can do except stand with him in my arms." This is another example of the mother's ability to gestate, wait, and give adequate support at the right time. She talks to her son, asking if he feels better. He relaxes and falls asleep.

> Maiara was silent for some time, taking care of her son. At times she looked at us, but she was busy giving her full attention to Raoni. Meanwhile, Anahi slept quietly in her crib.

Now that he is calm, Maiara puts him into his pram and says, "He really is more active and wants to participate in everything", looking at him and smiling; "He was like that the whole weekend, going from lap to lap because that's the only way he calms down, while Anahi sleeps." This behaviour becomes a distinguishing feature of the twins. Raoni always wants to be satisfied immediately, while Anahi remains peaceful. It must be remembered that Raoni's greatest weakness was revealed at birth, when he required more attention and special care from the environment, which became a pattern in his first months of life.

When the babies are three months and twelve days old, the observer is greeted by the maternal grandmother. They have had a two-week holiday, and the house is different and very messy.

> Maiara is in pyjamas, her hair is uncombed, and face looks exhausted . . . the babies are in their prams and also uncombed and unwashed . . . For a moment I felt strange because the environment was inconsistent from what I had seen so far.

Maiara has a cold and is taking antibiotics. She says that in fifteen days she will go back to work and tells the observer that she should ask the building janitor to open the gate for her, since the grandmother will not be able to go down to let her in. Could the end of her maternity leave and, consequently, the separation from her babies, be the reason for Maiara's poor health and disorganisation at home? Maiara is quiet and her eyes are tired as she struggles to stand up. Her mother talks endlessly with everyone there. At one point she says she misses Raoni, and says she thinks he confuses her voice with his mother's. Maiara reacts quickly and forcefully, saying, "Of course not! They know very well who is who! They can tell apart every little thing!" "Really?" says the grandmother. The mother looks for confirmation in the observer's eyes, who agrees with her in her facial expression.

At the next observation, everyone is in good health. The observer hears some whining and guesses it is Raoni, which is confirmed. Anahi was sleeping in the bedroom. During this observation the mother breastfeeds the two babies: while one nurses, the other waits. The mother lifts Anahi from her pram and positions her to nurse. The baby latches on quickly and starts sucking loudly and strongly. While feeding her daughter, Maiara feels this is the right time to talk about her emotional state when she found out she was expecting twins. She shares that she and Moacir had not been sure if they wanted to have more children, but their families had pressured them. As time went by, they decided to try for another pregnancy. She says, "I remember it as if it were today. I found out I was pregnant on the third week, because my menstrual period is super regular, so I soon figured out I was pregnant. I went for an ultrasound early on and found out there were twins . . .When the doctor told me there were two babies I felt something I can't explain . . . I started to cry and couldn't stop. A lot went through my mind: what would it be like; how scary; will I have to move? Will I be able to handle it? I was scared of the delivery, the pregnancy, of everything all together." Maiara's ends her outburst when Anahi finishes nursing and burps. Maiara says, "Oops, let it all out, that's right sweetie." They are in tune with each other, and the environment repeatedly reinforces how Anahi is just like her mother.

At three months and twenty-five days, Maiara is nursing Anahi and says she had given her daughter a doll on the previous day: "She was was so happy! I never thought she would like it so much. She's such a girl." She is a mummy's girl, which she had liked from the beginning. When she gave the doll to Raoni, he did not care, and the father said, "Everything is in its right place." He was given a car and loved it.

Maiara says she has decided to postpone going back to work, explaining that she still needs to be with her children so she could look after them better. When the time had come for Maiara to go back to work because her maternity leave was ending, she changed her plans: "I used some holiday time, I want to delay my return for as long as possible. I still have a lot to do here at home" (four months and two days). The babies also feel the approaching separation, which the mother translates as: "They need more attention. They've just started with the supplements, but Anahi still doesn't know how to use the bottle . . . All this requires helping them to keep trying. And they've just started eating fruit, which they didn't really like. Everything has to be done slowly. All this takes time."

At the next observation, Maiara reports that Raoni does not really like fruit, so she needs to be patient: "Everything has its right time" (four months and nine days).

The babies are discovering themselves:

> She observes her own hands, touching her nails and skin, shows great interest in discovering herself (four months and nine days).

Later, Anahi becomes a little agitated and Maiara

> puts her hand in her daughter's pram and caresses her face with gentle movements. Anahi calms down and proceeds to play with her mother's hand and to explore it as best as she can.

The babies also begin to relate to the people around them:

> Anahi pays attention to her mother and brother, staring at them and observing everything they do.

The relationship between the twins and Jandir also has its own pace. Initially, the two watch Jandir carefully, and he feels proud of being observed. Maiara reports that she is happy with Jandir and Raoni's interaction, "He loves his brother, and laughs at his tricks." When Jandir plays catch with his father, the babies "laugh so hard they lose their breath . . ." (four months and two days).

Maiara says the babies are organising themselves, "Can you believe it? When one sleeps the other one wakes up, you don't even need to check, just go in and the other will be awake and waiting. So they have me going all the time. I don't know how they manage to organise themselves like that! I know each one has its own rhythm, but this doubles the demand on me" (four months and twenty-two days). The mother treats each baby uniquely in this rotation, thus sustaining the dyad illusion. The place and space of each one that had been previously registered in intrauterine sensations are now in the home, the family, and in their future relationships with others.

The possibilities that Maiara and Moacir offer their children to help them grow are reflected in every stage of their development. They create space for spontaneity and are able to validate what the babies feel and respect their individuality and their rhythms. The way they deal with time and rhythm becomes more defined in their relationship with the observer. Frequently, upon her arrival, the observer has to wait five or ten minutes until someone opens the door, because one of the babies needs attention.

The space where they live increases in value and their plans to move to a new flat are coming together: ". . . We'll move this Saturday or the next, I can't stand the wait any longer" (four months and sixteen days). An agreement is made to interrupt the observations until after the move. However, the new flat is not ready as scheduled, which seems to disorganise them. A month goes by without any contact with the observer.

When the observations resume, still at the old address, aunt Ana is taking care of the babies. She adapts quickly and gives herself fully to them, interacting and talking to them while feeding them fruit one at a time; when she is caring for one the other sleeps, showing real harmony. When they both are awake, they seem to tolerate being alone very well, distracting themselves with their hands. The twins' interaction is also recognised and verbalised by the family. Anahi makes sounds that are answered by Raoni, and Ana says: "They are talking!" (five months and twenty days). The mother has gone out for a longer period for the first time because she had taken care of the paperwork for going back to work.

Anahi takes a long time to wean. She is six months and four days old when her aunt comments, "She is finally taking the bottle, but it was a struggle. The other day Maiara and I let her get hungry, so when I gave her the bottle she took it. It was painful but it had to be done, otherwise she would never get the hang of it." When Ana feeds her niece, she talks to her calmly.

> Anahi smiles between bites, making noises with her mouth and playing with her saliva. The aunt allows the girl to go at her own pace as she feeds her the fruit (six months and four days).

This carefulness and respect during feedings continue as the babies develop.

After a long period of observing themselves, Raoni and Anahi start to interact more actively with each other in their play:

> Raoni repeats the game of pushing a cube so I would take it. Anahi stretches out her hand. I give her the cube and she takes it firmly in her hand, turning it around to see the colours. Then she extends the cube to Raoni but doesn't let go, and they hold the toy together for a while. They look at each other and laugh (six months and fourteen days).

Later on, these games include their bodies.

> Raoni is quiet, sucking his dummy. Anahi watches her brother seriously for a long time, then approaches him, grabs him by his shirt collar, and snatches the dummy from his mouth. He looks ready to cry, but doesn't. He reaches out toward her as if to react, but instead they touch and recognise each other (nine months and eight days).

The babies gradually notice the observer and begin interacting with her. They frequently welcome her arrival with smiles and exclamations. Their interaction with the observer has its own particular rhythms, according to the personality of each one. Raoni is the first to connect with her: he watches her and smiles at her in the first months. Anahi, on the other hand, is shy and reserved, more like her mother, but eventually she also communicates with the observer. As the twins grow, their specific ways of interaction continue to differentiate them.

> Raoni smiles more emphatically and more often, and Anahi is more discreet and smiles softly (six months and fourteen days).

At around six and a half months, Maiara goes back to work and the babies begin day care. They start playing *fort-da* games (Freud 1920g) during this period of practising and reliving separation. This is clearly noticed at the first filming.

> The twins are playing and looking at the camera, and they smile when someone says something. Anahi was very active, grabbing her doll and putting it on the floor. She starts a game with me where she puts the doll on the floor and then waits for me to give it back. She smiles at the game (six months and twenty-nine days).

Maiara's attitude during the first day of filming the babies is of note. She leaves the living room and stays in the kitchen preparing soup for them. She gives the babies space, but is present from a distance: the observer can smell the vegetables cooking in the kitchen. Besides being connected to the needs of the babies, she also accommodates Jandir, but with established limits: she lets him play videogames during filming, but without the sound.

At the thirtieth observation, the babies are eight months and seventeen days old, and the family is already established in their new flat. The space for the babies expands significantly in the new house. It is a beautiful, recently constructed building, and the flat is cosy with a lovely view. When the observer arrives, she notices that the prams have been replaced,

> They aren't the ones for small babies any more, but those that allow children to be seated.

In the living room, there is a corner set up with a playpen for the babies. At the next observation, a fluffy blanket and pillows have been substituted for the playpen to make the place safe. Several toys are scattered around. Anahi is placed there and she begins to explore the environment, picking up toys, turning them, moving them around, putting them in her mouth, and making noises. She loses her balance as she plays, but she tries to remain seated by propping herself up with her hands. The twins interact by touching and looking at each other, and then the boy lays his head on his sister's lap and stays that way for a time. Touching, leaning, and feeling are familiar to Raoni and Anahi from when they were in their mother's womb, which seems to continuously reconstruct itself in their relationship.

At nine months, Raoni can drag himself all over the house, while Anahi is less active and prefers to have fun with her toys. They touch each other, look at each other, and even scratch each other. Sometimes Raoni lies down and rests his head on his sister's lap and stays that way. She takes the dummy from his mouth, pats him on the head, and gets up in a kind of interaction similar to what was observed during the obstetric ultrasounds.

Days later, he crawls around nimbly and explores everything. The observer writes,

> Raoni looks at me and smiles. He is now crawling skilfully, unlike last week when he was still dragging his body. He crawls over and circles around me, smiling happily at being able to go wherever he wants.

After the holidays, when the babies are thirteen months old, everyone is together in the living room for the first time: Raoni, Anahi, the father, the mother, and Jandir. Raoni is very active, riding his little motorcycle. He smiles and puts his hand on the observer. Anahi, who is skilfully riding a wooden horse, is serious as usual, although she soon gives in and smiles. The adults talk about the holidays and the twins' first birthday. The mother looks stronger and says, "I feel more secure now about going out with them. We went to Santa Maria over the weekend and everything went fine. They're bigger now."

The observer reports that the parents are attuned to each other as they verbalise the differences between the babies. Moacir says, "Anahi can keep herself entertained and play longer with one particular thing. But for Raoni, there's no way; he's much too agitated and always wants to switch games." Maiara confirms this, saying, "That's exactly how it is. But on the other hand, he is like a little clock, while Anahi can't follow any kind of schedule." The father continues, "He can't comfort himself like she can, but she is less steady than he is, and sometimes, when she's sitting, she'll tip over to the side. But she can crawl really fast!" The mother laughs and says it is true.

Maiara shows the observer photos of the twins' birthday and gives her one as a present: Anahi is wearing a pink dress and Raoni is wearing matching shorts and shirt with a bow tie. She tells her about "Anahi's mischief". The father had lain down on the comforter in the living room with her to put her to sleep, but he fell asleep instead. She was crawling freely around the room when Maiara found them. "She put her father to sleep . . ."

During their holidays the twins were let loose and they walked around everywhere, in the grass and in the sand: "At first I was a bit afraid that they might not like it or get sick, but nothing like that happened. On the contrary, they are strong and eating well" (one year and one month).

After a time, they put a plastic toy house in the children's corner. The two play there a long time. They like to play with the nebuliser cable (a cord).

> They get all entangled in there, then they fall down and get up again (one year and three months).

Anahi and Raoni's game in this space reminded us of the pair's interactions during the ultrasound exams. Even the observer's reports of this game are similar to the descriptions of the babies in the womb:

> The toy house is big enough for them to enter, sit in, and play in, but it is also quite small and cosy.

Raoni is very attached to his father and sometimes gets jealous; Anahi is quiet and polite, and likes to eat from a plate. For a family outing to the park, the mother dresses Anahi and the father dresses Raoni. Jandir follows behind them. The father comments about how "Anahi is very detailed and calm and does things with precision, while Raoni is more about moving and not thinking about what he wants." Anahi seems both flexible and secure, like her mother. Once she is dressed and ready for the park, she picks up her doll and waits at the front door. Since the rest of the family is taking a while longer, she sits on the floor to play. Raoni, on the other hand, does not tolerate changes or the arrival of new people. The observer writes,

> Jandir takes the ball away from Raoni, who cries loudly and screams.

Another time, a game exemplifies how the children compete for their father's attention, looking for his support:

> He [the father] swings Anahi back and forth by her hands while singing a children's song. She likes this kind of game and smiles up at her father. Raoni sees this, goes toward his father and screams, wanting to play too. Moacir finishes the song and says it's the boy's turn next. He says, "Watch how she gets mad!" He plays the same game with Raoni, and Anahi stands close, staring and serious. She crosses her little arms and stares at her brother. When the song ends, she pushes her brother away and takes her father's hands. Moacir smiles and repeats the game with her. Raoni goes to the kitchen looking for his mother.

The father is very involved with his children and helps with their care by bathing, feeding, and playing with them, saying he has a lap for two. He begins a campaign to clean up the park and surrounding areas to improve the environment. As a result, he was able to obtain permission to do this and round up volunteers to help. He seems to extend what is in his home to outside his home. The observer, who sees the changes in the park, registers what Maiara says: "It's amazing how everyone supports him. People are constantly coming by to offer their help." At this one year and six months' observation, Anahi is curious and comes running to see who has arrived. She soon interacts with the observer and plays hide and seek with her. Raoni had also come running, but when he saw the observer, he ran to his father's legs. The father represents a safe haven.

Maiara can count on the father as a carer who is present and in tune with the needs of the children. They create an introspective environment that transmits peace. The mother is in the kitchen doing her things, the father is watching television and concentrating on his programme, Anahi is entertained by her ball and the hair that is stuck to it, and Raoni is in his pushchair. They are all together but not clinging to one another, which enables them to play alone or together.

Although the parents are proud of their children's development, they are concerned about their language skills. The mother is bothered by the fact that her children still do not speak, and are only able to pronounce disconnected syllables: "Do you know they haven't said a word yet, these naughty kids? Just the other day I joked with my mother and told her they were mute. She said they scream too much to be mute. They even say syllables like ma and pa, but they haven't said any words yet" (one year and five months). None the less, it was possible to observe that the babies try to imitate Jandir's attitudes and words, which confirmed that Anahi and Raoni were using a sort of communication typical between children in this stage of development.

As the babies' perception of the world broadens, Jandir becomes more involved in their play. The boy treats them affectionately and clowns around to make them laugh, feeling fulfilled in this relationship. Later on, the way they include each other in their play becomes more active:

> The three children are in the room and Jandir starts to interact with him [Raoni]. Eventually he climbs on to the roof of the toy house and starts talking. Raoni stays close, playing behind the house . . . Anahi, who had been watching television, gets down from her pushchair and joins her brothers . . . She watches what Raoni is doing [imitating Jandir] and then tries to climb on to the toy house too (one year and seven months).

At one year and nine months, they all go to the park, and the mother dresses them both. They take a bike, a doll's pram, a ball, and some toys to the park, and the mother laughs, saying: "Look at this family! We're like a great big family with all this stuff just to cross the street and go to the park." They really are a big family built by the force of nature, and sculpted naturally. The observer leaves with a sense of satisfaction, wellbeing, and tenderness, and wishes she could stay longer.

Even as the babies get bigger, the parents continue differentiating them. Maiara tells about an episode with her son: "Raoni is so shy! This is the latest thing he does around people. Yesterday we were down there waiting for Moacir to come home. Raoni was playing by the door when he saw a neighbour. He did a double take and came racing over to my lap."

For their next holidays, when the babies are almost two years old, the parents decide to spend the summer at the beach. They conclude that this year the children will be able to enjoy it more, but that they still need security, so they choose a place carefully. They intend to include everyone in this choice. When they decided how the babies would bathe, the mother says, "We put them each in a different little swimming pool, that way they each had one.[14] It was great!" (two years). From this we can infer that their differences are already well established, and that the parents see the twins as separate individuals. The mother points out their differences: "He always does everything quickly and she does everything calmly and slowly. He's always going at full speed." The environment they have created has always encouraged individuality and space for each one.

The mother shows the observer the photos of their second birthday party, and Anahi sits beside her to see them too. Raoni, who is very attached to his father, becomes restless and cries when he leaves. The mother holds him in her arms and soothes him, walking him to the window so he could see his father going down the street.

The twins' second birthday party theme was the Flintstones, which portrays this family well: their Stone Age sense of raising their children with attention and care without exaggerating, and how Pebbles defined the little girl prototype, and Bam-Bam the boy.

Throughout this case, this family reminds us of the indigenous culture (also represented in the mother's and babies' names) in how the children are raised to be free but not disconnected. The parents are very connected to their children without being overly attached. They give the children enough space to explore their environment. Neither do the parents stop being themselves in order to raise their children. They continue their activities, a fact that encourages the children to grow beyond their parents, grandparents, aunts, and nanny. We imagine that in the future these children will be able to successfully, safely, and creatively circulate in the world.

Final considerations

The observations of Maiara and her twins, conducted over ten years ago, have taught us a great deal and generated numerous ideas and group discussions. At the very first meeting, the observer was surprised to see the space Maiara had that was able to hold two babies and, at the same time, offer them unique and discriminated growth: although they were twins, each baby had its own clearly defined "cave".

Maiara's natural, simple, and receptive manner both surprised and affected us, since that is so unusual nowadays. In her own way, she established a spontaneous relationship with her babies. Another one of her outstanding characteristics, which permeated the entire developmental process of the babies, is her capacity to discriminate and patiently welcome each individual in its own time: each of the babies, her older son, her husband, the observer, and the sonographer. This feat was due to Maiara's ability to be in touch with herself and to give herself the necessary time for things to happen in a mature manner, without drama. Her active silence, which is typical of someone who is connected, was maintained throughout the babies' development.

As Winnicott (1988f) says, ". . . the tiny things that happen between the mother and baby at the beginning are significant and not less so because they seem so natural and seem to be best taken for granted" (p. 29). In another text, he states that those things—the most significant—are not words (Winnicott, 1988e). For him, the most important thing in early life is what he calls contact without activity, which is very well illustrated in the case of Maiara and her babies:

> . . . the essential constitutes the simplest of all experiences, that based on the contact without activity, where there is opportunity for the feeling of oneness between two persons who are in fact two and not one. (Winnicott, 1988c, p. 7)

From the time of her pregnancy, Maiara always knew who was who. She was attentive, emotionally present, and she reacted when she did not agree. She knew how to meet each one's needs and recognised each one's personality, each one's cry, each one's gestures and movements, and she accepted that each one's maturing process would occur spontaneously. Maiara is a true presence, her interest is real, and her actions are human, personal, and her own. These conditions provide the basis for a reliable and facilitating environment that promotes integration in time and space.

We observed a well-defined sense of continuity between the intra- and extrauterine environment that facilitated the babies' going on being. Over time, we watched with satisfaction as this womb-cave transformed into a "place" for the babies, and later into a large "family-belly" that included the aunt and grandmother, which gradually became a house with enough space to accommodate growth, and which, finally, with the father's help, extended to outside the home space.

The father, Moacir, is on board with Maiara from the beginning. They are a couple with smiling eyes that fit together in such a way that they help and complement each other. Moacir holds and shares with Maiara the huge responsibility that comes with the arrival of two babies. During delivery, he was concerned about moving to a new house to make room for the babies, without forgetting his firstborn son. He exhibits a clear pattern of care that adapts to the needs of each developmental stage of the babies and is transformed during the evolutionary process.

Maiara was immersed in the vulnerability of the babies when she identified with them, but was able to emerge within a few months. She had the flexibility to come and go without this being a threat. She was not passive, but, rather, she reacted to changes (twin pregnancy, change of observer, the approaching birth, the babies' care) both in her physical body and her psyche and confidently gestated the feelings brought on by the new. The confidence Maiara felt in the external environment was a reflection of her inner world, her character, and her emotional maturity. This reliable relationship is vital to early life in order to produce full psychic development.

Psyche and personality develop gradually from simple to more complex. This is a process that is achieved through constant repetitions that gradually build the baby's sense of feeling real, and, thus, enable him to face his inherited maturation processes.

The firm and respectful environment that was neither rigid nor invasive, and where each had his/her place—where Raoni and Anahi had the opportunity to develop—allowed free emotional expression. Conflicts between love and hate, jealousy, and competition could be expressed and lovingly supported. This is very clear in how Jandir, the older brother, relates with his parents, how the parents relate with Jandir, and with how Jandir relates with the babies.

The experience of observation allows us to draw analogies between the function of the mother with her baby and of the analyst with his or her patient. It is a unique experience to enter the house of a family (patient), to feel and experience the intimacy of their home (inner being), to touch the most primitive emotions (patient and analyst), to dive into the smells, colours, and sounds that involve an unique relationship in its own environment, and to participate in a non-intrusive emotional experience that is respectful and receptive. The transference experienced by patients in analysis during some periods of regression to dependence refers back to the initial mother–infant relationship, when in the presence of the subjective object. The analytic setting becomes more important than the interpretation. In borderline cases or in the psychotic phases and moments that occur during the analysis of neurotic patients, the analyst has experiences that are similar to those of mothers as they care for their babies. The patient and the "good enough" analyst must experience growth gradually. The qualities of the good enough mother, which allowed the going on being in early life, now help the analyst recover the natural tendency towards the integration that had been interrupted in childhood, and to resume its development.

In Maiara's home, feelings were allowed to be expressed. Maiara was always there, even if not physically present. Not everything was wonderful in the life story of the twins. There were internal and external changes, surprises, anxieties, weaknesses, and discomforts. In fact, things are not always wonderful in the back and forth between a mother and her baby or between an analyst and his or her patient, especially in periods of regression to dependence. The silent psychic activity of the mother who makes herself available to care for her baby is very intense, as it is for the analyst. Maiara's story, told through the observer, enabled us to translate some of the intensity of the experiences and demands placed on her as a mother of twins—not only in welcoming them, but also in discriminating beween their differences—without neglecting her firstborn, who was still young and had his own developmental needs.

We have much to learn from this simple life story, this encounter, this mother–infant relationship. To feel truly free and devoid of rigid defensive categories, to be a natural analyst who is real, human, respectful, and good enough has nothing to do with sentimentalism, like Winnicott, who said he was not sentimental about mothers. A mother's internal availability, consistency, and predictability provide a setting that facilitates the development processes, especially integration, thus guaranteeing the baby's going on being (Winnicott, 1987a). Maiara demonstrated how her flexibility, receptivity, and firmness provided good enough conditions for the babies to grow at their own pace in a way that supported and facilitated the maturation process. Maiara's abilities teach us about the abilities that are essential for an analyst in the therapeutic process with a patient. Thus, we believe we have much to learn from the maternal function in order to better understand the analytic function and go beyond interpretation to the place where words lose all meaning.

CHAPTER FOUR

Lucia and her twins, Daniela and Renata: the birth of fraternity in the struggle against maternal indiscrimination

Pregnancy

We followed the story of the twins Daniela and Renata by observing six monthly ultrasounds between the thirteenth and thirty-fourth–thirty-fifth week of pregnancy and the delivery, followed by forty-six home observations until the twins were three years old. They are fraternal, dichorionic, diamniotic twins.

Lucia, the mother, is thirty-one years old, beautiful, tall, and athletic with light-coloured eyes and hair. The father, Roberto, is thirty-four years old, dark complexioned, handsome, and athletic also. He attended all the ultrasound sessions. Both are teachers and have a youthful appearance. This is their first pregnancy and their contact with the research group begins in the thirteenth week of pregnancy. Lucia says that this is already her fifth ultrasound: "It's nice to see the babies. It has to be like this because we are still not sure what they are. Will we be able to tell?" The couple seems receptive and accepted our invitation to participate in the study. Lucia likes the idea of "being able to see the babies more frequently . . . and to be observed" (thirteen weeks).

In the course of written reports, we will see that Lucia and Roberto's uncertainty as to whether there is room for both, their insecurity, fragility, and helplessness when told they were expecting twins, their wish that it was only one, their confusion, indiscrimination, and failed attempts to differentiate the twins will be part of the first three years of the babies' lives, which the couple transmits mostly non-verbally. The detachment between the parents and the babies, especially between the mother and the babies, is communicated non-verbally to the observer throughout the pregnancy until the end of the babies' third year of life, and is carried over to the observer's writing. The first reports are poorly written, fragmented, and lacking in clarity and detail, which hindered our ability to follow and understand the ultrasounds. There was a lack of affection, or something that would invite us to enter and join the babies' development. The observer begins the written report as follows:

> The mother is prepared for the exam . . . the father is sitting close to the mother . . . the mother has a hoarse voice and she seems friendly; the father is somewhat serious, athletically built, and wearing a T-shirt and jacket.

At the first ultrasound, Lucia says, "The other one is easier to see . . . the one over there keeps moving, its heart is racing; it's no wonder, the way I came up that hill . . ." The couple always forgets to bring the previous examinations and never knows how far along the pregnancy is. They get confused. At the second examination at fifteen–sixteen weeks, the intention is to confirm the sex of the babies. The mother thinks they look big and says, "But they have no genitalia yet, right?" The sex was confirmed: the foetus on top, with its little hand on its forehead, is a girl. She is facing forward and the sound of the lub-dub of her beating heart increases. The parents look at each other and the mother says, "What a big foot." The image zooms in on the other foetus and the mother says, "The one on the other side is really stretched out, it's so long . . . Look at that big toe", and the father says, "Look at that big foot." The second one is also apparently a girl, although the image was not clear. The confusing environment affects the sonographer, who says she is not sure which child she is looking at: foetus one weighs 141 grams and foetus two, 147 grams.

At the next examination, the couple wants to know for certain the sex of the foetuses, and it is confirmed that both are girls. The father says that the image is fuzzier today and that he cannot see the babies. The mother identifies the little head of one of them. One weighs 456 grams and the other 524 grams. Although the doctor has informed the couple from the beginning that the girls are fraternal, dichorionic, diamniotic twins, she needs to explain all of this again because the parents are confused and do not remember. The mother asks to see them and the doctor proceeds to show each one's face, kidneys, legs, bottom, spine, heart, and genitals. The mother wants to know which one is which. She suddenly says, "They're going to come out of my throat." When their genitalia is visible, she says, "Poor thing . . . she doesn't like it." After seeing both girls, the mother asks, "Is there less separation between them? And what's that over there?" "It's the heart", the doctor replies and turns on the sound so they can hear the heartbeat. The mother is amazed and covers her mouth with one hand, and the father says "Gosh!" Although there are numerous attempts to differentiate the foetuses, this does not calm the parents: "Is she the biggest one? . . . There are two placentas, right? Was it like that from the beginning?"

In numerous situations during the ultrasound exams, Lucia conveys, mostly non-verbally, her doubts and insecurities as to whether she has enough internal space to hold two babies. She mentions a mother who gave birth to twins at forty weeks and with normal weight. She exclaims, "The poor mother" (thirteen weeks). On another occasion, she tells Roberto, "Yeah, it better hold two . . ." (twenty-two weeks). At the last ultrasound examination, her feelings of fragility and inability to carry the twins to the end are explicit when she refers to one of the babies: "She's coming!" (thirty-four–thirty-five weeks), to which the sonographer responds, "Don't even joke about it . . ." Lucia continues, "Do you think I'll have to go until the fortieth week?"

On another occasion, Lucia repeats the comment made by the first sonographer who had examined her before she joined the study, who said that one of the embryos had not survived. Thus, she reveals her drama of having to carry two babies: "In the first ultrasound it looked as if one of the gestational sacs was not developing . . ." (fifteen–sixteen weeks). Lucia repeatedly used this sentence, seemingly to communicate her desire for one of the babies to disappear, which would be an easier "weight" to carry.

While, on the one hand, Lucia strives to differentiate the foetuses during the examinations, she also wants to give them equal attention. When the doctor says, "Let's look at the other one'', Lucia says, "Good, because we always spend too much time on the first and we don't want the other one to be jealous or feel rejected . . ." At the first examination, the doctor had said that it was easier for them to touch each other because there was space between them. However, the mother interpreted their movements as aggressive. "For now, the boxing ring is separated. We'll see what happens when they have their gloves on. You [sonographer] say they poke and push each other. What's worse is that later they'll do that to me" (thirteen weeks).

On another occasion, she measures the babies' growth by the pain they cause her: "They've grown . . . they're kicking me" (thirty weeks), implying that that the babies are hurting her, not just moving like all babies do. One of the babies turns upside down, and the mother says, "You're going to get a kick!" The father comments, "She has to learn to defend herself" and "If there were three of them, things would get really complicated." All movements are seen as aggressive and affecting the mother. These types of comments were repeated throughout the observations and indicate the mother's projection of aggression, rivalry, jealousy, and envy on to her daughters, based on her difficulty in making room for two.

The father also demonstrates his anxiety and confusion. He wants to know about the units of measurement the doctor uses to weigh the babies because he cannot imagine measurements that are so small but use such big numbers, like a lottery prize. He tries to visualise the baby when the doctor says, "This one is 859 grams, she's yawning and facing the monitor." The mother cries, and the father asks, "Is that her ear?" ''It is,'' replies the doctor. The father continues, "Does she already have eyes? Is her nervous system fully developed?"

On some occasions when the sonographer reassures the parents that the babies are doing well, the two exchange glances and hold each other's hands. Here, we find an example of how the doctor often unknowingly functions to unite the couple, an important step in the transition to parenthood.

It is noteworthy that, towards the end of pregnancy, Roberto focuses his attention almost exclusively on his wife, to the point of forgetting the babies. We think that the proximity of birth made the father more aware of the reality of having to care for two babies. This is clear in the fifth ultrasound. Lucia was uncomfortable in her position, and all his attention was focused on her, ignoring everyone else present: the observer, the sonographer, and the babies. It seems that Lucia is his only concern (thirty weeks). Foetus one now weighs 1,510 grams, and foetus two 1,481 grams. The mother is worried about their weight and about how their feet and bottoms hit against her belly. Lucia feels ill during the examination and is instructed to turn on to her left side so that she faces away from the monitor, meaning that the husband is the one looking at the images. Again, Lucia comments about how big the problem would be if they were triplets.

Everything looks good, including the results of the Doppler ultrasound. The father attributes the successful pregnancy in part to the fact that Lucia is athletic and has not stopped exercising. He also says that there are some small dumbbells at the gym waiting for the babies, and that many people panic when they see Lucia exercising and pregnant. It important to mention that Lucia's "turning her back" posture will continue in the next examination, and the postnatal observations will reveal that this becomes a pattern in the mother–daughters–observer relationship.

At the next exam, thirty-four–thirty-five weeks, the couple had apparently decided ahead of time that Lucia would keep her back to the monitor. The husband said, "Let me look." Foetus one weighs 2,137 grams and the mother exclaims, "I thought it was more", as if the girls feel heavier than they are. Foetus two is low in the belly, and the mother says, "She's coming!" She weighs 2,250 grams, and her heart, head, belly, kidneys, legs, feet, and bottom can be seen. The mother is visibly uncomfortable with the pregnancy, and seems to want to get rid of the babies as soon as possible.

Delivery

The obstetrician schedules the twins' delivery near the thirty-seventh week of pregnancy. Because she is carrying twins, the doctor recommends a caesarean section. Roberto informs the observer, as agreed. Lucia and Roberto arrive at the last minute after the observer, "sweating and tired" because Lucia had felt ill and had to wait a while before climbing the stairs. The two seem at a loss about what to do, demonstrating their helplessness. When the nurse directs Lucia to enter the room to begin the preparatory procedures and leaves Roberto to fill out the administrative paperwork, the couple seems distressed by the separation. Roberto is "frightened and confused". He accepts the observer's offer to hold Lucia's handbag and hospital bag. The couple's behaviour showed they were unprepared and feeling helpless.

The lack of discrimination the parents had transmitted during pregnancy, and their doubts as to whether there would be room enough for two, continued at delivery. When filling out the check-in papers for the hospital, the father gave the information for just one daughter. The grandparents asked who was going to sit on the throne, assuming it could only be one.

Roberto's parents are the first to arrive, just a few minutes before the scheduled caesarean section. Once he has filled out the necessary paperwork and is with his parents, Roberto "cannot hold back the tears". His parents are affectionate and understanding with him. Some time later, Lucia's parents and one of her sisters arrive. Roberto cries a lot and Lucia's mother says, "If you keep that up you're going pass out in there, I think it's better if you don't go in." He looks at the observer, seeming to ask for her support, and says, "But I want to try. You'll be there too, right?" Finally meeting his daughters seems to be very difficult challenge for Roberto. At the penultimate ultrasound he had apparently been willing to look at the ultrasound images while Lucia kept her back to them. Yet now, faced with the "flesh and blood" babies that would soon be on his lap, he reacted in desperation.

Meanwhile, the doctors, Lucia, and the observer are already in the delivery room. It is understood that anaesthetist is a family member when she says, "I'll do exactly what I do with my other patients, as if I were not family. And you, too, whatever you want to ask me or tell me, go ahead . . ." After the anaesthesia is administered, Lucia lies back and begins to cry,

> She cries uncontrollably, like Roberto did.

The anaesthetist tries to calm her, stroking her face and saying that everything is fine. Distraught, Lucia asks for Roberto, who has not yet come in, and the doctor says he is talking to the paediatrician and would be there soon. As soon as Roberto enters the room, the two embrace and sob compulsively and uncontrollably. Their abrupt separation when they entered the maternity ward had not been easy. Moreover, they seem to have only each other to help bear this stressful moment of childbirth. Lucia, still sobbing, says she is feeling so sick that she will vomit.

The first baby comes out with the umbilical cord round her neck and whitish in colour. The second baby also has trouble coming out because it is in a difficult position in the uterus. Roberto cries and Lucy wants to know how her daughters are and if they are perfect. Hesitantly and insecurely, the father asks to touch the babies. The paediatrician lets him touch and weigh the girls. Although he is still crying and shaking, he is able to carry them to the scale, seemingly feeling relieved at having succeeded. The babies do not look well immediately after they are born, but then they soon react favourably. The feeling is that the delivery did not go smoothly.

When Roberto comes back to the delivery room, he calms Lucia, saying that he held their daughters and that they are fine. They hold each other affectionately for some time, after which Lucia seems calmer and stops crying. The father still has bouts of crying, but they are less intense and more spread out. He comments to the observer, "I don't know what is happening to me, I can't control the urge to cry." He searches the observer's eyes, as if making sure she is there and perhaps trying to get some holding from her. The paediatrician asks the father to help him bring in the babies so the mother can see them. While the father holds one, the other is placed with the mother. The first one is more awake and whimpers, while the second one sleeps. The mother worried about these differences, as she had during the pregnancy. As we shall see later, differences between the two girls will continue to cause ongoing anxiety and concern for the mother.

At this time, the anaesthetist, who is the couple's relative, says they must decide which baby will be Daniela and which will be Renata. They seem disconcerted and not ready to name or differentiate their daughters. The parents speak quietly to each other and then the father says he needs to see them. The doctor says it is not possible at the moment, so she will tell them what to do: the blonde one, like the mother, will be Daniela, and the darker one, like the father, will be Renata.

Daniela and Renata had their names determined by the anaesthetist, who based her choice on external characteristics—the colour of their skin, eyes, and hair. Daniela supposedly was like her mother with her light complexion, and Renata was like her father with her dark complexion and slanted eyes. This non-discrimination always made the mother refer to the same external resources rather than internal ones to differentiate the girls, revealing her internal–external mismatch.

Soon after the delivery when Lucia was preparing to leave the room, she asked the obstetrician if she could breastfeed her daughters. Like the father, she asks for permission as if she were not authorised to be the mother, as if the babies were not hers. The doctor responds affirmatively, commending the mother's wish and offering to help. The two embrace each other. Lucia seems to need a mother at that moment, and the obstetrician takes on that function and confirms her support should anything become difficult. Lucia did not count on her mother, who at no time showed her support. Towards the end, when Lucia goes to her family to announce that her daughters "are beautiful", she reaches out her arm to her mother, who ignores the gesture, turns around, and walks out of the room. It was a very harsh yet significant scene that clearly demonstrated that Lucia could not rely on her mother for emotional support, and helped us understand that Lucia's "turning her back" posture, which had been visible since the end of her pregnancy, was part of this family's mother–daughter relationship pattern.

The first three years of life

The observer reports she had no problem arriving at the couple's home since she has been to that *cul-de-sac* street before. The family lives in a small but comfortable flat on the ground floor of an apartment building. The observer made few descriptions of the environment, although she emphasised a sense of "indiscrimination" and "lack of communication".

> I buzz the intercom and immediately two people approach and the gate opens. I do not understand if these people had opened the gate, perhaps because they live in this building, or if it had been Lucia . . . I realise that there are several entrances on the ground level . . . I proceed to the last entrance and buzz the intercom again. This time the door opens but no one says anything . . . I ring the bell and Lucia opens the door.

This "who opens for whom" kind of communication is strange and confusing, and is repeated throughout the three years of observation.

On the first visit, the twins are twelve days old, and Lucia and her mother are present. The maternal grandmother holds one of the babies on her lap in the living room. The mother introduces the baby, "This is ... [hesitates] Renata. Daniela is sleeping." The first impression of "who is who?" continues.

The observer thinks the grandmother knows what she is doing by the way she holds Renata. She soon addresses the observer, pointing out the differences she sees between her granddaughters: "This one eats a lot ... she is feisty ... you have a split second to put milk in her mouth before she screams. The other one is really quiet and calm! My, children have such psychological differences, don't they?" The observer agrees. The baby starts to move her head and the grandmother puts her little hand in her mouth to suck on, which she does. The grandmother, in command, continues, "Look at that, she wants to nurse again!" As Lucia prepares to nurse the baby, she touches her breasts and seems confused: "I lost track of which one has milk, I nurse so much I don't know any more ..."

Lucia is insecure and asks for help from her mother, who positions herself behind Lucia, giving opinions and criticising, telling Lucia what to do. Here, we can observe the continuity of the prenatal, childbirth, and postpartum periods: Lucia's insecurity and trouble sustaining an internal space for two is aligned with her own mother's lack of internal space for her.

Lucia's mother takes charge and continues speaking intrusively, "Did you know that the paediatrician advised her to give the girls supplements?" Lucia counters, "Giana [Lucia's sister] told me she knows a mother with twin daughters that she breastfed for four months. Only breast milk." Her mother retaliates, "Yes, but some dairy cows give thirty litres and others give fifteen!" She turns and says, "You know, Daniela got a nappy rash ... it's because Lucia was nursing her and didn't notice that she had pooped, so she spent four hours with a dirty nappy." The grandmother's tone of voice is often critical and denotes a lack of caring for her daughter, who is experiencing a delicate moment of adapting to motherhood.

The grandmother invites the observer to meet Daniela, who is sleeping in the bedroom. She says they sleep together in the same cot, which she had suggested to Lucia since it would make things easier.

The second cot is full of nappies and ointments. Already, in this first report, the observer transmits the difficulty of looking at two and the fear of giving more attention to one than the other, which the mother also transmitted during pregnancy:

> When we entered the room, I was tempted to look at Daniela, and didn't know how to divide myself so I can look at both. Then I thought, I already saw Renata, now I want to see Daniela! And I stood next to Daniela's cot for a little while as she slept peacefully.

The observer comments about how the girls are physically different: Daniela looks like her mother and has her features, while Renata looks more like her father and has slanted eyes. Despite their differences, Lucia has trouble differentiating between the two, and seems to fuse them into one. She asked her sister to be the godmother for both daughters: "I think she'll be the one for both of them . . . we like her and want her to be our daughters' godmother. There are no rules for this kind of choice" (twelve days). Later on, we will see that she begins breastfeeding her daughters simultaneously and sometimes uses the same breast to feed both.

The fusion of these two into one, the difficulty of holding two, the desire to get rid of one, all of which had already been observed during pregnancy, are enacted by the grandmother and communicated non-verbally to the observer during the first observation. When Lucia falls asleep, the observer picks up her handbag to leave. At that moment the grandmother brings Daniela from the bedroom and asks the observer to hold her:

> She looked at me with my handbag in hand and says, "Hold her for me" . . . I take the girl from her arms and rock her, she cries softly . . . I'm confused, I don't know if this one is Daniela or Renata! I try to remember who was in the living room earlier with me and I can't remember, I'm really in doubt . . . The baby is so fragile and small, she weighs next to nothing. I'm afraid I'll drop her . . . then Lucia comes from the bedroom and says she will nurse her a little before giving her the supplement.

After this observation, the work was interrupted indefinitely for nearly four months. Lucia "turned her back" on the observer, repeating the familiar family pattern. The father told the observer over the phone that, "Lucia is very tired." After the observations are resumed, the same arrival procedure is repeated: the building doors are opened without any communication. The mother looks depressed and complains about how tiring it is to take care of twins: "It's not easy. I've been locked up inside the house for four months with these two." Nothing more was said about the last four months, which turned out to be a pattern of communication that was maintained throughout the three years of home visits. The observer reported:

> The girl [we are still confused and do not know which one] has grown, her face is very round, her eyes are just like Roberto's, but lighter in colour. She stares at me unsmiling, and I look back at her smiling . . . The maid watches me out of the corner of her eye . . . Lucia was eating lunch . . . she eats very quickly, like her daughter.

The mother says, "Daniela nurses as if she's never been nursed before in her life." Lucia makes this comment without realising that she is mimicking her daughter, eating voraciously.

The mother talks about Daniela's vomiting problem, which requires special care and lasts until she is about eleven months old. The vomiting seems to be a symptom that embodies the conflicting aspects of the mother–baby relationship. The mother is reluctant to use the medication for Daniela because the paediatrician told her it is banned. Daniela's vomiting changes as she develops, going from the act of expelling to the act of hitting. Renata, on the other hand, develops the habit of putting her thumb in her mouth to soothe herself, and has become more withdrawn. After she is weaned, she puts one thumb in her mouth and the other in her mother's, father's, or nanny's mouth.

Lucia asks if the observer wants to see Renata. "She's sleeping in our bed; do you believe that if I put her in her own bed, she cries?"

> I see Renata sleeping, surrounded by several cushions. She is also bigger and very different from her sister. She looks more like Lucia and her maternal grandmother.

Throughout the next three years, the observer makes frequent physical descriptions of the babies in an attempt to discriminate them, but which only cause greater confusion.

Confusion permeates the whole family. Later on, the mother tells the observer about an episode where Roberto confused the two girls: ". . . it was getting close to the time when Roberto comes home, so I put a cap on Renata that their aunt had given them and went out to the front. When Roberto saw her, he quickly parked the car and came over to kiss his daughter. He asked me, 'And Renata, where is she?' He hadn't realised that Renata was the one with us and that Daniela was inside."

The non-differentiation and fusion of the two daughters into one is also apparent in how they are cared for. Daniela is given a serum and breastfeeds between short intervals because of her reflux. Renata does not need such care. However, the observer reports,

> Daniela starts crying, so Lucia says she will feed her. Lucia goes into the kitchen and gets the serum she had prepared and gives a spoonful to Daniela. She does the same with Renata, claiming that she will be jealous if she doesn't get any, because whatever one does the other has to do too (five months and three days).

Another time, the mother asks the nanny, "Which one did I give medicine to? I can't remember, was it Dani?"

Lucia is worried about Daniela's vomiting, especially her muscular responses: "I am nervous about Dani. A few days ago I went to a birthday party with Roberto and I left them with my mother. She was terrified because Dani went all stiff; her whole body was hard and she wouldn't stop crying for one minute. I called the doctor last week and he said that maybe she's picking up something from me . . . but I know I'm not that bad, I know myself. It's not easy, being locked away at home for four months with these two. I am depressed, and they'll just have to know that their mother is like this . . ." Lucia was expressing that the babies had to adapt to her, and not *vice versa*. Despite her greater resemblance to Daniela, the mother has a closer affinity with Renata: "It's possible that Dani notices I have more affinity with Renata. Renata is stronger and more determined. Dani is quiet and much more sensitive: all those diseases, well not really diseases, those viruses that little kids get, Dani got and Renata didn't."

The mother regularly nursed the babies together. During one observation, she told the observer she would see what it was like to breastfeed. She settled on the sofa with two pillows, one on each side for each baby so they could lie head to head. "Are you all right there, Daniela? Are you all right there, Renata?" Breastfeeding both babies simultaneously demonstrates a type of relationship where the singular space and time each baby had with the mother is blurred. This pattern of relationship/contact that fuses two into one and cancels out differences is seen repeatedly throughout the observations. At six months, the observer's slip of the tongue reveals how, for Lucia, only one baby seems to exist:

> When she is arranging the pillows to breastfeed the girls, Lucia puts *Renata* on the left and *Renata* on the right.

We believe that the observer's lapse reveals not only that the two babies were being breastfed as if they were one, but also how the mother duplicates Renata's image, the one she claims to have more affinity with, thus excluding Daniela. It is worth remembering how, at the first observation, Daniela's exclusion was enacted when the grandmother gives her to the observer as she was about to leave with her bag in hand. At seven months and five days, Lucia follows the pattern of fusing the babies into one during breastfeeding. The observer describes:

> Lucia continues to breastfeed with one on each breast, even after they are bigger and no longer fit on the pillows.

Lucia decides to wean her daughters early so she can resume her antidepressant medications. She tells the observer: "Yesterday I was at my sister's psychiatrist. I wasn't doing well . . . I've taken meds [antidepressants] since I was a teenager. When I got pregnant I stopped, but now I need them again . . . The psychiatrist advised me to stop breastfeeding the girls . . . Gosh! I felt so bad . . . I can't imagine not breastfeeding them now. I don't know what it would do to me. The doctor said I'm too dependent on them, and I think they are dependent on me. But I'm the one that really needs them. It's true that I'm so attached to them that I feel angry when someone else picks them up . . ." (four months and nineteen days).

Lucia cannot see her daughters as separate from herself. She latches on to Daniela and Renata to ensure her own existence. In another situation, Lucia says she wishes the girls would not grow up because that meant being separated and that they would have their own desires. She says, "I do not want them to grow up, no I don't . . ." (five months and ten days). Another time, she describes her relationship with her daughters as follows: "Oh, I do not know what it will be like when I go back to work. They are so dependent on me. Actually, I don't know if they are or I am, since I am so needy, you know? But it's such a good feeling . . . it's nice to feel them so connected to me . . ." (four months and five days).

Lucia's mother criticises her, and in one situation she complains that her granddaughters are hard to comfort, insinuating, "Maybe they're stuck at home too much . . . Lucia spoiled them; she got them used to the nursing. I don't know what it will be like when she goes back to work. It's dreadful every time that girl [Lucia] leaves the house" (seven months and five days).

The observations are permeated by confusion in terms of time. An example is when Lucia asks to cancel the first filming, to which the observer agrees and transfers it to the following week. Even then, Lucia only showed up at the end. Upon their arrival for the rescheduled filming, the observer and her colleague are received by the nanny, who reports that everyone, including the mother, is asleep. They wait until five minutes before their time to leave, when they hear a small cry.

> Lucia comes into the room holding Daniela. She briefly talks to me and I tell her we can't do the filming at this point. The mother leaves, handing Daniela over to the nanny, and goes to take a shower! I leave a message with the nanny that we will do the filming in two weeks.

This brief report clearly demonstrates a type of communication that is characteristic of this home, which registers neither arrivals nor departures. Additionally, Lucia displays a childish attitude of disregard to others, revealing her emotional inadequacy and detachment. This makes us think of the high levels of expectation placed on the observer in her function of providing emotional support.

The filming finally takes place at the next observation. The father, Roberto, is present, but Lucia had an appointment scheduled for the same day and time. The filming begins with only one daughter, in keeping with the couple's pattern of excluding one:

> Daniela is sleeping on her father's lap while Renata is asleep in the bedroom. The film starts with Daniela sleeping deeply and peacefully. Then she slowly awakens and starts interacting with her father and imitating the sounds he makes: "brr, brr". She moves her head, watching everything that is happening around her. The father argues that the bedroom where Renata is sleeping is too dark and he doesn't think it will be good for filming. We decide to film her another time.

A colleague will return to film the ten remaining minutes when the babies are together. According to the observer's report:

> A few minutes before the observation ends, Lucia arrives . . . "Hello, mummy's little princesses! Did you miss mummy? Where you all right while mummy was gone? . . . I want to know how you behaved! I want to know! Is it true that when the mice are away the cats come out to play?"

This inversion of the saying is interesting. Why did Lucia feel like a mouse inside her own home, and not like a cat? Possibly, she felt threatened with being eaten by the kittens. Her first experiences with her babies were permeated by insecurity, low self-esteem, and depression.

The father's insecurity is also visible, as well as his lack of support for his wife. Shortly before the filming, Roberto gives Daniela to the observer, saying, "Hold her and let's see how you do." This reminds us of when the babies were born, which had been so traumatic for him. He had asked permission to touch them and hold them, and had wept copiously and uncontrollably during the delivery. Thus, the father's gesture of handing his daughter Daniela over to the observer possibly still expresses his need to free himself of the very real commitment of having two babies in his arms. The gesture also reminds us of the grandmother's attitude at the end of the first home observation when she gave Daniela to the observer as she was about to leave.

The difficult "three-in-one" relationship between the mother and the twins and the need for emotional support are seen in Lucia's reaction to when the observations are changed from once a week to once every two weeks, and then to once a month. She begins seeing a psychotherapist and using antidepressant medication. Thus, it is evident that the constant presence of the observer had a supporting therapeutic function for Lucia as a mother. When the observations became less frequent, she "replaced" them with appropriate therapeutic help. These decisions confirm her initial statement when the ultrasound observations began, that it felt good to be "observed" in her transition to motherhood.

Although she had already been preparing herself, the weaning occurs abruptly and without elaboration. Lucia tells the observer, "I decided to stop breastfeeding. I've been nursing them for eight months already. It's time. It's just that I have to start taking antidepressants again, you know? And the doctor said I had to do it for them, because they are at a stage where they require a lot from me. And I can't be feeling down and depressed; I did it for them! . . . But look, it wasn't easy! I suffered a lot. I spent the whole night up crying, and the other day I was feeling really bad and spent the whole day in bed! . . . Daniela is feeling it much more; she's suffering a lot. You should have seen her. She spent the whole night crying . . . Renata took a while to realise what was going on. She only cried after the second night of not being breastfed" (eight months and twenty-three days). The separation of the three seems unbearable. Daniela and Renata react physically to being weaned. Daniela runs a fever and both develop allergies. In the observations after they are weaned, the twins are less active, apathetic, and cry more often. According to Lucia, "They still haven't accepted being weaned. Can you believe Daniela was looking for my breast yesterday?" (nine months and twenty days). On this occasion, the observer reports,

> There were two framed pictures turned to face the wall. Lucia explained that they were photos of the girls breastfeeding. She said her daughter wanted to see the pictures, but she could no longer show them to her [nine months and twenty days].

Here, we can see the typical pattern observed since Lucia's pregnancy, where she "turns her back" to magically make things disappear.

In keeping with her intrusive pattern, the grandmother gave the observer the news about weaning the babies. She says she bought a machine to pump milk from her daughter. She gives the impression that she is talking about a dairy cow, which reminds us of the first home observation when she made a comment to her daughter, in a competitive tone, that some cows produce thirty litres and others fifteen. Lucia maintains the ongoing competitive environment, stating, "I've pumped tons of milk with this machine." This comment seems to express both her satisfaction and her horror at having a lot of milk.

When the babies are eight months and nine days old, the observer is received by the nanny, who says everyone is sleeping because Renata had a fever the night before.

> I take the time observe the home and think about how the girls are already eight months old, but it was still very difficult for the mother to give them the freedom to grow. I think of how it's three o'clock on a Friday afternoon and the three of them are sleeping, even though they are already eight months old . . .

Lucia's reaction to the separation brought on by the weaning is seen in her intensified depression, absences, and isolation. During this period, the three of them revert to sleeping a lot, as they had in the first observations, going into a stage of regression. Lucia put a "Do Not Ring" sign over her doorbell and called the observer to let her know.

In a later situation, Lucia says that Daniela has become angry and aggressive, which she associates to problems with weaning. She thinks that when Daniela starts preschool, she will be "very angry, and will shout and hit [the mother]" because of her frustration about the weaning. Lucia projects her separation difficulties on to her daughters and they correspond, often being attuned to her. Weaning also marks Lucia's increased control and inhibition of the children's exploratory behaviour. For example, when Daniela is put in a baby walker and moves away from her mother, Lucia complains and orders her daughter to stay close. She is always between the girls, acting as an intermediary and hampering their exchange. It is important to clarify that early on, in the first few months, the babies did not exhibit the expected behaviour of twin sisters. They barely interacted, did not recognise each other, and seemed to be one person. Lucia is a kind of mother who finds it difficult to allow her daughters any distance so they can have the space to separate themselves and become independent. Another time, the observer reports,

> I saw the following scenario: Lucia is sitting on the floor with her legs forming a circle around Renata that establishes limits. She had placed selected toys inside the circle. I notice that this provides very limited space for Renata to explore her environment (eight months and nine days).

In another situation, Lucia repeats the same behaviour:

> She sits on the mattress and encircles her daughters with her legs, adding some toys to the space for the girls. Daniela rolls to one side of the mattress and Lucia grabs her with her hands . . . (eight months and twenty-three days).

When the girls are around ten months old, their interaction finally becomes a little more frequent and some closeness begins to develop. The observer reports,

> I noticed that Renata looked at Daniela once, very quickly, but she definitely looked at her sister.

These situations are quite rare. The few times the twins do interact by touching or looking at each other, they are interpreted in the same way that was described in the ultrasound exams: they are either fighting or competing about something, with Daniela considered the aggressor and Renata the victim. For example, the following scenario was reported:

> Daniela touches Renata's face and she begins to cry. The nanny says Daniela pinched Renata. Renata screams (ten months and eighteen days).

Thus, Lucia, her mother, and the nannies interpret most of the girls' interactions as either Daniela being aggressive towards Renata, or as a competition between the two for objects, which the adults respond to by preventing their interaction and by reprimanding them. Another example:

> When Lucia stands Daniela up in her chair, the girl notices that Renata had a straw in her hand. Lucia says, "Don't fight with your sister." Daniela looks at Renata's straw and Lucia says, "Don't take it from your sister, wait until mummy gets you another" . . . Daniela tries to take the straw from her sister and Lucia tells her not to hit her sister. She gives the girl another straw.

We notice that the parents attribute the girls' supposed sibling rivalry to their relationship, not recognising that they are the ones who have provoked the rivalry since pregnancy with their problem of not being able to open space for two.

Although their interactions continue being interpreted as mostly fights or aggressions, after their first year the twins begin to interact more often and more independently. For example:

> Maria [the nanny] gives a bottle of tea to Renata at the same time as Daniela leaves her mother's room and they meet half way. Daniela seems to want the bottle of tea, saying, "give, give, give". Renata holds the bottle in her hand and says "no, no, no", shaking her index finger (one year, two months, and seventeen days).

On the same day, the observer reports that the two play "make-believe":

> Renata makes food and tries to feed it to Daniela, who in turn wants to take Renata's plate.

The mother's difficulties with regard to the babies' separation continues after their first year of life. When they are one year and twenty-six days old, the observer reports that Daniela stands up and then falls, causing the mother to pick her up and say, "You can't walk, mummy is not ready to see you walking." Later,

> Lucia gives her a bottle, but holds it herself. Then she repeats the same pattern with Renata. While the mother is busy with Renata, Daniela picks up the bottle, and Lucia says, "Let mummy give it to you." Lucia pulls the bottle from Daniela's hands and feeds it to her. I notice that Lucia uses one hand to hold the girl's hand to keep her from grabbing the bottle (one year, two months, and fourteen days).

Thus, even though the girls are able to hold the bottle themselves, their mother does not allow it and continues acting as the essential figure in their feeding routine, which stimulates their dependence. Hence, the pattern of a mother who is not prepared for daughters that are developing and becoming independent continues.

When they are approximately one year old, Daniela holds herself more firmly, keeping her body upright, unlike Renata. Even so, their different characteristics are not enough for the mother to differentiate them as two separate babies. This non-discrimination of the twins carries over to the nannies who take care of them, who, like Lucia, either prevent or do not notice the individuality expressed by Daniela and Renata. In one situation, for example, when they were one year and seven months old, the nanny calls for Renata but Daniela answers, showing that the two are developing in a very undifferentiated environment. The observer comments on the lack of differentiation between the babies in another situation:

> I immediately think back to the last observation and confirm that Renata is dressed in the same clothes Daniela had worn last week, and that Daniela is wearing the same blouse Renata had been wearing.

The indiscrimination in this case is intense and encompasses both emotional and physical aspects. Even the physical environment of the house demonstrates this indiscrimination. The observer describes:

> There are large baskets full of toys, many toys of various types including dolls, clowns, and inflatable puppets that take up nearly the entire living room. They are on the sofas and scattered across the floor. There are two of each toy, varying only in colour.

We reflected on how this description of the environment and the duplicated toys is revealing of this mother who both invalidates differences and denies reality.

Although this atmosphere of non-differentiation is prevalent, sometimes the twins are described in a manner that is stigmatised and polarised. Daniela is described as more active, more responsive, and more aggressive, while Renata is more passive and submissive to her mother's wishes. There is no flexibility or middle ground—they are either completely undifferentiated, or differentiated to the extreme. Lucia describes Daniela as more obstinate, saying, "Daniela is stubborn, she is capable of hitting Renata on the head with this bottle! . . . Daniela is terrible; yesterday she hit Renata because of a toy. She's going to be horrible!" (ten months and four days).

When the girls are one year and six months old, the observer reports that Daniela is throwing temper tantrums, gets extremely angry, hits her sister, cries, and stiffens her body, which worries the mother. The mother calls Daniela's behaviour hysteria, saying it is caused by the weaning process that had been too sudden and had a negative impact on her. We think about how Daniela's behaviour has intensified and how much this is associated to her relationship with her mother. First, she spewed out milk as a way of showing her dissatisfaction and of protesting her non-existence to her mother. The mother wants the paediatrician to prescribe an anxiolytic for Daniela, seeming to have chosen her to be her successor: the weaker one, the sick one who needs medication. It should be noted here that, by suggesting medication for her daughter, Lucia resorts to the external containment typically used by the women in this family to replace emotional support.

Lucia's separation issues cause her daughters to react when she leaves or withdraws. Lucia follows her customary pattern of "turning her back" and typically leaves without saying goodbye. At the observation that takes place just before the girls turn one, Lucia has to go out and leaves her daughters in the care of a nanny. When she is gone, Renata plays with a box, putting her hand inside and pulling it out, which makes the observer reflect:

> I think that this game Renata plays in her mother's absence can symbolise her feelings of separation.

The girls seem to begin working through the separation issue using "fort–da" type games (Freud, 1920g) that symbolise their mother's abrupt exits and help them bear her absences. This also occurs when Lucia leaves the house and

> closes the door so quietly you can't hear the sound of the key. When Lucia leaves, Daniela points to the door and says, "Mummy!" (One year, two months, and seventeen days.)

Although there are people around her, Lucia receives very little real support and is often helpless. None the less, she is able give her daughters some space to develop in a healthy way. As she comes out of depression, she is able to emerge from the long and painful "three-in-one" process, albeit carrying its marks. She continues to be absent or to forget the observations during this period. At the observation marking two years, three months, and twelve days, the observer arrives at the house at the same time as the mother, who does not see her. The mother is carrying some bags and the observer approaches her and greets her. The mother says. "I was wondering why you never came back." The mother's disconnection is astonishing; it is as if they had never set any sort of schedule. In the penultimate observation, when the girls were two years and nine months old, the mother once again forgets the observation and, when she sees the observer she says, "Gosh, I completely forgot!" She asks that the observer remind her ahead of time before the next visits, because she forgets. Lucia "turned her back" as much as she could in this period. Towards the end, we think of the mother's disconnection as something authentic that provided gradual differentiation for the daughters. As the mother spontaneously withdrew, the girls became closer and started playing more with each other. In spite of the non-discriminated female environment, Renata and Daniela's development progressed and they found ways to differentiate from each other.

Once the twins turned two, their interactions expanded. When they are filmed at two years and nineteen days, the observer is puzzled to find the sisters playing inside a little cabin in a very natural and spontaneous way, and reports,

> I'm sitting on the sofa watching Daniela and Renata's spontaneous play (two years and nineteen days).

Towards the end of their second year, these kinds of interactions become more common. Another example is reported:

> Lucia goes outside saying she has to park the car. Renata starts screaming and crying for her mother. She goes to the door crying while Daniela sits with a doll in her lap. Daniela goes after her sister and says something I don't understand and strokes Renata's face (one year, ten months, and seventeen days).

The twins not only interact, they also establish a mutual relationship of giving care and comfort in distressing situations such as their mother's absence. They also begin to include the observer in their playing, which she describes:

> Daniela and Renata play hide and seek with me. They look for me with their eyes and smile when they find me, then hide again behind the sofa, continuing the game (one year, eleven months, and fourteen days).

In another situation,

> Renata was watching me very seriously from the living room, where she was drinking a soft drink. Renata joins her and both run to the laundry area, laugh when they see me, then run to the kitchen door and smile again when they see me. I join their play, saying "hi" when they find me . . . At one point, Daniela slams the kitchen door then opens it again, smiling when she sees me. Renata imitates her sister's actions and says "come Nana" (two years, three months, and twelve days).

Still on that same occasion,

> Renata says "Come on Dani, let's take the balls to the bedroom" and Daniela does what she asks.

At the next observation, the twins are two and a half years old. The observer reports,

> Daniela and Renata walk to their parents' room where they stay for a while. Then they come running back into the living room towards me. They pretend they are giving me chocolates and sweets, telling me they have sweets in their hands. I pretend that I'm eating the sweets. The girls repeat this game countless times.

Maintaining the setting along with the constant presence of the observer most probably helped in the mother–babies differentiation process. When the girls are one year, nine months, and fifteen days old the observer arrives to find the girls sleeping and thinks, "I have to keep my mind active so I don't tune into the mother's depression." In the observation reports, it is clear that the observer looks for reference points to discriminate herself from the environment and to stay in motion. For example, at one year, nine months, and thirteen days the girls are not at home, so the observer describes the noises she hears, as if seeking the sounds that give life to this home. She also connects to the most constant person in the environment, Maria, the maid. She says,

> Again I pay attention to Maria and her movements and work. I realise that I'm also connected to the sounds that echo outside the house, to the sound of people's footsteps inside the building, the noise of keys when they are inserted into locks, and once again to the ticking of the clock.

The last observation is conducted with this family when the girls are three years and fifteen days old. A scene is played out that represents Lucia's progress in differentiating her daughters and how much the twins helped and confirmed this process.

> Lucia walks into the kitchen and then returns with two cups in her hands, one yellow and one green. Lucia gives the yellow cup to Daniela, and Renata says the yellow cup belongs to Daniela, and the green one belongs to her [confirming the mother's actions]. The mother asks Renata again which is her cup colour, and she answers.

Towards the end of this last observation, the observer reports,

> The girls approach me and I give them their gifts—a doll for Renata and a plastic beach bucket with shovels for Daniela. Lucia helps Renata open the box with the doll, and Daniela asks for her mother's help, too ... When Lucia realises the gifts are different, she reassures the girls, saying they can play with both toys on the beach. I notice that this made her anxious.

The observer's gesture of giving two different gifts seemed to have an interpretation effect that surprised the mother. But, as they had been doing recently, the daughters reassured her by showing they were comfortable with the differentiation.

> Renata held the doll in her lap and played with it. Daniela pretended she was digging the floor with her shovel. Renata says that when she grows up she will drive her mother's car, and Daniela says she will drive her father's car.

Now they are able to differentiate. Now the three can truly be three.

Final considerations

The case of Lucia and her twins has much to teach us about the maternal challenge of dealing with differences and the threat of exclusion that accompanies it. The case also allows us to follow the birth of fraternity that came as a result of the twin sisters' joint effort to differentiate. Confusion permeated the entire family during pregnancy. The twins are not often seen, and when they are, it is always as body parts. They are not differentiated or remembered according to their physical characteristics or location in the uterus. The mother sees them as an extension of herself—foetus one and foetus two—and does not name or discriminate between them. Any distinction seems to break a fragile emotional balance. They are a "three-in-one" unit. Even in the midst of this confusion, the twins consistently show their differences, starting at the first ultrasound. They have different rhythms and styles of movement, which are distinctly evident in all the exams. One is always active and the other is more passive. This difference is noticed by the observer from the start, but is not seen by the mother:

> Right now one is more active and we can see it swallowing liquid, its spinal column, and its beating heart . . . the other baby was quiet, seemingly asleep. Then it moved slightly and yawned (thirteen weeks).

During pregnancy, the mother maintained a fantasy that one of them would disappear *in utero,* always commenting that in the first ultrasounds it had looked as if one of the gestational sacs was not developing. It should be noted that before the first examination, our research project conducted in her thirteenth week of pregnancy, Lucia had already had four ultrasounds in an attempt to clarify what, in fact, was occurring inside her, and the fact that she still did not know was very distressing to her. She agreed to participate in our research, saying she could see better . . . "Will I be able to see?" The mother's ambivalence made her oscillate between fearing that the presence of two babies would be confirmed and fearing that one would disappear. Her anxiety was communicated non-verbally to the sonographer, who unknowingly started several of the examinations by stating, "Let's see if there are still two of them." At other times, she was affected by the confusion, which was not typical of her, saying, "Let's see if I've got the right child. Sorry for the confusion, it's that sometimes we get lost."

The confirmation that there are two girls seems to have added to the confusion. The father has trouble seeing the images, that he now says are blurred. The mother is totally lost and asks about body parts . . . "Do they already have genitalia? A brain? Poor thing, it's a girl . . ." Her difficulty in holding two and her desire to either fuse them into one or exclude one of them is all very intense, which leads us to think that the presence of two girls sharpened her fear of being excluded herself, something that was very real in her family history. She grew up in an indiscriminate female environment that was coincidentally made up of two daughters, she being the undervalued and excluded one. Lucia felt threatened with repeating this same pattern with her daughters. As we have seen throughout the babies' first three years of life, Daniela ends up being the one that is always threatened with exclusion because of her alleged resemblance to her mother and because of her personality.

The intensity with which the couple experienced the delivery leads us to think that the reality of having twin daughters shook them deeply, making it a traumatic experience for both. Once they were born, the couple could no longer sustain the doubts they had during pregnancy, the fantasy/fear that one would not develop. The various ultrasounds that were performed were not enough to prove the actual existence of the girls, who were seen in parts. What to do with two? (It is worth remembering that the father filled out the administrative papers at the hospital for only one daughter.) Both sobbed endlessly, showing they were unprepared and helpless, as if reacting to the many separations and losses that were inherent to the birth of their daughters. They lost their status of being merely children and siblings and were now required to assume the function of parents in a very real situation. The mother had to face the separation issues of the girls, and the couple reacted to the inevitable changes in their relationship. (When the nurse called Lucia to begin the proceedings, the observer noticed that the couple was upset by the separation.)

They were confused about how to assign the names they had previously chosen for the girls, leaving the paediatrician aunt to determine which was which according to their physical characteristics: the one that looked like the mother was called Daniela and the one that looked like the father was called Renata. At the first observation with the daughters after they were born, the mother, following a pattern that she maintained throughout the first three years of the girls' lives, held only one in her lap and worried about their differences, about why one was awake and the other one asleep.

The first home observation is a precise example of the mother's tragedy: she was weak, ambivalent, discredited, and criticised by her own mother and sister in an intrusive and indiscriminate pattern from which she feebly tried to defend herself. At the end of that first observation, the grandmother dramatises Daniela's exclusion by handing her to over to the observer as she was about to leave, her handbag in hand. She seems to enact the desire to get rid of the negative aspects related to her, Lucia, and the family, and, thus, try to find some relief from her anxiety, powerlessness, and sadness. Daniela's destiny was to be the repository of things unbearable. She had to be excluded. Hence, it was common for her to stay in the bedroom during the observations while the sister remained in the living room.[15]

The approximately four-month interruption after the first observation makes us think the twin birth experience was extremely intense for the mother. The observer faced a major challenge in sustaining this long period of silence, the lack of communication without knowing what was going on, despite wanting news. At one point, the father informed her that the mother was tired, indicating that she most certainly was trying to digest the presence of two babies she now had to take care of. To succeed, she had to fuse them into one and, thus, exclude the ominous difference. The observer's physical presence threatened this indiscrimination and created a wedge in the symbiotic mother–babies relationship and, hence, she needed to be kept away from the observations.

The observer's patience, supported by the supervision group, allowed her to withstand the situation and remain emotionally attached to the family. Although the observer was denied entry by the mother not only during this period, but continuously over the babies' first three years (it was common for the mother to forget the observer or not see her during the observations), she established an unconscious partnership with the mother and babies that helped dilute their anxieties and, in the long run, helped support the mother–babies differentiation process.

At the next visit after the observations resumed, the observer felt she was entering a difficult environment that had been complicated by their long and silent separation. She faced a striking scene of the tired mother nursing both babies simultaneously, which had become routine. At the same time, the presence of the observer seemed to serve as a catalyst, causing the babies to begin differentiating themselves more. It is interesting that, in an unconscious partnership, Daniela's reflux symptoms began at the same time Renata started sucking her thumb and withdrawing. These patterns remained until the girls were approximately eleven months old. Daniela reacted by expelling what was being projected on her: not existing and being considered "two in one" with her fragile, sick, angry, agitated sister who, according to the mother, had been on anxiolytics (continuing the women's pattern in this family) since she was a newborn. Renata, on the other hand, dramatised the fusion with her mother, which calmed her somewhat.

Once she was weaned, Renata continued sucking her thumb, but now she added putting the other in her mother's, father's, or nanny's mouth. In this manner, she maintained her function of internalising, of connecting and not breaking. Daniela's spewing turned into aggression. She acted out, on the one hand, by hitting her sister, her mother, and classmates at school, but, on the other hand, she took initiative in things such as including her sister in her play and exploring the house and discovering the excitement of surprise and new things. Renata was able to "hold" one thumb outside her mouth, or rather, inside another, without losing herself. Daniela was able to hold in feelings and experiences without spewing them out. Thus, one was able to "push" the other in their process of separation, which was so incomplete in this case, and enjoy life, play, and creating. They begin to demonstrate creativity in their playing and their relationships, including in how they interact with the observer.

Theirs was a long, hesitant, and painful process of mother–baby separation that did not match their evolving needs. The pattern that developed was that of a mother who was never prepared for the different stages of her children's development. Additionally, it became clear throughout the observations that the babies frequently could not count on their mother, who inversely relies on her daughters for her transition into motherhood.

A number of situations demonstrated how the daughters were put in the position of mothering their mother, of having to meet her demands for affection, comfort, and containment. Lucia often asks the babies to hug and kiss her, even when they are too young to do so, placing their little arms around her own neck (Renata is the one put in this more submissive position). At other times, the babies submit to Lucia's desire for them to nurse nestled beside her, thus emphasising their dependence on her. They seem to comfort and care for Lucia, who feels undervalued and alone.

Roberto, the father, was no longer on the scene after the babies were born, which intensified the mother's dependent, "three-in-one" relationship with her two daughters. It was inevitable that the three be as one for a time. Lucia kept the babies from demonstrating spontaneous behaviour, thus causing them to adapt to their mother's needs. An example is when Renata comforted herself, as she often did, by putting her thumb in her mouth, and Lucia scolded her because she thought she was rejecting and substituting her breast, saying, "You can't nurse with your thumb in your mouth! Get that thumb out of your mouth. Don't you want your mummy's milk any more? . . ." (five months and three days).

Having to meet the mother's needs extended the separation process and delayed the girls' development towards independence. Lucia's attitudes created an abyss between dependence and developing independence for the babies, and circumvented every kind of differentiation. Crawling, standing, walking, and weaning were all difficult transitions for Lucia, who was experiencing certain levels of unbearable uncertainty, helplessness, and abandonment. We think that the mother's needs and projections were so intense that they permeated the observer to the point that she was at times too confused or identified with Lucia to see or describe the rich and decisive steps the girls took in their development.

The environment was one of confusion and a lack of discrimination. The twins slept on a single cot for a long time, at the suggestion of the maternal grandmother. The cot was later replaced by a double bed mattress, which continued the pattern of sleeping together. The girls did not have their own separate clothes or medications (only Daniela required medication for her reflux). Their names were often switched. Their toys were all duplicated, occasionally varying only in colour. Lucia's sister was chosen to be the godmother for both. Clearly, it took a long time for them to be born and become distinguished.

In addition to observing this pattern of confusion and non-discrimination, the observer also experienced the family pattern of "turning her back" (Lucia's mother also "turned her back" to her), especially in her relationship with the mother. Lucia acts like a child. Because she lacks the courage to take charge, she runs away, disappears, and becomes even more forgetful of the observation days. She uses her tough projected identities to communicate to the observer and the girls her anxieties and dramas related to separations, and her need to be free of them. This makes us think of the defence mechanisms mothers adopt during this period that function to alleviate their fear of the unknown and separation, and to relieve anxieties.

The way the mother switched on–off, or became confused or disappeared, did not favour differentiation, a process that had been interrupted in her own life. The discontinuities and lack of communication were intensely experienced by the babies and the observer. When the observer arrived at the family home, the building doors were opened without any sort of communication. On numerous occasions, the mother would only arrive near the end of the observation, or would forget them completely. When the babies were a little bigger, she began to leave home secretly or without warning—she simply disappeared. Weaning was abrupt and erratic. The post-weaning period relived the separation and the mother's depression that had been experienced in the first four months of the girls' lives. The observer encountered the "Do Not Ring" warning sign taped to the doorbell, which recalled the initial period when the mother kept her away from the observations. The observer often had to wait in the empty, silent, and non-communicating house while mother and babies slept.

The observer very clearly described being alone in this environment, looking for some sort of reference point, whether they be noises or the presence of the maid to keep herself lucid and discriminated. The fact that she kept herself apart from the confusion and maintained her function and the observation setting allowed her to be used by the mother and the babies. She held the mother's absence with her presence. She provided time and space. She empathised with these babies who had to make a team effort to find their individual places, since the mother continually blurred their differences and singularities.

It was a beautiful experience following the development of this sibling relationship. Daniela and Renata formed a partnership that facilitated their separation from the mother and enabled them to continue developing towards independence. Indeed, the girls were required to make a significant effort to withdraw from the mother's symbiotic attachment, which she considered undoable. The twins helped each other by complementing their strengths, roles, separation, and growth.

This interaction that occurred between the girls since they were babies produced a sense of despair in their mother, as if she were threatened with being excluded from the trio, which made her prevent their contact. She systematically placed herself between them as a constant intermediary, which was exhibited in her simultaneous breastfeeding of the two, and by not allowing the girls to hold their own bottles despite already having the full capacity to do so. The same happened in their play or sleep (it was common for Lucia to sit her daughters within the boundaries of her legs). Yet, at the same time, she turned her back on them in order to cut them off, leave the scene, and not see them together and individualised. "If I don't see, I won't suffer." The girls are penalised with abandonment and loneliness. They gradually begin to observe each other, interact, and play together, comfort and support each other, and symbolise and expand their relationships with the nanny, the observer, and at school. They were clearly discriminating themselves. "The home clock began to tick" (in many observations, the house clock had stopped). They were growing up, whether or not the mother acknowledged or approved it.

The observer had the wisdom to wait and follow the twins' natural evolution towards independence. At the right moment, when the babies were near the end of their third year of life, she expressed her thoughts that the girls had finally been able to achieve greater differentiation without it being a threat to themselves. When she said her goodbyes, she gave each girl a different gift as the mother watched, still clearly threatened by the differences and visibly uncomfortable. But Daniela and Renata try to reassure their mother by each playing with her own toy. Renata says that when she grows up she will drive her mother's car and Daniela will drive her father's car.

Daniela and Renata's story makes us think of the strength of human nature and its tendency to integrate and mature. A sense of confusion related to time permeated the observation work with this family. During pregnancy, Lucia never remembered how far along she was, and always forgot to bring the previous exams. In the post-delivery observations, she did not notice her daughters' growth and forgot practically all the scheduled observations. Her difficulties in dealing with the passage of time often caused her to schedule two things at the same time. But, through their play, especially their different versions of hide-and-seek, each of the girls progressively tried to build a bridge that both separated and united. The babies teach us that maturation is more than a natural tendency; it is an achievement. They also teach us that solutions cannot be predicted. As their play expanded, Daniela and Renata helped each other find solutions to their daily problems and to find ways of comforting each other. Watching the relationship that unfolded between the sisters teaches us to value the fraternal nucleus in human development.

CHAPTER FIVE

Tânia and her daughter, Julie: the creative recovery of discontinuities in a tailor-made space of protection, care, and mutual growth

Pregnancy

Julie's story was followed through observations of six monthly ultrasound scans conducted between the mother's fourteenth and thirty-fourth weeks of pregnancy, her birth, and forty-seven home observations during the first three years of her life.

The observer arrives at the clinic early for the first scan and finds the couple already there. The feelings of anticipation and urgency that permeate that first examination remain throughout the entire pregnancy, to the surprise of the observer, who is at times confused and called upon to do things such as set dates, exchange phone numbers, and make plans. Additionally, the parents ask the sonographer obscure and ambiguous life-and-death questions.

The first impression the observer has of Carlos, twenty-seven years old, and Tânia, twenty-six years old, is a strange feeling of superficiality, as if they were putting up "a front"; nice, but provoking surprise. The first contact by phone had been amicable, making the observer anxious to meet them and more willing and stimulated to participate in the research. They are smiling and have a fragile, almost scared, look about them. During the scan, the movement of the foetus perplexes them, as if that were something unexpected. Each new piece of information given by the doctor caused them to exchange looks and smiles and ask questions, as if something mysterious was about to be revealed—a somewhat theatrical behaviour that seemed to cover up fears and concerns.

Both were very anxious and insecure, yet happy and smiling. Nothing was clear; in fact, everything was strange, according to the observer, who could not tell if their feelings were of happiness or sadness, satisfaction or frustration, certainty or doubt.

The couple's reaction and dialogue when they saw the first image is confused.

> The image of the foetus appears on the screen, the couple's eyes immediately light up, and they become somewhat euphoric:
>
> Mother: "Look at that, dear!"
>
> Father smiles and says, "Look at it move!"
>
> Mother: "It's moving, dear, look."
>
> Father: "I know."

They seem distressed and at a loss, almost angry at the image, as if there were something stuck in their throat and they were asking themselves: is it in there? No? Is it alive? Is it moving? Is it dead? Isn't it moving? A lot is said in that short yet intensely expressive dialogue, yet other things are left unsaid. Their exchange is choppy and frightened. They seem excited and surprised as if they had never seen anything so magical. Tânia has trouble seeing and is confused with what is in and what is out, saying: "Can you imagine that it's going to be in that position in here?" pointing at her belly. She spoke as if the foetus was not in her uterus. Yet, she comments about the "thin skin" that covers her belly and the organs of the baby, mixing up her body with that of the foetus. She appears frail and very afraid of not being able to carry the baby to term.

The doctor is aware of the parents' unspoken anxiety and tries to alleviate it by explaining the scan and the different images of the heart and spine, and the size of the head. She is very patient and understanding, respecting the pace of the couple. To really be sure that there is a life pulsing inside her womb, besides hearing the baby and seeing it on the monitor, it is important to touch it. Carlos says, "I can hear the heartbeat just by putting my hand or my ear on Tânia's belly, it's amazing."

Although the observer started her job enthusiastically, as the scan progressed, she describes,

> I feel left out and awkward. I hesitate to enter, despite being willing.

The doctor asks if they want to know the sex of the baby and the couple immediately agrees. The mother says, "The father here says it's a boy. He even has a name. Look at his feet and big head. He takes after his dad. Aunt Beatriz, his obstetrician, said he was a big baby, and you won't believe this: he was born with two teeth!" she says, pointing to her husband. Everyone laughs and the atmosphere relaxes considerably. The mother continues, "Imagine his poor mother trying to nurse him—with teeth!"

After a while, the doctor says she thinks the foetus is a girl, but it is just a guess because it is still too hard to know for sure. This will be clarified at the next ultrasound.

When the couple's participation in the research was confirmed, they seemed very excited and emphasised their need to be observed, understood, and helped throughout the pregnancy. They were filled with emotion when they talked about a very traumatic experience the mother had gone through when she observed another woman giving birth. The mother remembers the panic she felt at how fast things progressed. "I have already gone to the hospital with someone having a baby, and it was terrifying. We went to one hospital, and they sent us to another one. When we got there her waters broke and she had the baby. Just like that. I heard all the screams, it was horrible!" There are a number of latent fears regarding the rapidly growing life in her womb and of the foetus that might not develop; these fears come to the surface and reveal the couple's ambivalence. They want the baby, but they do not think they will be able to carry it through to term and keep it.

The father was present during the entire exam and as the scan progressed he moved closer and closer to his wife and the monitor. The communication between him and his wife made it hard to grasp the couple's story. They were enclosed in a kind of confused exchange, as if they had created their own code.

The observer, involved in this tumult of emotions, later found it odd that that, at the first examination, she so quickly addressed the subject of the birth, the hospital, and even arranged with the father how she would be notified, exchanging telephone numbers "so there wouldn't be any trouble in case of an emergency", all in a fast sequence of verbal exchanges, as if everything would be happening right then.

At the second ultrasound scan, the couple was anxious to see and know the baby's sex, saying other family members were waiting expectantly to have confirmation. The mother says, "That's right, baby girl, everyone wants to know. Mummy is going to buy you the proper clothes." The father says, "Stop hiding," and the mum responds, "Turn around and show your us your twinkle, baby girl."

The movements of the foetus made it very difficult to confirm the sex, which kept the couple tense. However, they could see it had grown. The doctor says the baby weighs 241 grams and the mother exclaims: "It's really grown! And gained weight! The last time it only weighed 120 grams!" The mother's expression was always ambiguous about this: sometimes she would be excited and gaining weight was something good, and at other times she seemed distressed, as if it were something bad.

It is interesting how those present demonstrated satisfaction at seeing the foetus swallow, open and close its tiny hands, and even responded by waving at it. The mother asks tensely, "Why is it that when they are so small and still in the belly they can swallow, but they can't in the end?" The doctor, as usual understanding the anxiety of the parents, answers all their questions and says the foetus can swallow until the end of the pregnancy. The observer describes feeling that the baby could die if it did not swallow liquid, and simultaneously the father starts talking about the birth, asking if only the observer will be there to watch, or if the sonographer would be there, too, as if the birth could happen at any moment. The observer answers that she will certainly be present for the birth and restates all the arrangements, confirming that she will contact the obstetrician. Understanding the need of the parents, the sonographer frees the observer and stays a while longer to see if she can determine the sex of the foetus, which turns out to be a girl.

At the next scan—twenty-two weeks—the parents are riveted when the foetus appears on the screen. Right as they are watching and talking happily about their chosen name, Julie, the baby moves, as if confirming that she is alive. Tânia smiles in a mixture of happiness and fright. She addresses the doctor: "Your profession is so wonderful, to be able to give life . . ." Tânia seems to have removed her own ability to procreate; she does not see her fundamental function in maintaining the life growing inside her womb. Instead, she projects this ability on to the sonographer.

During the scan, the observer describes herself as feeling paralysed and not very sharp, asking the parents if they will stick with the name they chose, which they confirm. The doctor continues describing Julie to the parents, showing her kidneys, brain, and the image of her beating heart. The mother asks if that is really her heart. When the answer is yes, she becomes emotional. When the measurements of the foetus are taken, the mother asks about the weight—487 grams. She is both impressed and worried, saying, "But that's already double! It's incredible how she's grown! I can't see how she's going to get out of there." The baby's intrauterine growth is a relief, but it also worries the mother. She seems terrified that the foetus will stop growing and die, while at the same time hopes it will be born quickly so that it survives. She feels threatened and doubts her intrauterine space is reliable enough to ensure good development for the baby. This mix of feelings, fears, and confusion creates a constant concern that something might not go right and that the baby will die.

At the fourth scan, Carlos keeps very close to Tânia. She says, "Ah, my child, if you knew how crazy everyone is to see you arrive. We can't wait!" The doctor says, "Yes, but for now you stay there a little longer, Julie, it's too early to come out." Everyone laughs and the mother asks, "It's amazing how she can swallow, isn't it?"

Doctor: "What have you eaten today?"

Mother: "I had ice cream just now. She must be getting mad at me, I spent hours without eating this morning for the exam at the obstetrician's."

Doctor: "That means she's having a shake."

Mother: "Can she taste through the liquid or through the umbilical cord?"

The doctor explains that she tastes through the liquid, but that food comes through the umbilical cord.

The curiosity and fear about the growth of the foetus are significant aspects of this couple. They are concerned with the weight, length, and size of the baby, and repeat the same reaction to each new piece of information: pride and satisfaction at the growth, and significant anxiety that this development could be interrupted at any moment.

At the next scan, Julie is more active, and, according to the mother, "She's a lively one who won't stop kicking and moving from one side of my belly to the other." If she stops, the father "pokes her non-stop". As always, the mother wants to know the baby's weight—1,230 grams—which the observer notes as kilos, and length—thirty-one centimetres. Tânia says, "You're growing, baby girl", surprised by the image of the foetus. A short while later, the observer asks the couple about some arrangements for the research, which they accept without question. They ask that she use the name Julie in the documents, which she does.

Thirty-one weeks into the pregnancy, Julie measures thirty-seven centimetres and weighs 1,908 grams, which the observer once again registers as kilos. She is bigger and can only be viewed in parts on the screen. The foetus seems to be doing well and there are clear views of all her organs, spinal column, and genitals. She moves a lot. The sonographer increases the volume so everyone can hear her heartbeats. Everyone is silent, giving Julie space. The father remarks that her position is "low and settled", and asks if there is any threat of early labour.

At the end of this scan, the observer mentions that some of the images of Julie moving her little feet are funny: "She spreads her toes, moving them up and down as if she's waving." Everyone laughs and seems to say good-bye to this intrauterine stage. The doctor points to the mother's swollen feet, iterating that she should see her gynaecologist. The father wants to schedule the next examination, and the mother says: "Do you think it will be the last ultrasound?" Then, pointing her finger at the observer, she says in a tone of summons, "Are you ready to watch the birth?" The observer, surprised, says, "Yes, I'm ready", and looks at the father to remind him that he is responsible for letting her know, regardless of the day or time. He laughs and agrees, and the observer continues, "I intend to be there an hour early. I'll contact the obstetrician and the hospital ahead of time." He adds, "Oh, there's the film, we want it filmed!"

The next ultrasound takes place in the thirty-fourth week of pregnancy. The observer arrives at the clinic with the mother and writes,

> I almost don't recognize her, she's so swollen. She has anasarca. When she sees me, she gives me a big hug.

They conduct a Doppler examination and the observer describes that during the exam she felt intense heat that made her sweat profusely, she could not catch her breath, and had a tingling sensation. The doctor asks the mother if the baby had moved that morning. She answers not much. Carlos asks if everything is all right. The doctor answers that her circulation is good, but the amniotic fluid is almost gone. The observer feels sick, pressured by the heavy silence, and notices the mother's profound disappointment. She was sent to the obstetrician, who, when shown the results of the examinations, had Tânia hospitalised and prepared for labour.

Premature birth: "What can you do?"

After the obstetrician's evaluation, Tânia calls the observer and tells her that she is going to the hospital. The observer says she is already there, waiting for her. Tânia is silent, then says, "I don't believe it! Really? You're there?" The observer tells her that she still needs to finalise a few things for filming and watching the birth. Tânia already knows she will have a caesarean, since she no longer has any amniotic fluid.

Fretful about the forthcoming events, the observer describes what happened at the hospital to solve administrative issues in order to follow Julie's birth. As with the pregnancy, she felt the weight of anxiety. Maybe Tânia was more prepared for this than she knew. She calmly helped the observer, who, in her nervousness, had forgotten her handbag, which she had left on a chair at hospital admissions.

From the bed, the mother says, "She's got personality, that's for sure. It has to happen her way . . . What can you do? Miss Julie doesn't want to stay inside any more . . . I just worry about her being so tiny . . ."

It is important to note the mother used the expression, "What can you do?" at that moment when the continuity of the mother–baby relationship is being broken. As we will see throughout Julie's first three years, this expression shows how Tânia confronts reality without drama, simply determined to find a solution. The observer asks about the filming, but they say they do not want it any more. The father says, "It's because it's going to be by caesarean . . . she's coming early", and the mother adds, "It's because I didn't bring her clothes; the closet and her cot aren't ready either. She's coming early."

While Tânia is being prepped, some people exit the delivery room, leaving only the obstetrician, who looks at the observer and states, "Yes, there's nothing you can do, it's nature that decides. They must have told you that they had a miscarriage earlier and a month later she was pregnant again. If the other baby hadn't miscarried, Tânia would be in her ninth month, having the baby now."

The observer feels run over, shocked. The harsh delivery of this information reveals the reason for all the apprehension, anxiety, and insecurity during the entire pregnancy: Julie had developed "on top of" a dead foetus; the couple felt hounded by this ghost that might reappear at any moment. The uterus in which Julie grew was haunted and dangerous. And now the parents are faced with this strange baby whose life only a few hours ago had been diagnosed as being in serious danger and who required surgical removal from the maternal womb. The couple becomes serious and embarrassed, and the mother keeps looking at the monitor: "I think this machine is crazy. It keeps changing numbers. She reached 240 heartbeats per minute."

Tânia calmly looks at her husband and laughs, saying, "You look cute dressed like a doctor", to which he laughs and replies, "I work the medical shift." Everyone laughs. She becomes thoughtful: "I'll only leave this place with her in my arms. This business of leaving her here and me going home, don't even think about it!" The couple are united and ready for this birth, early or not.

Once they remove Julie, the anaesthestist raises the mother slightly so she can see her baby, born weighing 2,305 grams, measuring 43.5 centimetres, and with an Apgar score of 5–9. The paediatrician quickly takes Julie to her mother so she can see her better. Tânia cries and touches her tiny nose saying, "They're being mean to you, darling! Don't be mean to her, auntie."

The nurse puts a little beige cap with a red bow on Julie: "I can see she is a petite, round, cutie-pie." She wrapped her up and took her back to Tânia so she could have one more look, and then took her to the neonatal ICU where she remained for a week. The observer went back to Tânia to say her good-byes and thanked her for allowing her to observe and said she would call the next day. Everything was turning out well. The couple thanked her and said their mobile phone would be turned on. Tânia asked the observer to give the news to the family members that were outside waiting. When she gave the news, the observer again mistook grams for kilos, saying Julie weighed 2,305 kilos. Realising her mistake, she immediately justified herself, saying the baby was a big strong girl, that's why she increased her weight so much. Everyone laughed. The experience was so intense for the observer that she felt lost in time and space as she left the hospital. The situations she had experienced seemed to acquire a new dimension:

> I remember that the whole time I had the feeling the birth was imminent. But I really didn't have time to prepare myself for all this. I had to say good-bye but my departure hasn't reached full-term. It's part of life, I know. At first, I thought we hadn't reached the end of the pregnancy. Then I thought: the end of the pregnancy is as far as it goes, and we followed it to the end.

From pregnancy to delivery, we followed the mismatched steps of Tânia and Julie, who had to be born ahead of her time. The pre-eclampsia, prematurity, and life-threatening risks increased the gap in the mother–daughter rhythm at birth, which provoked a huge challenge to their survival and continuity.

The first four months: constructing the maternal setting

After she was born, Julie spent seven days in the ICU. The observer for this phase makes her first visit to the hospital and meets the father, who politely tells her the hospital room number. She is surprised that Julie's name is not on the door, but, rather, the name of a boy. When she enters, she sees a mother with her husband and child; it is Tânia in a bed surrounded by visitors. Tânia transmits a feeling of uncertainty, fragility, which seems, somehow, ambiguous. None the less, the observer feels welcomed and rapport between them is immediate. She brings a gift for the baby, which is well received by the mother. She will put it in her daughter's incubator, since she does not have any toys with her yet.

A few days later, the observer calls the parents. The mother sounds radiant. She transmits joy and security, as if she can finally feel confident now that she is holding Julie in her arms and taking her home, leaving the failures behind. The observer reports a different Tânia, as if the ghosts of death and the threats and failures have been left behind, giving way to the mother's happiness, security, and willingness to invest in the baby and continue the process of becoming a mother. It is as if, now that she has the baby in her arms, she can be confident, unlike when she carried the baby in her womb. Three weeks later, the observer contacts the parents again and they schedule a date to start the home observations.

Over the phone and in the first home observations, it becomes clear that Tânia has entered a state of primary maternal preoccupation, willing to live a "two in one" relationship, an experience of mutuality, in order to meet the needs of her baby. This condition provides a setting in which Julie's constitution and developmental tendencies can be revealed, thus guaranteeing her continued existence, which had been temporarily threatened by her premature birth.

On her way to Julie's house, the observer thinks the way is familiar, although feeling lost at the same time. She meets an older, rather invasive woman who knows Carlos and Tânia's family. She talks a lot, emphasising how frail and small Julie is: "The baby can't even cry, she has such a weeeaaak little cry."

To reach Tânia's house it is necessary to cross a yard, go past her mother-in-law's house, and pass several ferocious dogs of different breeds. Tânia lives in "a very pretty prefabricated house like her mother in-law's, both painted in similar dark colours". The house was in half-light, like a still-pregnant house–womb. Inside, the house is very clean. Julie's crib is neat and beautiful and has a pleasant smell, although she still does not occupy it. Besides the dogs there are two cats—a white one that belongs to the paternal grandmother, and a black one that belongs to the couple.

The same ritual with the dogs happens at every home visit: the observer announces herself at the gate and someone, usually the mother-in-law, goes out to lock up the dogs. After the observer enters Julie's house, the dogs are let loose, but then locked up again so she can leave. The dogs scare her, and on many occasions she thinks at some point one of them will jump the gate and attack her. Sometimes, the paternal grandmother screams at them and is violent when she locks them up: "Now you're going to get it! Come on, Laika! Down, down." She hits them with a belt: "You pieces of shit! You worthless pieces of crap!" She whips the belt back and forth. The grandmother does not measure her words or attitudes; she is always going off half-cocked. The observer says, "She does not mince her words. If she has something to say, she says it, and if she has to fight, she will." She is very present in Julie's family, albeit with her invasive ways and inappropriate speaking and behaviour. Although she gets furious with the dogs, she welcomes the observer with kisses and cautions her to be careful on the slippery ground. She questions the observer about diagnoses, mood swings, and bipolar disease. She also frequently questions the attitudes of the parents and teachers at the school where she teaches, asking for the observer's opinion and position. Sometimes, she is insistent and difficult to manage, but the observer is calm and firmly maintains her function. Over the following three years, this same grandmother will drastically change in her relationship with Julie's family, as will be shown in the progression of the reports.

Surprisingly, and interestingly, the first home observation occurs on the very day when Julie should have been born. In those forty-four days she has grown seven centimetres and gained one kilo. She is jaundiced and seems upset, crying and twisting until she is red in the face. The mother complains about how much Julie suffered and about how "t-i-i-i-i-i-ny" she was. She refers to her daughter's irritability in the first days in hospital: "She pulled at everything, she seemed angry and you couldn't keep anything on her or attached to her. She had such a tight grip that she yanked the catheters out of her little arms and feet. That's why they had to use the veins in her head. She suffered a lot, poor thing. So many things poking into her; she had three in each foot, three in each hand, and some on her head."

Julie's room is full of toys and stuffed animals. When they arrive in her room, Julie is crying. Tânia hands her daughter over to the observer without hesitating, then throws herself into her arms as well. The observer has become an important person to her and her relationship with her baby, having supported her during the transition to motherhood and in weaving a web of protection and comfort after the mother's pre-eclampsia and Julie's premature birth. Unlike the relationship with the observer during the first phase, who had been kept on the outskirts and silently ordered to perform, the second observer was quickly welcomed into the household. The two immediately establish a sense of partnership, respect, and trust. The observer can feel how difficult it is for the mother to hold this totally strange and fragile baby in her arms:

> Tânia smiles and says she's going to set the dogs loose. I'm alone with the baby. I try as best I can to make her comfortable, but my arms feel awkward holding her. I finally find a position that is comfortable for both of us, my left arm supports her little bottom, and my right arm her back and head. I hold her in front of me. I notice her jaundiced colour, the lack of hair on the right side of her tiny head, and that her eyes make me think of Down's syndrome. Maybe they are like that because of being born premature.

When the mother nurses her, the observer speaks quietly, but Tânia tells her, "Julie needs to get used to the routine in this house." Thus, she addresses the situation that affects everyone: the difficult task of knowing, getting used to, and adapting to the surprises brought on by Julie's presence, the relationships that develop between her and the family, and *vice versa,* and what the interaction with the observer will be like.

When the observer reports this episode, she mistakenly writes,

> Julie speaks as she nurses, which seems to bother the baby.

This sensitive slip of the pen in her writing reveals a mutually dependent relationship, a regression that unites mother and daughter, and the observer and mother–baby pair. Julie latches on to her mother's breast and Tânia latches on to the observer, talking a lot and using her to elaborate the intense experiences of the last several days. She–baby needs help. The connection between Tânia and the observer is impressive. The observer is aware of this and allows herself to be permeated in a natural and authentic manner.

Tânia mentions how

> she and her husband expected a very different baby than Julie turned out to be . . . "we expected a little blonde girl with light-coloured eyes and white skin". The mother says, "Today, this one here doesn't let me do anything, she just wants to be held . . . today is the day she was supposed to have been born, but she was in a bit of a hurry."

The mother rehearses getting to know this new baby, born premature, not blonde, and so different from what she had imagined. She describes her daughter as two different babies: the hospital one as a very angry little fury tearing out all her catheters, and the home one as soooo weak and sooo quiet—another baby. In this beginning of life, the ability of the mother's ego to support Julie's fragile ego is fundamental to her gradually becoming strong and capable of starting out as a new and unique human being.

At this first meeting at the baby's house, the observer notices that Julies whimpers and twists her body, turning red in the process. The mother gives the baby her breast to calm her, saying, "Are you hungry already?" The observer describes her sucking as different from other one-month-old babies that are born full-term. Her sucking is that of a newborn: very slow and requiring a lot of effort. She nurses a little on one breast and falls asleep. Tânia lifts the baby to wind her, tapping softly on her tiny back; she wakes up, whimpers again, curls up her little legs, and whimpers. Tânia cuddles her in her arms, placing her head on her left breast, and she falls asleep again. While nursing, the mother holds the baby in her left arm, which she leans on her leg for support, her hand not touching her body. She uses her right hand to lightly caress Julie's head with the tips of her fingers. Her fingers move delicately from the top of her head down her left cheek or temple, creating vertical and circular movements with the tips of her fingers back up to the starting point. When Julie falls asleep, Tânia gently places her on a cushion next to her. In this observation, it is clear that Tânia has divested herself of her personal interests and is willing to concentrate fully on Julie.

The observer is shown Julie's album. It takes a while to arrive at the current photos since there are many pictures of the hospital. There are others of the first month out of the hospital but they "haven't been developed yet", says the mother. She surprises the observer by stating that she does not think Julie can see yet. Tânia wants to see the ultrasound films because she wants to know what happened before her daughter was born, why this happened to her.

At the end of the first observation, the observer makes another mistake in her written notes:

> Julie wants to leave, but finds it difficult.

This probably shows how much she has made herself available to the mother in assuming different roles and being permeable enough to help Tânia relive what she might have experienced rather abruptly with Julie.

The connection between the mother and observer is so intense and primitive that the observer regresses to a sensory level that is typically seen in the beginning of life. As she leaves she reports,

> I have the feeling of being hollow, my head is hollow and I have no brain. I'm frantic that I might not remember everything that was said, because I feel empty.

The sensitive slip of calling herself Julie reveals an experience of mutuality (Winnicott, 1969b), a regression that unites mother and daughter, observer and the mother–baby couple. The moment marks the intense relationship and the therapeutic potential of observation conducted by a participative, yet non-invasive, presence that helps connect the disconnected and integrate the unintegrated.

On the second visit (one month and twenty-one days) the observer's attention is drawn to Tânia's amazing sensitivity in the way she has adapted herself delicately and thoughtfully to her baby:

> After Julie nurses, the mother affectionately tries to make her comfortable. Julie interacts and responds by smiling at her mother's smiles and sticking out her tongue. They hold each other's eyes for long moments. The connection between mother and baby is visible. Julie falls asleep cuddled in the nest of Tânia's arms. They complement each other. Tânia interprets some of Julie's behaviour—she extends her hand to be kissed.

There is a mutuality that allows the mother–baby pair to establish quality contact.

The mother tells the observer that she and Carlos spoil their daughter. As the mother speaks, she looks often at Julie, who stares firmly back at her mother. She caresses the baby, making small circular movements on her back and buttocks, and the baby responds with direct movements. The mother makes clicking sounds with her mouth, as if sending small kisses, and Julie looks and looks and tries to open and close her mouth. The mother smiles and Julie opens her mouth wide and nestles into her mother's body. The constant communication between the mother and her baby, and the proximity being built in their relationship is clear in the reported observations. The observer describes,

> she is cuddled between two cushions, one in front and one behind; she was comfortable from head to toe. Her security blanket was always touching her, especially her face. The mother offers me some juice, while cuddling her baby.

At the third observation (three months) the observer slips in the yard as she walks in, has an allergy crisis, and is scared of the dogs. She is frightened and Tânia "cares" for her by offering juice and trying to make her comfortable.

Tânia's attempts to accommodate her daughter and hold her, calm her, and snuggle her continue to increase. At two months and five days, the observer notes the baby's growth in her report:

> . . . the baby sleeps peacefully, wrapped in a pink blanket. She is much bigger than she was last week, practically taking up the entire pram that now seems too small for her new size . . . she has grown four centimetres and now measures fifty-three centimetres and weighs 4,280 kilos. [Again, the observer confuses grams and kilos.]

The impression is that Julie and Tânia are slowly becoming closer. Tânia waits for her daughter to wake up because she knows when it is time to nurse. When at her mother's breast, Julie has some trouble latching on. Both are patient and Julie finally nurses eagerly.

> Tânia picks up Julie, who is still crying, and invites me into the living room . . . she talks to Julie looking at her, "Is mummy's little girl hungry, is she?" Tânia gives the baby her right breast and it takes a while for the two to get settled. "Can't find mummy's tit, can you?" says Tânia. When Julie finally latches on to her mother's nipple she nurses so eagerly I can hear her sucking.

Since the observations began, it is interesting how Tânia is always knitting little outfits for Julie, because "She didn't give me enough time to finish, she wanted to come early." She makes beautiful pieces for the baby and says she will make a jumper for herself for when she goes back to work. Around the time when Julie turns two months, the mother offers the observer the place next to Julie, and then sits a little further away, knitting for her daughter. It is interesting how the mother–baby creative, tailor-made, and unique relationship gradually unfolds and how the process of integration that was taking place is translated by the mother. Tânia comments, "Look here, it's like I told you. I've already made the sleeves, and now I just have to sew them on. I still have to make the collar and then I'll have finished it." From the depths of her helplessness and creative capacity, Tânia is able to extract threads to weave a protective space where she can care for her daughter and form the basis for developing the complex mother–daughter relationship.

The house cats show up: the white one that belongs to the mother-in-law and the black one that belongs to Tânia. The black one is with Julie in one of the first photos displayed in the living room. Tânia responds to his constant need for attention and non-stop meows by telling him she cannot pick him up because she is busy knitting Julie's jumper. He jumps on her lap and tangles his claws in the knitting. In the end, she sets her work aside so the cat can lie in her lap while she pats its back, like she does the baby's. The cat falls asleep.

Julie is in the pram in front of her. She whimpers, squirms, and falls back to sleep. Tânia looks at her and continues petting the cat. Julie wakes up screaming and her mother moves the cat from her lap and picks up Julie to feed her. There is a misunderstanding between the two: Julie twists around and cannot latch on or settle down, which seems to bother the mother. The cat places itself again in front of Tânia and meows until the baby finishes nursing. She tells it she cannot hold it, but he meows and meows until she ends up petting it with the tip of her foot while Julie nurses. She puts the cat to sleep on a cushion and goes back to patting Julie's back in the same way. She falls asleep and Tânia goes back to knitting.

Another time, Tânia is petting the cat and when Julie wakes up crying, the mother puts the cat down and goes to the bedroom. When she comes back she seems rough and impatient in nursing the baby:

> Tânia's tone is more severe . . . "Come on, honey, settle down already, didn't you want to nurse?" Tânia is connected to the cat demanding her attention, so she twists and manoeuvres to satisfy it while holding Julie in her lap. As she feeds Julie she tells the cat, "Mummy can't hold you now, mummy can't."

Things are clearly changing for Julie and her mother: mother and baby act freer and more differentiated. Every context goes through alterations. At three months and two days, the observer arrives at the house no longer afraid of the dogs, and Tânia greets her with Julie in her arms. Her head is held high and she is alert as she surveys everything around her. She looks firmly at the observer, wanting to "talk": she smiles and gurgles, moving her mouth. The mother says, "Ah, she wants to talk, her thing is talking. You should see her, this kid is a chatterbox. The other day we went for a walk and she wanted to look at everything. She's a pistol, this girl. She loves the television and she loves Fantástico."[16]

The mother says, "Julie hasn't been sleeping much during the day and when she's awake she wants company and someone to talk to her. She likes to chat, right baby?!" The parents introduce CDs for babies that play bird and water sounds to help calm her and put her to sleep. The mother remembers that when she was pregnant she would listen to the birds on her way to work, and would rub her belly, telling Julie that those were birds singing. The water sounds are like a continuation of pre/post birth. When Julie gets agitated and waves her arms, her mother says she will "grow up to be a boxer . . . she's always punching the air."

Julie interacts with her environment and mobilises it. When she hears someone's voice, she strains to sit up and stretches out her little arms. She gurgles and talks and always gets responses from people.

The mother says, "She wants to participate in the conversation." The grandmother comes in making a scene, and speaks to the baby in a loud voice: "You want to talk, so talk, kid! Talk to this here grandma. Have you nursed yet? Because if your mum hasn't given you any, granny can"—squeezing Julie's belly—"why, that jumper is as cute as a button", then proceeds to complain that the reason Julie has thrown up is because Tânia has not positioned her correctly in the pram.

Once again, there is clearly some kind of competition between the two, with the grandmother always telling Tânia how to handle Julie. The grandmother says, "Why didn't you use pillows so she could sit up?"

Mother: "Because it won't work."

Grandmother: "Well then, lift the bloody pram!"

Mother: "Why don't you?"

During this exchange, the baby reacts by crying, but then calms down. The grandmother gets angry and does not think Julie should be left in the pram. She takes her out and holds her. The mother says,

"Oh no you don't. Leave her there." Grandmother says, "What? I'm going to hold her. Mum can sod off." Tânia calmly takes her daughter back into her arms. This aggressive atmosphere later leaves the observer feeling as if she has not said good-bye to the mother, and writes, "the dogs have invaded the house".

This example of a threat of annihilation that the baby experiences, which also has an impact on, and disorganises, the observer, repeats itself on numerous subsequent observation visits at varying levels of intensity and for different lengths of time. Julie will demonstrate increasing trust in her recovery and a progressive egoic capacity to confront and handle frustrations. Over time, the grandmother significantly changes her behaviour and her participation in Julie's life. She gradually becomes more respectful, more collaborative, and less invasive. She even said on some occasions that she was taking a psychology course to learn how to deal with children.

Julie's psychomotor development is excellent in response to her contained environment, which also stimulates independence and separation. She is very good at noticing people and looks at them attentively, smiling and wanting to talk as she tries to raise herself from her pram, stretching out her arms to be picked up. She is a pleasant and enjoyable baby. She watches and gestures at everything her mother does from her pram. When she sleeps, Tânia talks about things that are important to her: the miscarriage, how she had lived with her parents in the countryside of Santa Catarina—a beautiful place with a garden and even a waterfall, and how her father had been murdered while working at a club when she was five years old. She had been raised by her grandmother, whom she calls her adopted mum, and who is also Julie's godmother. In those first months, she visited her "mum" and felt comfortable and fulfilled at her house, where she would leave Julie when she went to see about going back to work.

At the ninth observation (three months and nine days), the dogs do not let Julie sleep. Tânia is aggressive with them and beats them on the head with a broomstick. The maternal great-grandmother is in the house and the husband is sleeping in the living room. Tânia is starting to fret about being away from her daughter since she will be going back to work and wants to take back some of her personal interests: "I want to see what it will be like when I start working." She feels threatened by her loss of control over Julie and tries to prepare for everything. Following her typical pattern of being prepared that has been evident since her pregnancy, Tânia seems to be subtly getting her daughter ready for this moment: occasionally, she will not listen to Julie and lets her cry, but not to the point of concern. Although she seems not to listen, she is really giving Julie space to express her dissatisfaction. As a result, Julie seems to adapt—making efforts on her own so she does not need her mother for everything:

> Julie sometimes lets go of her dummy [when sleeping] but then uses the top part of her hand to push it back into place. But when she can't get it back in, she cries. Julie lets go of the dummy and it falls past her face. She starts crying, opening her arms and moving her head from one side to the other, her eyes wide open . . .
>
> Tânia takes her time, comes back in carrying a cup of tea for me in one hand and a small bottle of tea for Julie. Tânia places Julie's hands around the bottle so she can hold it. The first time, Julie brings her hands together too fast and the bottle jumps. Tânia puts it back into Julie's mouth and repositions her hands around the bottle, but Julie has her own way, placing one of her hands underneath to serve as a support. She holds it for a good while. When the bottle starts to empty, Tânia helps her daughter by lifting it with the tip of her index finger. Tânia looks at me and smiles, which makes Julie turn her gaze toward me. When she sees her daughter is holding on firmly, she takes away her finger. When Julie takes her hand out from underneath, Tânia puts it back in place. Julie takes the bottle out of her mouth and stares at her mother. The maternal great-grandmother is impressed and satisfied with the baby's development. She says, "Lord almighty, she's really developing, isn't she? After all she's been through . . . look at that! Look how big she is, at 5.5 kilos."

The mother continues to worry about getting back to her personal interests and it is significant how she addresses this desire with the observer, and non-verbally implies that she counts on her. She says immediately at the beginning of the observation at three months and sixteen days, "Well, now I'm going back to work. I'm going to take advantage of the fact that she's given me a break and wash the dishes and finish cleaning, OK?" She puts Julie's chew toys in the pram with her so she can reach them if they fall. She talks about arranging the house for when Julie starts spending more time on the floor. She says:

"I'm thinking about changing the living room for when she spends more time on the floor, you know?" She also starts the weaning process: "Yeah, I'm already preparing her. Next month I'm going to give her cereal so she doesn't bother the person that's going to take care of her. She's already eating some fruit, she eats mashed bananas with sugar, etc." She mimics to the observer the faces the baby made when she first tried the fruit.

Despite all her efforts to organise a caring schedule with an aunt and the grandparents, the mother's sadness about the forthcoming separation from her daughter is palpable, because now that she is used to her, she does not know how she can stay away: "I'd like to stay like this together all day . . . it's going to be hard. I can't imagine not seeing her start to crawl, stand up, take her first steps, or say her first words, the cute things . . . I'll miss everything. Everything will happen with another person." Her eyes fill with tears; she feels very divided and has given a lot of thought to this. She says, "She was nursing so hard, wouldn't let go. My breast was this big . . . imagine how it's going to be when I go back to work and leave her with no one to nurse her." Tânia is suffering through the weaning process along with the baby. It is a complicated situation because she needs to work to help support the family household. Tânia clearly expresses the drama of motherhood and the demanding process required to first connect to, and then disconnect from, her baby without breaking the ties that keep them together.

At three months and twenty-two days, the changes the mother has made to the house are visible.

> I walk toward the pram and notice that the TV room is different. The TV is where the side sofa was; the three-person sofa that was on the side is now against the wall with the window, and the two-person sofa that had been at the window is in front of the TV. It looks pretty. Tânia has spread some cushions against the wall facing the window, and the sofas are covered in plaid blankets. On the two-person sofa are Tânia's knitting and a red pullover for Julie. Julie is sleeping in the front of the pram, belly and hands up. She almost doesn't fit in the pram any more.

Clear transformations and growth continue to affect both Julie and Tânia. Both flourish and expand simultaneously. Both create and inhabit new spaces, distinguishing themselves from each other and becoming more unique and authentic. The relationship of trust and respect is visible in the relationship they are creating, after the initial ruptures and uncertainties of overcoming the fear of death. The mother had to wait until Julie was out of her womb and in her arms before she revealed her rare skills as a mother.

At four months, mother and daughter are true communication vessels. The baby pouts and whines and looks at her mother. The mother says, "She just wants to be held." The baby cries and looks at her mother. They look at each other face-to-face and the baby makes talking noises, which the mother answers: "What's wrong, huh? What's wrong, honey?" Julie whimpers and makes noises, which the mother mimics. The mother puts the baby in her lap in front of the TV, dances with her, and then lays her down. She cries and the mother sits her up again. The successive attempts to accommodate Julie in her lap by nursing her, pinching her cheeks, and talking to her makes Tânia become emotional and her eyes fill with tears. "I can't imagine what it'll be like when I go back to work. I can't even talk about it, because it makes me want to cry."

Julie looks at her attentively, smiles, pouts, cries, tries to get her mother's attention, saying, "aaaaaaaaa . . . ooooooooo . . . brbrbrbr . . ." The mother talks back, making the same sounds. Then they go back to the television. Julie wants to remain sitting. The mother understands and puts her in that position. She strains to sit, following Tânia's movements. One of the changes the mother points out is Julie's loss of hair—the father has nicknamed her baldy. Tânia adds that today is her four-month birthday, although not exactly the right time of day, since she was born at night, at 7.10 p.m. The two continue making sounds, talking, and exchanging kisses.

The relationship of trust and respect that occurs between mother and baby is repeated between Tânia and the observer. When the observer arrives on the fourth month and seventh day, Tânia welcomes her, saying, "We've been waiting for you." It was bath time and she wanted to wait for the observer to be there. "I was going to give her a bath, but it was almost time for you to get here, so I thought it best to wait so as to not interrupt the bath. She'll have her bath now, right, to take advantage of the warm day."

As she goes to prepare the bath, Julie whines a little, but nothing out of control. She is kicking her legs and, from the kitchen, Tânia asks her what is wrong. When Tânia comes back into the room, Julie breaks into movement when she sees her mother, and raises her arms. In that sequence of events, mother and daughter are practising being apart, both tolerating only a certain distance. Tânia is going back to work in two weeks.

It is interesting to notice how Tânia fulfils herself emotionally through her relationship with her grandmother–mum and with the observer during this important time of separation. The following week, at four months and fourteen days, the observation take place at the great-grandmother's house. The observer promptly accepted when Tânia asked if the visit could be there. It is a partnership that works. Upon her arrival, the observer is welcomed by the mother, who seems surprised to see her: "Hi! You're early." She said she and her niece had been about to go meet her at the bus stop. She invited the observer to come to see Julie, who is sleeping, and says, "Don't mind the mess." This sentence is repeated several times in the next observations, which leads us to suppose that Tânia was communicating the "mess" that was settling around her with regard to her work, her separation from Julie, and her uncertainties about the care Julie would receive in her absence.

In the last observation before Tânia went back to work (four months and twenty-one days), Tânia welcomes the observer, commenting on the cold weather outside: "Inside it's actually warm, but out here, man! It's really cold!" The observer finds Julie nestled in her pram. It is significant that she sleeps through the whole observation. Tânia says her mother-in-law had wanted her to stay at her house because of the cold, but Tânia says, "It's our last chance to be together, so I think we'll stay here, just the two of us, so we can enjoy ourselves a little bit longer . . . I don't know what it will be like, but what can we do, right honey?" The expression, "what can we do", also used at Julie's premature birth, is her way of accepting and confronting the reality being imposed on her that requires a solution.

Tânia offers the observer tea and shares that she also wanted the chance to enjoy being with her in this warm, cosy, protected space created by the mother–baby pair. She once again shows how important the observer is in following her through the process of creating this space. "I was just waiting for you to have some tea. I thought, when Marina gets here, we'll have tea, just the two of us." She looks at her daughter and says, smiling to the baby, who is smiling in her sleep, "Look how big she is . . . do you remember how she was before, 'how tiny'! And how she developed, thank God . . . from what she was like in the hospital. Now look at her!" She talks again about the baby's hair loss and the peach fuzz that is growing in, subtly and non-verbally communicating the end of the intrauterine and postpartum phase and the beginning of a new one. There are many moments of silence during this observation.

Tânia demonstrates the helplessness of a mother who depends on someone else to care for her baby in her absence: "I still don't know what it will be like next week. My sister-in-law still hasn't given me a straight answer. I don't know what's so hard about just saying yes or no." She continues talking about all the options she has considered for Julie's care, and lists the inconveniences of each one: her grand-mother's house—her first choice—is far, and she does not have the financial resources to put Julie in a day-care centre or pay for some-one to stay with her. Tânia turns to look at Julie: "Oh my . . . just one week left . . ." Julie sighs deeply. Mother and daughter are on the same wavelength. In her own way, the baby is also experiencing separation.

Tânia recounts, smiling, how, the other day, Julie was sleeping beside her and suddenly let out a yelp, and how Carlos asked if she was dreaming someone was stealing her milk. She says her daughter is starting not to want to go with other people and "already knows who her mother and father are". She says that the other day they left her with her aunt for fifteen minutes to go to the supermarket. When they came back she had a big red mark on her head and her eyes were as big as saucers—motioning with her hands how round her eyes were. It was hard to calm her down.

Tânia places two cups of tea side by side on the dinner table, and picks up her knitting as she sits down. She says she's making a red jumper: "It's for me, because it'll be cold when I go back to work." "Uh-huh," answers the observer. Tânia is slowly gaining back other aspects of her femininity, while knitting a space for the mother–baby separation. She expresses her regret about being separated from the observer, too, again demonstrating how important their relationship is to her. The observer offers the possibility of doing the observations at the weekends, which Tânia immediately accepts, saying, "Why, it could be just at the weekends, if you can. I can, and would like it very much . . . I was thinking I'd never see you again . . . that would be so strange . . ."

From four to eleven months: a "messy" period of turmoil and instability

The next written observation reports demonstrate how the period where Tânia goes back to work is another break in the continuity of the mother–baby relationship that will require huge effort and will once more test both of their abilities to recover and survive. The instability in Julie's childcare network that Tânia had organised with such concern and dedication did not make for an easy transition in the weaning process of the mother–baby pair.

Tânia's sense of helplessness is palpable when she calls the observer on the night before the next observation to say it will take place at Patrícia's (her sister-in-law) house. The observer asks how they are doing, and Tânia answers using the now familiar phrase: "What can you do, right?"

The observer arrives at Patricia's house (four months and twenty-eight days), "a still unfinished house", with little difficulty because of Tânia's directions. She arrives at the same time as Regina, Tânia's mother-in-law, who mentions she is taking a course taught by psychologists. The sister-in-law takes the observer into the bedroom where Julie is sleeping. She immediately notices that Julie does not seem to be getting the same care that her mother gives her. The observer reports,

> She seems to have fewer blankets and doesn't seem to be wrapped up as well as when she is at home with Tânia looking after her.

Julie wakes up and recognises the observer, smiles at her and plays peek-a-boo with the sheet. The observer feels awkward and misplaced. Maybe this is how Julie feels. She describes the environment in detail; everything calls her attention. Julie seems to do the same.

> She keeps looking at her cousin, sometimes smiling at him, but mostly just looking.

Sérgio, Tânia's youngest brother, holds Julie in his lap. The observer describes the moment:

> Julie looked at me and her lower lip came out and her eyes filled with tears . . .

The baby clearly demonstrates that she has internalised her mother and feels her absence. She knows the difference between the mother and the observer, who is sensitive and demonstrates her awareness of the mother–baby pair:

> Right now, I'm thinking of Tânia.

The same feeling of instability continues in Julie's childcare network when Tânia once again calls the night before the next observation (five months and four days) to say that the next observation would be at her grandmother's house. The observer is welcomed there by Julie's cousin, Mariana, who lives with her grandmother and seems very participative and connected. Upon her arrival, she says to the observer: "Hi! I've been waiting for you." She tells her that Julie and Tânia have been at her house for three days, and, although it meant being far from Julie's father, it was easier this way for Tânia, who could get to work quicker. She says her cousin will love seeing her. She only cries when she's hungry. "She's a good little girl."

Julie's great-grandmother comes in and says, "Hi, you're here." She mentions her great-granddaughter had arrived with a slight cold and had been coughing a little, but was better now. She describes how she feeds the baby, seemingly attuned to her and her preferences. When Julie wakes up, the observer notices that she is a wearing a synthetic wool body suit that seems to cover a lot of clothing underneath, making her look warm. Mariana picks her up and asks her grandmother to hand her the blanket. The observer notices that she is warm and cosy in her great-grandmother's house, different from at her aunt's house. She hangs on to her security blanket and rubs her face with it while she waits for her great-grandmother to prepare her bottle. The observer reports,

> Mariana and the great-grandmother take care of Julie by holding her on their laps and watching TV, like her mother does at home.

This environment where Julie is being taken care of is closer to the one she has at home, as if it were an extension. Tânia's return to her mum–grandmother's house where she grew up is very interesting. There is no doubt that the care she received in this mother-house is what she takes to her own home. The grandmother's house functions as a kind of "auxiliary home" for both of them during this period of instability. The grandmother compliments Tânia, saying how she is a "careful mother. You should see her when she has to leave, she gives us a ton of recommendations . . . Poor thing, today she didn't even have time to eat breakfast. She nursed the baby, and then, instead of letting us change Julie's dirty nappy, she went and changed it, and then she ran out of time and had to leave in a rush." She adds that Tânia needs to work, because "Carlinhos can't support them."

There is a prolonged silence interrupted by remembering Julie's premature birth: "You know, I don't even know why I went to the hospital when she was born. I felt so bad I couldn't sleep that night, I didn't know if she'd make it or not. I've never seen anything like it. She could fit on the palm of my hand, and now look at her there." Mariana's father arrives, and Julie smiles at him and says "aaa". The great-grandmother wonders if Julie thinks it's her father, because "With her dad so far away, it's been days since she's seen him, poor thing." She introduces the observer as the "baby's psychologist".

Although the family does not know how long they will stay at the great-grandmother's house—everything is uncertain—the next observation (five months and eleven days) takes place there as well, on a Saturday. Upon her arrival, the observer sees a gathering of about six or seven women in front of the house with Tânia in the middle, who invites the observer to come in. The house is silent and Julie is asleep. She still has a cold, as on the previous visit. Tânia voices her satisfaction and relief that she spent the whole week at her grandmother's house, exhibiting again her sense of helplessness in this situation of instability in Julie's childcare network. "It's that this week I still didn't know what it would be like . . . Rose has to take care of the boy, who is not doing so well yet . . . one more for her to take care of. It's a lot, I don't think it will work, but I don't know. Carlos is coming today so we can go over there, but I don't know. If we could spend one more week here . . ." Once again she utters the familiar expression, "What can I do, I have to sacrifice for her."

The helplessness of a mother faced with this reality of total dependence on the outside to help take care of her baby is again exposed. It is a totally silent process for the mother; a demanding back and forth that requires huge effort. Tânia has been interlacing the thread that connects her to her baby and her story, using this auxiliary mother–

grandmother house as a space that will guarantee continued care and development for her baby. This period will once more reveal Tânia's genuine abilities and creative resources in dealing with the challenges of dependence. The Tânia–Julie pair teaches us about the importance of a mother's flexibility in adapting to changes and interruptions while keeping the mother–baby connection essential to the baby's development.

Tania says she feels more at ease at work knowing that Julie is being well taken care of at her great-grandmother's house. She mentions that she goes from lap to lap. "Everyone wants to hold her. She's the only baby; everyone else is an adult . . . Mr and Mrs X come to get her. These are good people here, who watched me grow up after I came here when I was little . . ." "Uh-huh", says the observer.

Julie smiles at her mother, buries her face in her blanket and falls asleep. Tânia says she feels confident about the care being given to her daughter, emphasising that, "She is growing like a weed." She tells about how she puts her on the mobile phone so she can hear her father and how she would "double over laughing and giggling . . . nobody would believe me if I told them." Tânia lays Julie in the pram and the observer notices how she always lines it with a blanket, "forming a softer and warmer bed".

After settling Julie, Tânia offers the observer tea and mentions that her grandmother thinks it is strange that the observer does not talk. The observer smiles and Tânia asks if she likes Japanese food. The observer answers, "Hmm." Tânia continues, saying that when she was pregnant her husband invited her to a restaurant to try some and that she had liked it. They had planned to go back, but the baby was born early and then they forgot about it. They had gone to another restaurant recently and she explains in detail the different dishes of this new culinary art that is becoming part of their lives.

The visit ends and the observer asks if it is possible to continue having the visits on Saturdays, to which she answers by repeating the instability and uncertainty of this period: "Of course, I would love to do them on Saturdays. It's great for me. But I don't know where I'll be, here, at my house . . . If anything changes I'll call you to tell you where we'll be, but we'll probably be at the Vila." Typical of Carlos since the pre-birth observations, he says he might not always be able to be present at the observations. Tânia rolls her eyes and smiles at the observer.

The observer's function was essential during this period of instability. She naturally followed the comings and goings of the mother–baby pair, from one house to the next, from one city to another, according to whatever the mother needed. Her flexibility, availability, and adaptability are important qualities for being a mother, as well as for the clinical analytic function with patient regression. The father complains about the absence of his wife and daughter during the week. Now at their house (five months and eighteen days), Tânia welcomes the observer and expresses her feelings about these inconsistent times. She starts by apologising "for the mess", then commenting about how cold it is, and that she cannot imagine how she would get Julie out of bed in the mornings. She settles the baby in the pram and offers the observer a cup of tea. "Nice and hot, right? It's cold today, they say it might even snow." When the mother leaves the room,

> Julie pulls at her blanket, touching it to her nose . . . she pushes the edge of the pram's security bar and makes a face as if to cry. She whines and her mother calls from the kitchen: "Mummy's coming, Julie." But she doesn't quiet down, and instead starts kicking her legs and arms and crying. Her face turns red and her cries intensify.

The mother tells her again that she's coming, but this fails to quiet Julie, who coughs and chokes. The observer picks her up and the crying diminishes and she stops choking. She looks to the sides as if looking for someone—her mother. The mother comments about Julie's weaning process, saying she is getting her used to nursing only at night, "so Julie won't bother those taking care of her". She mentions the connection she has with everyone who takes care of her, and that she probably is not recognising her own home, since she's been at her great-grandmother's house for the last three weeks. "You should have seen the crying that went on today when we tried to leave. Nobody wanted us to come here. They must be missing her, the only baby in the house, and you know how a baby charms everyone. She was the centre of attention, and then she left. They must be missing her a lot." "Uh-huh," says the observer. "Then I get here and there's clothes to wash, lunch to make, and Carlos doesn't do a thing . . . he's gone back to sleeping in his mum's bed." She looks at her daughter and says, "She's so big, I can't even remember how it was when she was little and I held her in my hands. I don't know how to hold a tiny baby any more."

She tells about nursing a one-month-old baby at work because the mother had no milk and could not heat a bottle. She said she could not remember how to hold a small baby, and that that baby she fed was really tiny "compared to Julie now. Look how big she is!" She strokes her daughter's body murmuring from time to time, "My chubby little girl. Mummy's chubby little girl." This conversation shows that the mother is proud and relieved to arrive at this point and of proving her ability as a mother, which she had so doubted during her pregnancy. Her panic about not being able to produce life or of not being able to sustain it had finally been overcome.

The next observation is filmed. Tânia invited the observer and her co-worker doing the filming to come in and tells them to "pay no mind to the mess", saying that they had been out all week at Julie's great-grandmother's house. She is placed in the middle of the living room and the father once again tells them, "Don't mind the mess." Julie complains and Tânia picks her up. The father plays the bird sounds CD that she likes and has listened to since she was in the womb. As usual, he leaves, saying. "I'll leave you guys to it." Tânia asks him to stay, but he disappears. She sits and holds Julie in the same position she used when she was smaller, "nestled in her lap . . . like a continuation of her own belly", and reminds the observer of how small Julie had been when she met her.

There is a lot of evidence that the mess has affected the couple and the family. At the next observation (six months and one day), the observer notes,

> This time not one dog came to greet me.
>
> Carlos opens the door and says he and Julie both have bad colds. Tânia says Julie is sleeping because she hadn't been able to sleep well that night, and she had to hold her through the night "like this", she says, holding her arms to her chest as if she were holding the baby, "until she fell asleep".

The instability in Julie's childcare network continues. Tânia still does not know where Julie will stay this week and says, "I'm not even going to unpack her suitcase, since we'll be leaving again anyway . . ." Julie seems to be fine for all the inconsistencies she's experiencing. This is most likely due to the mother functioning as the baby's auxiliary ego during this uncertain period. Julie also demonstrates the resources and patterns that are proper for this stage in her development. Julie has learnt to cuddle and can make her own *moquinha,* a term invented by the mother that means *nest*. Tânia calls Carlos over to witness this new development. "Hey Carlos, look at her! She made a really cute *moquinha* for herself." "Yeah," says Carlos. Smiling with pride, Tânia continues, "She must be really comfortable in that *moquinha* because there's no sign of her waking up. She made it herself; she just kept nestling in until she found a good spot." Carlos says, "It looks like she knows she's home", meaning she recognises this familiar space despite all the comings and goings.

It had been a long road to building this *moquinha*-house, which expands and changes over time into a "den", the family term used for Julie's space in the living room, and finally into a "cabin", the term used for her room, all of which have lots of creative space for mutual mother–baby growth. Julie wakes up and, as usual, smiles at everyone. Tânia and Carlos admire their daughter, whose eyes shine when she looks at her mother—the family says Julie is under her spell. Julie makes noises that Tânia repeats, demonstrating full motor development. She seems to connect feelings, movements, and perceptions in a sequence that demonstrates that her internal and external abilities are expanding. The observer reports:

> Julie plays with her rattle, but every once in a while she'll stop and look at me and smile, dropping her rattle. She doesn't pick it back up and instead starts playing with her legs, pulling them and letting go. She looks at the blanket fringe and rubs her little hands in it, pulling at the threads. She makes different sounds as she plays. She looks at her hands and plays with her fingers, holding them and letting go, putting them in her mouth, and then looking at them again.

Later, Tânia gives Julie a bath, during which she turned to look at the observer and smile several times. The mother comments that she already recognises the observer.

As the baby grows, the mother continually notes the changes in her weight and height, and makes other physical changes to their environment. At seven months, Julie is on the floor where she likes to explore and invent games. The observer writes,

> . . . I noticed that Tânia put a blanket on the floor and several cushions against the wall, and spread a number of toys on the blanket: a soft toy

> puppy, a rubber flip-flop that has a whistle, a coloured rattle cube, and the doll I gave her at the hospital.

When Julie sits like a "big girl", her mother calls to her, "Come, come, come over here to mummy." Carlos thinks it is too soon, but Tânia says she knows of a nine-month-old child that can walk: "You have to pull her along." Soon the father leaves, and Tânia tells her daughter that Daddy ran away.

Julie's prematurity is remembered each time a new phase in her development is conquered, and, over time, the mother's characteristics of a strong, emphatic, responsible, and brave woman become more pronounced.

At seven months and eight days, Julie weighs 8.2 kilos and measures sixty-five centimetres. The father asks the observer if she thinks the baby has grown and if she is doing well. The mother says, "I thought that being a preemie she would be smaller than the other kids, but I look at kids her age and see that she's bigger. Even her doctor said she's above average." Julie is a spontaneously happy, smiling child:

> Julie looks up at me from the carpet facetiously. She picks up her rattles and shakes them, puts them in her mouth, then babbles "brrr, brrr" and blows bubbles with her spittle.

The mother reports that Julie's first word was "Daddy", but that it should have been mummy. She adds that Julie now has two little teeth that she uses to break apart and chew biscuits. At times, the mother is very demanding and sharp, wanting immediate reactions from the baby to stay seated, to crawl, or keep still—commands to which Julies does not immediately respond. When she moves in a way similar to crawling, Tânia yells at Carlos to come quick and see.

> Julie babbles, lifts her bottom, and moves her legs as if she were crawling.

Carlos says she "just hasn't worked out she needs to move her arms", to which the mother responds that she will figure it out soon enough. They start training the baby to keep her arms firm and to move forward. Tânia says that they had spent fifteen days at her grandmother's house and that Carlos is complaining about their absences.

The next observations are not conducted at Tânia's house, but at her mother-in-law's house, which is on the same piece of property. After a difficult and unstable period with many comings and goings, Tânia is gradually returning home. At eight months and eleven days, Tânia greets the observer on the porch of her mother-in-law's house and asks her not to mind, but that she would not stay there with her because she had spent the weekend away and was trying to "organise her house". This is one of Tania's well-known patterns of wanting to prepare for changes ahead of time. In this case, she is preparing her house for her return with the baby. Some factors are complicating matters: misunderstandings between the great-grandmother, mum, dad, grandmother, and grandfather occur during the observation. Tânia's house is abandoned and, as she repeatedly says, "a mess". Carlos does not take care of anything. The freezer had broken down and he had not even noticed. All the food Tânia had frozen had gone bad and now she has to clean it up over the weekend. After some time at her house, Tânia returns to sit on the porch step beside Julie's pram and play with her daughter:

> Julie tries to get up in the pram. She smiles and stretches out her arms for her mum to pick her up, but when she doesn't, she sits back down. She slides around in the pram and has fun grabbing her feet. She holds both and makes a kind of swing, saying "ba ba ba".

The father and grandfather come into the yard, trying to raise a ladder to fix the television antenna that had broken off. Tânia keeps talking about Julie: she can already lift herself up in her cot and can sit by herself. The baby stops her playing and stretches out her arms to her mum, who gets up to hug her and kiss her head and hands, calling her "mummy's little chub". She says, "Right baby girl? Small misfortunes are no big deal."

Carlos and Tânia have a misunderstanding. He asks her to go into the house and check the image on the television. Meanwhile, Julie whines and the grandmother says that she is applying what she is learning in her psychology course to her grandchildren. Carlos bellows at his wife. She leaves the house, yelling back that she had heard him. And so go the misunderstandings.

Interestingly, in the midst of this commotion, Tânia remembers how her water had dried up, causing Julie's premature birth. Maybe she is communicating her exhaustion. The "mess" that has been referred to over the last several observations intensifies and becomes difficult to manage, threatening to divide the family. Tânia cannot count on her husband's partnership. Julie had not nursed, so the mother offers her coconut water. She refuses and the grandmother does not understand why, saying to Tânia, "It's coconut water. She likes it and it will keep her from getting dehydrated. When I was pregnant, I drank a lot of coconut water, but it wasn't enough because I dried right up, didn't I? You sucked me dry." This marks the end of the observation and, as the observer is leaving, Julie throws herself in her direction and the mother says her daughter wants to go with her.

At nine months and nine days, the observation is conducted at Julie's maternal great-grandmother's house without Tânia, who is working longer hours because of the Christmas season. The great-grandmother says the baby is curious and observes everything, and she loves eating biscuits. The observer gives her a soft toy doll for Christmas. The baby explores the doll from top to bottom, and then exchanges it for a biscuit. Several complaints about Julie come up: the great-grandmother says she is very angry. The father agrees, but the expression on his face changes and turns serious. The aunt arrives and says it is very difficult to take care of Julie because she cries and gets angry about everything: "You lay her down to change her, and you can't because she's angry and crying. It's getting harder to deal with her." Carlos is silent and the observer notes that the aunt seems bitter.

The next visit between the observer and Tânia happens after Christmas. Tânia had been nervous and apprehensive over the phone, saying she had been losing a lot of weight and did not know what to do. The baby is ten months and twenty-one days. She asks the observer for advice about a day-care centre, saying that there is nowhere else to leave her daughter. During the previous observation, both the grandmother and aunt had been very honest and straightforward about how Julie was becoming "angry" and hard to manage. In her usual pattern of dealing with the difficulties that came her way, Tânia accepts reality and immediately looks for a solution. She shows discernment, recognises limits, and is concerned about, and respectful of, her grandmother. She supports the frustration without retaliating and, thus, is able to maintain her relationship with her grandmother. As we will see further on, Tânia carries this pattern over into her relationship with her daughter.

When the observer arrives, there is a lot of commotion. Carlos has Julie in his arms and Tânia is rushing down the steps of her house wrapping a cover-up around her hips. She was wearing a bikini. Carlos opens the gate and the observer greets everyone. She notes that

> Julie looks beautiful with her hair longer and held back with barrettes. She smiles at me and gurgles a soft "aaah".

Carlos immediately asks if the observer thinks his daughter has grown. Tânia looks at Julie and says she still does not know if she will put her in a day-care centre or not, but that she will have to decide. She says Julie is already crawling all over the place, and can stand up holding on to the sofa. While she describes Julie's new skills, Tânia controls her daughter's walker so that she does not wander off too far. The fact that Julie eats well gives her mother satisfaction, and she describes her as a "good eater who eats everything". How they relate to food gives important indications as to their interactions as a family.

After her February vacation, the observer calls Tânia according to their plan and they made arrangements to restart the observations. The observer reports,

> Everything is going well. Tânia had been afraid that I wouldn't call and she wouldn't be able to give me Julie's invitation. I thank her and we schedule our visit for the following Saturday.

The day of the observations (eleven months and twenty-four days), Tânia apologises for her outfit . . . she's wearing a bikini and a cover-up, and has products in her hair. She says she is losing hair, like Julie, who lost her baby hair as she got bigger. Tânia is experiencing changes and is going through phases like her daughter. The couple tells her to not "mind the mess". The observer actually does think the house looks messy—there is a mattress in the living room where Tânia says the three sleep together. As Tânia talks, the observer understands that she has stopped working outside the home. Eventually she says, "So, I quit my job."

She explains that between her work and her daughter, she opted to be with her daughter. She reached an agreement with the company she worked for. She says this is the first time she has not worked since her childhood. She has never taken a full month vacation. She had only taken ten or twenty days, and "now she was going to see what it was like". As always, she asks the observer for her opinion about Julie, if she is bigger or developing. Julie now weighs ten kilos and measures seventy-five centimetres. Remembering her daughter's premature birth, Tânia is proud of her progress: "She was so tiny when she was born, and now . . ."

Tânia has put a gate up in the kitchen so her daughter will not go out into the street. Julie climbs the sofa to see what is outside the window and grabs objects her mother does not want her to have. Then she shakes her little finger in the air to indicate "no". Tânia also recounts how Julie is destroying the gate with her finger: she sticks her finger in a hole and pulls out pieces of wood. Each time she digs a hole, Tânia covers it with a piece of wood. The mother–daughter relationship is clearly becoming richer and more complex. There is an increasing, albeit temporary, egoic integration of emotional experiences connected to feelings of anger, ambivalence, anxiety, and conflicts that challenge the pair. Throughout the observations until the end, when Julie is three years old, all of this is confirmed in surprising and delightful development, creativity, and uniqueness.

While Julie sleeps, the mother talks about the photos they took on her birthday—it was stressful—and of the beach: "She loved the beach." She would sit Julie in the sand where the water was shallow, but then she would crawl out towards the ocean and would get cross if someone stopped her. She screamed because she wanted to go in the water, even when a strong wave came that could cover her. "She wasn't afraid, she did this"—Tânia spits, imitating her daughter. "In the swimming pool it's the same thing—she screams because she wants to get in. The neighbours already know her by her screams. She has a set of healthy lungs! And to think that when she was born she had lung problems . . . but now, she certainly can bellow!"

When Julie wakes up she smiles at her mum and Tânia points out her four new teeth that had come in at the same time. There is music playing and Julie claps her hands and dances. She raises her leg to try to cross one of the barriers that keeps her from going out of the door of the house.

The mother slaps Julie's bottom to keep her from doing something to hurt herself in the same way she does it to motivate her development.

Tânia encourages Julie to climb the sofa: come on honey, you can do it.

At the end of this observation, Julie climbs on her mother and sits on her belly, poking her finger in her belly and pinching her. The mother shows her the marks left by her pregnancy, and tells her daughter, "This is what is left of you, a chubby mummy." The observer says it is time for her to go and Tânia says, "Already?" Julie whines and her mum adds, "Next week Marina will spend a lot of time with us because it's your birthday."

Twelve to thirty-six months: Julie and Tânia's mutual blossoming

Tânia's decision to leave her job and stay at home to take care of Julie brought intense transformations to the mother–baby pair that once again revealed its strong capacity for growth. From this point forward, we will follow a clear and emotional blossoming of the two in ways that are both mutual and creative.

The spaces inside the house are changed as part of the changes taking place between Julie and Tânia. Both expand and differentiate their spaces, while respecting each other's individualities. Julie now has her own corner in the living room for her various toys, a space she owns called the "den". There, she throws herself on the cushions, plays, sleeps, and hides things.

Tânia also expands to open a creative workspace at home. The dining-room table is now covered with handicraft materials: glue, paint, varnish, bags, small straws made of rolled newspaper, clothes pegs, completed newspaper baskets, plastic pots, and the beginning of a square basket made with newspaper straws. Tânia comes into the room smiling. She talks about selling flip-flops, the newspaper basket sales, and her plans to make costume jewellery. She is excited about her new work and an order a store has placed for one of the baskets for Mother's Day.

She describes the details of her work, demonstrating satisfaction and pride in her new activity.

Julie and Tânia are "working" together. Julie plays beside her mum while she works. The mother's handicrafts are selling successfully and Julie watches her create these objects attentively. Tânia shows the observer several very pretty pieces of costume jewellery and asks her to choose one. It is a meaningful gesture, especially because Tânia was giving her a Mother's Day gift. It is possibly a way of her communicating how important she has been during this motherhood process. The observer's constant presence and availability to follow the comings and goings of the mother–baby couple most certainly helped to sustain a sense of going on being amid the discontinuities and ruptures. The relationship between Tânia and Julie grew at the same rate as the relationship between the pair and the observer in terms of her function.

Julie very actively walks around and explores her environment, and the mother interacts with her constantly. The girl follows her mum with her dummy and security blanket. Tânia shows a certain independence, demonstrating how it is possible to keep a mother's idea and care alive over a period of time. At the same time that Julie blossoms, her mother reveals her creativity and discovers something for herself that fulfils her professionally. She is very excited about doing the handicrafts. She takes classes and makes plans to join the Artisan House to sell her pieces. She is proud and self-confident about this.

At one year and three months, Julie's interactions expand to include the observer. Julie starts to play at putting her dolls to sleep and everyone—she, her mum, and the observer—participate in the game. The mother puts away her work material and Julie places her doll inside the big basket her mother made. Julie has been talking a lot. At one year and four months she walks quickly and likes to tease. She runs short distances, using tiny steps and smiling. She loves the observer's red sneakers, and is always looking at them and admiring them in her own language. The mother has bought Julie her own pair of red sneakers.

Julie loves her den. When Tânia cleans and takes out the cushions, Julie quickly reorganises everything. Tânia continues to grow professionally. She commented that on the previous Saturday she had taken the entrance examination for the Artisan House and passed. So now she has her credentials, which gives her the right to issue invoices. While her mother talks, Julie also talks and plays: she throws herself on an enormous pink and white cloth mouse. She gets up and falls into a sitting position on the mouse. The mother and the observer drink tea and eat cornbread that Tânia made. Julie gets up, gets a doll, and asks the observer to put it to sleep; she sings a lullaby to the doll and then returns it to Julie, who says: "It's for mama." She gets up from her little stool and takes the doll to her mum. The mother is happy because Julie has grown seven centimetres in four months and is now eighty centimetres tall.

At one year and five months, the observer reports a new fence at the door of the house, placed to contain Julie better, and a pink wooden table with a little chair. Julie sits by her mother for a few seconds and then climbs down from the sofa and goes to sit in her little pink armchair. She compares her feet with the observer's and her mother's. She smiles and says she never forgets her red tennis shoes, even when she's not wearing them. She plays with the cloth mouse, turns somersaults, throws herself back on to the cloth mouse, calling out, "Mummy!" The mother says Julie has used a complete sentence. Julie takes the observer by the hand and leads her to sit beside her in the pink armchair, gives her a doll to put to sleep, and calls the observer "mummy". Then she leads the observer to the kitchen and asks her, in her still unclear but understandable language, to reach the biscuits. After getting some biscuits, she goes back to her den and lies down on the carpet, lifting her legs and holding her feet. She remains in that position swinging slightly, until she says, "poopy, poopy, poopy". Tânia says Julie warns her when she has to poop, and then does it, of course.

Julie repeats a gesture of opening and closing her hands toward the observer, and the mother says she means she wants to be held. The observer puts her in her lap, and she continues the gestures toward the door to the street, saying "Daddy, Daddy", and the mother says, "She wants to go outside." When they go out on the porch, the father is just entering the yard. "Wow", says the mother, "she just talked about her dad. Seems as if she knew he was coming." The observer smiles.

The filming day at one year and six months is stressful. Julie walks through everything, laughing, running, climbing up and down stairs, throwing herself on Chico the monkey in her den, calling mummy and daddy repeatedly. They go to the yard where the grandfather has come in on horseback to invite her for a ride. This time, she does not want to go. The mother remembers the differences between other filming shoots when she was smaller and less active. The observation ends with Julie trying to stick a doll through the hole in the porch screen so that it would fall into the yard. The mother tells her to stop, but because she keeps trying, she gets a spank with a flip-flop. Julie takes the doll out of the hole and Tânia angrily tells her to put it away in the box. Julie makes a face as if to cry as she takes the doll inside the house. Tânia follows, slapping Julie lightly on her little bottom as she goes, as if she were steering her with the flip-flop. She takes her inside the house and Julie puts the doll away. Tânia goes back to sit outside and Julie goes after her, asking to be picked up. The mother answers that she is angry and that she knows that when mummy is angry there is no holding.

Julie goes into the house and returns with her dummy and nappy in hand. She hovers around Tânia, looking towards the yard. Then she points towards the stereo, meaning she wants her mother to turn it on. Tânia goes to the living room and turns on the sound system, saying she did not know if the CDs inside belonged to Julie or her father. When the music starts, Julie begins to dance. Tânia collects the dummy and nappy, telling her daughter she will not need them any more, but if she did, she could have them back. Julie did some simple choreography: when the song talked about hands, she touched her hand, if it mentioned feet, she stamped her feet. She circles, twists, and balances her little body, and hugs her mother's legs. The song also has the word bottom, and Tânia tells her that she has to show where her bottom is. Julie climbs on her mother and taps her bottom and the mother says, "Is there poopy in your bottom?" Julie says no and keeps dancing.

When Julie is one year, seven months, and eleven days, the observation takes place at the great-grandmother's house in Cachoeirinha, because there will be a debutante party for Mariana. Julie comes to the door and loudly says "Hi! Hi!" and waves to the observer, who waves back, says "Hi", and smiles. She gives her a small present for Children's Day. The mother explains this to Julie, who closely watches her mum open the package. She puts her hand inside the package. The doll is stuck inside the box and Julie waits to get it: she hugs it and says, "baby". She cradles it saying "beddy-bye" and the mother repeats, "Ah, sing the baby to sleep" . . . Tânia says that the box that the doll came in can also serve as a bed and Julie places the doll back in the box-bed, saying, "Beddy-bye, baby." The mother and the observer smile. Then Julie takes the doll back out of the box-bed and walks around the house; minutes later she is swinging the doll by its cap. The doll has a rattle inside it, so the mother tells her to be nice to it and not shake it so much. Tânia shows her by holding the baby and rocking back and forth, saying, "Be nice, be nice." Julie strokes the doll while her mother talks . . . Julie puts the doll back in its box and then takes her out and tries to sit on the box as if it were a chair. The mother says she is too big for that box, but that she can sit on the little chair next to the sofa. But she decides to take the box and put the doll inside and then take her out and take her to the sofa, where she says "baby" and rocks her for a while.

While she does that, Tânia shows the observer the new crafts she is making using serviettes and painted tea-towels with Christmas themes. She says she made them last week when her grandmother was there and could help her: "The house was like a little factory. You should have seen it! Grandma crocheted and I painted." Everything seemed to flow and the grandmother was back on the scene, demonstrating a creative and handicraft partnership with her granddaughter and a partner to Tânia–Julie. While Tânia took a painting class, Julie stayed with her grandmother. Tânia has exhibited her work at a craft fair and she sells at the school where her mother-in-law teaches, at her old work place, and at some small stores that put in orders. She explains new techniques like biscuiting and jute baskets, among others, and how she needs to increase her production so that she has enough money to go to the beach in the summer. Julie pays close attention to her mother's conversation and also wants to show, mess with, and touch the pieces, all the while looking at Marina. Tânia says she wants to participate and show her mum's work.

Several facets of the mother–Julie–father relationship show up:

> She approaches her mother and asks for tea. Tânia answers that she can't go to get it, and that she'd have to get it herself. The girl gets a bottle that contains tea or a soft drink (there were bubbles). She hands it to her mother, who says she won't open it, and if she wanted some she'd have to open it herself. Julie takes the bottle and shakes it, dropping it on the floor. Tânia yells and shifts to the front of the sofa, reaching for her flip-flop. She tells the girl to pick up the bottle. Julie widens her eyes, makes a crying face, and picks up the bottle and its lid. She gives it to her mother, but does not drink it. She goes to the living room table and gets her nappy that was rolled up and gives it to her mother. Julie opens the nappy and gives the dummy to her mum, who says she doesn't want it. Julie puts the dummy in her mouth and holds her nappy.

Tânia shows the observer pictures from Santa Catarina and Julie positions herself between the two. The photos of the aunt's small farm are beautiful. There are many pictures of Julie with pigs, calves, and cows, and there are many comments about the event. Julie names all of them in her still unclear language, and when pictures of baby animals come up, for example, a calf, she lays her head on the photo and says, "cutie, cutie". The girl looks cheeky and happy in all the pictures, and when she sees herself or her mum or dad, she points and says, "mummy, daddy". Her mother asks, "And the baby in the photo, who is that?" Julie taps herself on the chest.

Carlos enters the living room from another part of the house, and as soon as Julie notices him, she says "Daddy, Daddy" and runs to be picked up. He picks her up and greets the observer. Carlos sits in the armchair next to the mother with Julie in his lap. The couple talk about a party, but the observer notices an air of animosity between them . . . the mother asks the observer if she would like some tea, which she accepts. As soon as the mother gets up to go to the kitchen, Julie climbs down from her father's lap and follows her. In the kitchen, she asks Tânia for some "tea-tea", and her mother says she will make her some, but that first she will prepare tea for the observer. Julie goes back to the living room with her cousin Fabiana, who sits next to Carlos. Julie goes back to her father's lap and Tânia holds the bottle so she can drink. Julie drinks her milk then leaves her father's lap to go and play with her doll and her teenage cousin.

The next month (one year, eight months, and seventeen days) Julie makes rich associations using mimicking, games, and her own language with the observer. When she arrives, Tânia walks down the steps with Julie in her arms, calling to the dogs so she can tie them up:

> They come up the yard. Tânia greets me and opens the gate. I smile to Julie, who is all smiles. I greet Tânia and say hi to Julie, who points at her finger and says something. Tânia says she's asking about the ring I'm wearing. I stretch out my hand for her to see it. She continues talking and Tânia translates, saying hers is inside the house.

While Tânia goes back outside to "let out the dogs", the observer notices how much bigger the girl has become. She is wearing a blue dress with little embroidered flowers and colourful ponytail holders in her hair, and her feet are bare. The mother comes back in saying she had just been working, and picks up where she left off. Julie circles the observer who is sitting on the sofa. She shows her foot and then points to the observer's foot and calls to her mum, who is working with earrings and stones at the table. She goes to her mother and stamps her foot on the floor, pointing at Tânia's foot and to the observer, babbling. Tânia answers that she is not wearing sandals, but that the observer is wearing sandals like her [mum]. Julie continues talking and proposes playing "beddy-bye baby" with the observer. She finds a cloth Santa Claus, says something, and then clearly says "Santa Claus" . . .

Tânia gets up to go to the kitchen to get some fruit salad for the observer. Julie takes the observer by the hand and leads her to the kitchen, talking non-stop. There, she insists to her mother that she wants to put on her sandals, like the observer, and the mum says no because the two are not going for a walk. Julie leaves the kitchen and goes to the porch and Tânia says she went "to get her sandals". She comes back with only one sandal, and her mum asks where the other one is. She returns with both sandals in her hands and the mother warns that she should not put them on now, and that there is a bottle of juice ready for her.

The scenario repeats itself and Julie gives up drinking her juice, going instead to play with the observer. She takes her by the hand and pulls her into the living room, still babbling in her own language. She picks up her doll, sings to it, and gives it to Marina so she can sing to it, too. They do the same with Santa Claus. Julie sits next to the observer. She puts the baby doll beside her and Santa Claus between them. She strokes Santa Claus and takes the observer's hand and moves it as if to pat Santa, saying, "Beddy-bye." The observer does what she wants while Julie looks on and strokes the doll. Tânia goes back into the kitchen and comes out with the bottle, commenting on their "deep conversation".

The mother keeps working and when the daughter starts to circle the table, she asks, "Where's Lulu?" Julie goes to her den to look and brings back the doll that the observer had given her for Children's Day. The mother comments how "Lulu is really something, because ever since Julie got her, she carries her around everywhere." The mother asks about other dolls, which Julie finds and brings over. She seats them and tells them to stay put: "Stay, stay." Tânia continues working, producing one earring after another until Julie asks for her bottle. The mother removes the lid from the bottle and gives it to her. The girl drinks a little and drops it. The mother asks if she wants some chocolate cereal balls and the girl says yes. Tânia closes her boxes and tells Julie to sit on the sofa, and then brings a plate full of little chocolate balls. The girl eats some and offers some to her mother and to the observer. The scene is repeated.

Julie takes her mother's hand and puts it on her groin. Tânia smiles and Julie takes a cereal ball and pretends to put it in her mum's hand, but instead puts it between her legs. Tânia gets cross and says that is not nice and threatens her with a flip-flop. The girl replaces the cereal ball, but flips the plate over spilling its contents all over the floor. One falls between her little sofa and her mother's. Both go to pick up the cereal balls from the floor. Julie eats some and the mother doesn't mind, saying that she will not get the one that fell between the sofas. The girl pulls the observer's hand, but her mother says the observer will not get the cereal ball for her either. Julie sits on the sofa and eats the cereal balls that are on the plate.

At the end of the observation, Tânia gets up and says she is going to get her daughter's sandals so they can both follow the observer to the gate. When Tânia leaves, the girl asks to be held. The observer stretches out her arms to her, but Tânia interrupts: "She has to put on her sandals first." As soon as she finishes putting them on Julie, she says she is going to tie up the dogs, adding, "Imagine if I'd forget." Julie goes with her. After the dogs are locked up, the observer comes down and Julie and Tânia walk her to the gate. When the mother opens the gate, Julie does not want the observer to leave. Tânia decides they can go with her a little way further so that Julie can have a walk. In the middle of the street, the observer says good-bye to the two and wishes them a good weekend. Julie demonstrated that she is in the process of organising defences and developing patterns that are defined by her mother's personality.

At the observation marking one year, nine months, and eight days, Julie has got into trouble and has been put to bed, where she is now sleeping. Tânia said she got angry with her because she was being very difficult and stubborn, so she sent her to bed. When they enter the living room, the observer notices a sewing machine and a lot of material for making tea-towels. Tânia says she has already sold everything she had painted and her grandmother had embroidered. Julie wakes up and comes into the room with her dummy in her mouth and nappy in her hand. She runs open-armed to the observer. The observer leans down to hug the girl and then sits beside her on the sofa. Julie imitates the observer. When she gets up because the mother invited her into the living room, the girl gets up too and follows quickly. She shows the observer their Christmas tree, and says, "Christmas". She leaves to go find Santa Claus and comes back carrying an inflatable version. The observer gives her a present that the mother opens, and Julie stands close making little shrieks of delight. The gift is a Monica[17] cube with a variety of orifices for inserting differently shaped pieces. The mother shows her how it works and the girl, through trial and error, discovers how to play with it. This keeps her entertained with the observer.

Julie asks for a "bat", and her mum translates, saying she wants a bath. She tells the girl to go and get her towel, and Julie runs ahead and pulls the towel off its hook in the closet of her room and takes it to the couple's bedroom. The mother chooses the clothes she will wear to the party and separates a pair of sandals, placing them along with the dress. Julie switches the sandals and looks at her mother, saying: "Daddy". The mother adds, "Yes, Daddy gave you those." She picks them up, looks them over, and says they might work. They all go to the living room and Julie goes to her den, sits down, and smiles at her mum and the observer. Both smile back. Julie gets up and goes to take the observer's hand, pulling her to the den. She puts her hand on the blanket and the mother asks if she wants the observer to sit down. Julie looks up and says "Malina" and points. She calls her mum, too, and the three of them sit in the den. She asks Marina to "beddy bye-bye" an old doll from her mother's childhood, and then asks her mum to do the same. The observer reported,

> I noticed Julie felt her mum was nervous and was trying to soothe her, to care for her.

When the observer telephones to organise the next observation for after the summer holidays, Julie listens in and asks who it is. The mother says it is the observer and hands the phone to her. She says "Malina!" On the set date (one year, eleven months and sixteen days), Tânia says Julie is sleeping because she spent the morning playing in the pool. The house had been painted and the porch looked attractive with its white fencing contrasting nicely with the wine-coloured roof tiles of the house. While the two walk towards the house, they hear a heated argument between the paternal grandparents.

When they enter the house, they go towards Julie's bedroom and the mother whispers that she has been fixing up Julie's room. Because it is dark, the observer cannot see the details, but noticed new curtains, a single bed, and some toys that had typically been kept in the living room. The mother comments that her daughter has grown a lot. Mother and observer go to the living room and Tânia tells her that they had spent some time at her grandmother's beach house and that they had just returned a few days ago. Julie did not like the ocean at first, but then had gradually become used to it. By the end of the season, they had to be careful so she would not go off into the open water. Since Julie had been spending the days in her bikini, they had decided it would be a good time to potty train her.

Tânia says she has been very busy and worried about changes and about keeping the house clean. Some things had to be substituted, for example, the curtains in her daughter's bedroom. She had not been able to find the old-style lace curtains she wanted, so she bought curtains to match her daughter's new bedroom layout: "It wasn't the length that I wanted, but it seems they don't make that kind of curtain any more." Grandma Regina had given her the bed. It was second-hand and very cheap. Tânia had sanded it and decorated it with her own designs. "I performed a miracle with that R$10 bed! It was a lot of work; I spent days on it." She recounts how Julie can say everything now. Tânia hears her daughter speak and goes to her bedroom. The observer sees her taking Julie to the bathroom "to tinkle".

While she waits, the observer looks through the summer photo album Tânia had shown her. When Julie arrives, they greet each other with kisses on each other's cheeks and the girl points to the people in the photo. The first person she shows, pointing with her finger, is "Juju", then daddy and mummy . . . "Juju's daddy" . . . she calls the fish dolphins when she sees one on the beach. Another picture shows Juju and Pedro, her cousin—both the same size, although he is a year older . . .

The father arrives and she runs to him, asking to be held, saying, "Daddy, daddy, hold me." She gets a hug and he puts her back down because he is going to visit his mother. Juju had taken Lulu the doll, an old present from the observer, to the beach and had dragged her everywhere. "Where's Lulu?" Juju finds her and brings her to the observer and asks her to rock her to sleep, which she does. The mother says she tried to move Juju's den to the bedroom, but she had it back out to the living room. Julie takes the observer's hand and shows her the new bedroom. When they enter, she throws herself on the bed, as she had always done in her den. Mother and daughter show her the details of the paint job on the bed, the sheets, the coverlet painted by Tânia, the big soft toy animals on the edge of the bed, placed to keep Juju from falling on the floor, and a sheepskin carpet. They go into the living room and Julie goes back to her room to get her dummy and wants to sit on Tânia's lap, where she sits with her legs hooked around Tânia's waist. She leans against her mother's chest, and Tânia says the girl misses nursing, that sometimes she touches her breasts, smells them, and misses them. She hugs her daughter. She feels her daughter's panties to see if they are wet, but they are not.

Before leaving, the observer reminds Tânia that, starting with the next observation, the visits will be quarterly: Tânia says, "Only every three months! Ahhhh", and hugs her daughter. Growth hurts and brings losses, absences, and transformations, but also "a new bedroom, panties, etc."

At the next observation (two years and nineteen days), the observer noticed that there was dog faeces spread all around the gate entrance. This had never happened before. Regina appears and apologises, chasing off the dogs so Tânia can lock them in the basement. The observer and her co-worker, who is along to film the day's observation, go into the garden. Julie is near the pool and when she sees the observer, she approaches.

Tânia decides to do the filming inside the house rather than in the garden. When they enter the house, Julie says some things that the observer does not understand, but the word "Keka" is clearly understood—Keka is the witch in the Xuxa television show called *The World of Imagination*. Julie had seen a witch's hat when she had been out with her dad, and the two had gone into the store. "Now look at her," says the mother, "Now all she can talk about is Keka." She talks faster and faster, walking quickly about the house looking for an elephant, looking for "Bush". Then she throws herself in her den and turns around and smiles. She goes back to talking about Keka, asking the observer with inquisitive eyes, "Do you have Keka?"

A little later the observer gives Julie her two-year birthday present: a large, pink, soft cloth rabbit She takes the bunny and hugs it, then proceeds to walk around dragging it by its ears. She comes close to the observer and gives it to her, who returns it to Julie. She latches on to the bunny and goes off to her den. She sits with the rabbit on her lap, looking into its eyes, squeezing it in her arms, and talking to it in baby talk. The mother goes into the kitchen to get drinks to go with the presents, and Julie goes in after her, dragging the rabbit by its ears. Tânia says they also have a little gift for the observer: a keychain with a tiny plastic sneaker with bells on the tip. Occasionally, Tânia is tough with Julie, usually when they are disputing the command of a situation and measuring each other's power.

> Tânia gives me a keychain as a gift. As soon as Julie sees it she comes to me with her hand extended. Tânia tells me not to let her have it. Julie looks at me while her mum goes to the handicrafts cupboard, saying she would get another one for her. Julie asks for the keychain in my hand. Tânia once again tells me not to give it to her. Julie looks at me, tutting. Tânia returns and gives her daughter another keychain, but she won't take it and goes back to asking for mine. Tânia tells Julie to take the other one, but Julie starts crying and asking for my keychain. Tânia raises her voice, saying that keychain was for me, and then asks me to put it away while she exchanges Julie's keychain for another one. Tânia goes again to the cupboard and Julie, who is at my side, starts screaming. Tânia tells me not to give her my keychain, and Julie cries so hard she howls. Later she kept circling her mother, who didn't pay her any attention. Tânia shows me her new projects: table runners, plastic bag holders, and different painted tea-towels with crocheted borders that she learnt how to do from her grandmother while at the beach. Later on, Tânia comments that she's thinking about putting her daughter in a day-care close to her house: "Just in the afternoon for a few days. It will be good for her to have other children around and I can work in peace."

When they say good-bye, the observer confirms the next observation date and Tânia says, "Yeah. . . . not until July . . . it's a long time . . ." and tells Julie that the observer will take a very long time to come back. After the dogs are locked up, Julie leads the way holding her mother's hand until they reach the gate and they say good-bye.

Three months later, after the ritual with the dogs at the entrance to the house, Julie comes out with a sleepy look on her face. Her mother comments that her daughter was resting because now she is going to day-care and is more tired than usual. She is in ponytails and a red jumper that highlights her pink cheeks, and a pink tracksuit. Cute as a button! The observer greets her with a smile and leans down to give her a kiss. She is warm—a nice kind of warm. Julie tells the observer that she had been lying on the sofa where she has a blanket and a pillow. Tânia tells her about Julie's adjustments to school, the June parties, and that Julie has pleasantly surprised her teacher with her fine and gross motor skills. She is able to sing all the little songs. She tells stories to her group and they pay attention to her. She came home the other day with a bite mark on her arm. "There was a mark of a child's full set of teeth on her arm", which was hard for Tânia to look at. She went to her daughter's school every week and had seen her hitting another child and her cousin João. Tânia asks her daughter to tell the observer a story, so she goes to her den, selects a book, and sits beside Marina to show her the witch.

For a good while she "talks about the witch". Then she goes to her pink table and asks to draw. After a while, the grandparents call her to go and ride the horse with her grandfather, who trots Julie around the yard several times. She seems to have a lot of fun. When they come back inside the house they go to the kitchen, where Tânia prepares coffee with milk and tells about the parties they have been to. Julie asks to sit at the table and Tânia helps her, saying they always have their meals together. Julie sits looking at the observer and "tells" her various things; occasionally the mother helps by translating some words.

In this way they have their coffee with milk and biscuits. In the conversation, the mother talks about her work and the Latin American fair. She demonstrates a new technique that she has learnt that is very beautiful, along with tablecloths and serviettes she has painted and crocheted. During this exchange, Julie goes to her pink table and asks her mum for coloured pencils, which she hands to her one at a time. Julie shows her drawing to the observer, who compliments her. At the same time, Tânia shows her other new projects, making the observer feel divided between the mother and daughter. Julie gets up and goes to the sofa, where the mother and observer join her. When the three are seated, Julie gets up and brings two plastic chairs and leans them against the sofa. She climbs on one and asks her mother if she can fly. Tânia says no, and Julie says, "Yes, mummy flies", and then lies down in the den. The mother says, "This one turned out better than a work order." The mother is the witch that flies.

At two years, six months, and thirteen days, Tânia locks up the dogs so the observer can enter the yard. The observer notes her harsher tone of voice when she does this. Julie is sleeping and Marina notices that Tânia had been painting towels. She comments about her daughter's growth and about the exhibition she has been able to do of her work, which is really very beautiful. At the exhibition, she meets other people and gets to know other places. She says she will keep working and trying to improve. Julie's father wakes her up and she comes into the living room still sleepy. The observer is taken aback when she sees her, thinking, "She is losing her baby look and is becoming a little girl." They greet each other with kisses and the mother, noticing her daughter's messy hair, says, "Come here and let mummy fix that hair", and, as usual, does it expertly.

Tânia and the observer sit on the sofa and Julie on her little sofa next to them. She takes the present the observer had given her for Christmas several months ago—the Monica toy for inserting shapes—and plays. She gets some right and some wrong, but keeps playing and getting past the hard parts. After a while, she throws the parts in the air and while she and Tânia pick them back up, Julie says she wants to stay home with her mum. She has a distant look in her eyes and asks why she has to go to school. Tânia explains, and then shows the observer her daughter's schoolwork, which the observer says are very pretty:

> Julie answers emphatically: "They are not pretty." Tânia gets angry and chastises her, saying she shouldn't talk that way. Julie pouts and looks down, crossing her arms. She looks at me with her head down and her brow furrowed. The mother tells her to lift her head and not look that way: "Don't do that, Julie! Lift your head!" The girl refuses. Tânia insists, "Lift your head, Julie! Oh, you're not going to look up, are you? Uncross those arms, child!" Julie keeps her frown until Tânia lifts the girl's head with her hands, saying in a loud voice, "Lift your head, girl!" Julie whimpers and says she doesn't want to. Tânia insists and pushes Julie's head, which bangs against the wall. Even so, Julie, who is now close to tears, says no, but ends up lifting her head.

Tânia backs away a little and goes to the kitchen to get some fruit salad for the observer, telling her daughter to follow her. The mother says tells Julie if she doesn't behave she'll get a spanking, "and just because Marina is here doesn't mean I won't let you have it." As soon as the mother leaves, the girl goes back to her frowning and lowers her head. The observer watches her, which does not affect Julie. A few minutes later, she is still impassive and her irritated expression is clear. She kicks a cushion in front of her with her feet. The mother returns and notices the cushion is out of place and says harshly, "Did you throw that cushion at Marina, Julie?" To break the ensuing silence, Marina says that she had not. Julie goes to the television, the mother makes comments, the observer says her "uh-huhs", and the tension in the air begins to dissipate. There is a clear dispute between the mother and her daughter, who fights for her space when the mother requires her to perform.

After eating her fruit salad, Julie takes a doll and walks around with her a little. She hands it over to the observer to put it to sleep . . . she takes two more dolls and places them on the sofa with the observer. Julie says it is time to go to sleep, but that there is a witch. She lies down with her arms around the dolls because the witch is coming. She stretches her legs to lie with the dolls, leaning her face against them. I look at her nestled with the dolls and smile. Tânia and Carlos comment about how the observation project is coming to an end.

At the second to last observation (two years, nine months, and six days), the dogs bark until they see it is the observer and then stop. Tânia comes to lock them up and open the gate while Julie stays on the porch, waving to Marina. The observer has a present for her, since it is almost Christmas, but keeps it hidden. When she comes into the house, she gives it to Julie and the mother says Santa Claus had stopped by the observer's house and at the school party. While Tânia opens the present, the observer notices that the living room is decorated for Christmas and that Tânia had been working on T-shirts. The present was a Barney, which Julie hugs. The mother says, "Now I've seen it all! She's going to be dragging that thing up and down all over the place." The girl had been given another Barney, but it was too big and difficult to carry. Hugging the smaller one, she says this one is good and the big one is bad.

She goes to her den, which now has only a few cushions and a few toys: the big Barney, almost as big as her, the soft toy mouse, which is even bigger, and an extra-large inflatable Santa Clause. After playing, the mother insists that Julie tell the observer her news: "It's that a spider peed on my dummy." The mother continues, "Yeah, the dummy fell beside the sofa, and then a spider peed and pooped on it, so how are you supposed to use it now, huh?" Julie confirms, repeating her mother's words. The mother is happy, saying her daughter does not need the dummy any more . . . Julie takes the smaller Barney and goes to the sofa to lean against her mum. The girl sits with her legs open, and the mother tells her to close them so her panties do not show. "You're already a young lady and can't show your panties." The mother insists and repeats, and her daughter closes her legs, but then opens them again. Julie repeats the same situation with Barney, saying, "Close your legs, or your pantsies will show." Mother and daughter play with the big Barney and the baby Barney, and Julie talks about a stepmother who stole a baby in the eight o'clock soap opera. Tânia says this event in the soap opera has caused an impression on Julie and she talks about it a lot.

The last observation is also filmed. Julie is three years old and twenty-one days. During the ritual with the dogs, the observer considers the smiling girl who is now so big and beautiful. When the observer introduces Tatiana, who will do the filming, Julie says: "Tati". Everyone smiles. Inside, the girl goes to the sofa near the window. The observer sits beside her on the sofa where she always sits during observations, and "Tati" sits on the opposite side, so that Julie is in the middle. She gets up and goes to sit on the other sofa between her father and mother, who tell her to go and fetch what she is learning in school: scribbles, letters, words. Tânia writes and Julie traces. Tânia says her daughter is ahead of her class, a fact the teacher has confirmed. She still tells stories at school and Tânia insists that she tell the observer one.

Julie tells several stories about Hansel and Gretel, Cinderella, Little Red Riding Hood, and others, in her own fashion: there is always a witch and she mixes up the stories, which her parents correct. The mother talks about a professional at her grandmother's school who evaluated Julie's IQ. The observer listens and says "uh-huh" several times. Julie grabs her nappy and says she's going to sleep. Her mum says sleeping is for the bedroom, and asks her daughter to show the observer her room. It is a very girly room full of enormous soft toy animals, a sheepskin carpet on the floor, toys on the shelf, and a little cabin—all very neat and tidy. Julie throws herself into the soft toy animals, hugging the big Barney. Her mother tells her to find the little Barney, which is inside the cabin. She takes it to the big Barney saying that one is the mummy and one is the child, and then proceeds to sniff the dolls' bottoms. The mother says, "That's not nice, Julie!" but she keeps doing it.

Even on the last day, Tânia serves drinks, first to the visitors and then to her daughter. Everyone has juice and then Julie asks her mum for some books to read. The daughter wants her mum to read the stories, but she says she has already told her those stories and that now it is her turn to tell them. When the mother leaves the room, Julie leafs through the storybooks saying that in her stories there is always a witch. Tânia and Julie stack and put away all the books before going back to the living room. The observer gives her a doll with hair just like Julie's. Tânia has trouble getting the doll out of the box because part of her hair is stuck. So she curls the hair around her finger and pulls out the part that is stuck. The three of them—father, mother, and Julie—are there with the observer and her co-worker during the shooting. They ask with interest about the research, and then they all go out to the yard and to the gate, where they say good-bye.

Final considerations

Tânia and Julie's story allows us to closely follow a captivating story of the progressive and creative blossoming of a mother–baby pair that overcame the challenges of discontinuities, which, despite everything, did not threaten the continued existence of either mother or baby during the first three years.

The story of this mother–baby relationship is marked by rupture (premature birth) and a risk the parents dramatically and wordlessly revealed to the observer early on at the first ultrasound scans. Julie's circumstances during pregnancy became more discernible as the pregnancy developed. Although the parents wanted the baby, they acted strangely, demonstrating high levels of anxiety and fear throughout the entire pregnancy. The atmosphere during the scans was always perplexing, as if important aspects could not be revealed; they were mysterious, challenging, and secret. No matter how healthy Julie was, recurring subjects like labour, prematurity, excessive worry about amniotic fluid, weight and foetus size, and numerous fears permeated the exams. They seemed to have been preparing for the pre-eclampsia, anasarca, lack of amniotic fluid, and Julie's premature birth. At the same time, they felt a certain euphoria, which the observer identified as false, and which functioned as a protective schism during that period.

The observer was strongly affected by this context, which made it difficult for her to perform her duties and to report her findings at the weekly supervision meetings. Her few and succinct reports placed us in direct contact with the silence of what could not be communicated verbally throughout the pregnancy. During the supervisions, the observer always tried to use more words in an effort to translate what was being felt but that could not be verbalised. The predominant form of communication was non-verbal, with the parents transmitting euphoria on one hand and the observer, paralysed, counterpointing with what could not be communicated: the terror of not being able to produce life or not being able to sustain it.

There were two babies being carried simultaneously: one alive and one dead. The dead one was hidden, creating a heavy atmosphere that the observer captured during the ultrasound scans and then bore along with with the sonographer. The doctor frequently pointed out signs of life in the foetus to the parents, yet the mother did not seem to believe in the safety of her internal intrauterine space, or that it could produce life. In the end, the absence of amniotic fluid and Julie's premature birth confirmed the mother's fantasy that the foetus's life could only be guaranteed outside her womb, because inside it was dangerous. The demands placed on the observer of carrying a dead baby throughout an entire pregnancy were very heavy, which helps us understand her constant feeling of being kept on the outside and of being a stranger with bizarre feelings, despite her willingness to enter. The supervision group played a key part in supporting the observer so she could maintain her surrogate function in this complex pregnancy.

Only when it came time to deliver was it was possible to understand a little of the shadow that hovered over Julie since the beginning of her story. The obstetrician abruptly, and without the consent of the family, revealed that Julie was arriving on the very day that had been set for the birth of a first baby that the mother had lost before completing her first trimester of pregnancy. The mother became pregnant with Julie one month after the miscarriage, without any sense of mourning or loss. Thus, the second pregnancy carried powerful ghosts that could not be brought to life through words, and therefore remained hovering over the ultrasound examination room. Parallel to Julie's gestation was the first pregnancy, which had to be expressed bodily because it had no psychic closure. Therefore, when that first pregnancy would have come to term, Tânia's body sprang into action, announcing the need for Julie's premature birth, which took both the place and the timing of the other. Not dealing with the first loss is what came into play in this case.

During birth, similar to other moments during the pregnancy, Tânia projected her angst on to the observer, who absorbed them to protect her from having to deal with them. Julie is born, is welcomed by her mother, and then sent to the neonatal ICU until she can go home. The observer says her good-byes with the feeling that she is also leaving prematurely, yet at the right time for performing her function of helping bring to term and bury a dead baby and close that phase.

The therapeutic function of the observations for the mother during her pregnancy is well illustrated in this case. Tânia and Carlos were able to count on a faithful partner who willingly and continuously offered the psychic space they did not have. The observer was a faithful trustee of their nameless anguish who posed no risk of returning any of it prematurely or of questioning their medical history in a way that would force them to think the unthinkable.

The sonographer also played an important therapeutic function in calming the parents and alerting them to the mother's clinical state of anasarca in the second-to-last scan, which had put both mother and baby at risk.

We believe that it was especially important to have a different observer for each phase in this case. Tânia was able to connect with two very special partners that met her unique and specific needs in the pre- and post birth phase.

By observing this case longitudinally, we can confirm that it is only as life progresses that we can know which direction development will take. It cannot be predicted, be based on preconceived ideas, or be singled out. Therefore, by implementing Bick's infant observation method in a specific setting, we were able to follow the relational patterns that emerged and the development of Julie's personality as she interacted freely with her carers. We were also able to follow all the mother's efforts to adapt to the needs of her daughter and to re-establish the continuity that had been interrupted by Julie's premature birth.

Tânia's return to work brought additional discontinuities—physical changes, carers, angry dogs, attempts to adapt to the grandmother's and aunt's houses, changes in schedules—all of which were bravely faced by the mother–baby pair. Tânia was not a depressed or sad mother; she latched on to her partners (grandmother, observer) and naturally and courageously faced the real circumstances that her life presented without dramatising them. The observer's flexibility and willingness to keep up with these changes were crucial in this period. She adapted herself to the needs of the pair and participated in all the instabilities the mother and daughter experienced. She changed her observations to Saturdays and to different locations without thinking of it as detrimental. On the contrary, it formulated a creative work environment that added value to the partnership.

Once the secret that had haunted the couple and the team throughout the pregnancy had been revealed, the possibility of life opened up: with her life, Julie helps her parents bury the dead baby and the ghosts hovering around Tânia's womb, and is born to face what life has to offer. Mother and daughter experience a very real relationship marked by a liveliness that carried over to the mother–observer relationship as well, creating an immediate bond between the two. The observer had first telephoned the mother right as she was leaving the hospital and could sense that she was radiant, now holding her baby in her arms, totally different from how she saw her at the hospital on her first visit.

The ritual of "locking up the family dogs" in order to allow the observer to enter the house, letting them go during the observation, and then locking them up again to allow her to leave depicted a central theme: containing aggressiveness. The mother needed to test her capacity to contain her aggressiveness. On the first observation that had been scheduled for the exact date Julie was expected to be born, the mother gives the baby to the observer to hold while she goes out to the yard to let the dogs loose. When locking up the dogs, Tânia frequently alerted the observer about the possible risks they posed: "Imagine if I forget to lock them up." Or when the observer was about to leave, the mother would comment that if she did not hold the dogs back, the observer would "leave the place dead". After about three months, the observer reported no longer being afraid of the dogs, and in one harsh confrontation between the paternal grandmother and Tânia, the observer was confused and wrote, "The dogs invaded the house".

In this new phase, Tânia's "dogs" can emerge. She does not deny their existence, but learns to control them, locking them up and setting them loose when necessary in order to maintain the baby and the observer safe. Tânia regresses, mixing herself with her daughter without fear of her "brutality", using the observer to dilute and drain her affections. Besides counting on a third party to help her in this function, Julie reinforces that her mother's fantasies, so frightening during her pregnancy, now have no impact on her life. Julie's vitality not only diminishes the mother's fantasy of destruction, but also confirms her ability to create and sustain life.

On several occasions, Tânia is harsh and demanding with her daughter. She wants her to grow, walk, learn to do things, be independent, like she is. What is incredible in this case is not the lack of failures, but how these failures appear gradually, showing Julie how life comes in small doses. This true relationship gradually offers a model for Julie to also construct a space that is just hers, where she can contain her own dogs and learn to tame them.

We learn from the authentic way Tânia lives her life and from how she helps Julie live her own life. This case helps us elucidate the fluctuations of real life, not only its beauty and charms, but also its brutalities and failures. Julie's house is a stage set up to show the conflicts of daily life.

The mother's capacity to discriminate and accept development and separation became evident when Julie was very small. For example, at the first observation, Tânia tells the observer that her daughter has to get used to the noise and sounds of the routine in the house. When Julie was almost two months old, the observer noticed a security blanket placed near Julie. At three months, the mother was already stimulating the baby to hold her own bottle, and had started creating spaces in the house for the baby's motor skills development. Thus, the house changed to reflect the growth of the mother–baby pair.

When Julie was six months old, the observer witnessed the creation of a *moquinha*, which revealed signs of the baby's own sense of discrimination, and how the mother accepted both their individualities. At the right moment the *moquinha* expanded to become a "den"—a corner in the living room with cushions, a mattress, and toys—that changed over time. In this space, Julie had the opportunity of administrating the dramas of her life by integrating her aggressiveness, dealing with conflicts, and exercising the art of playing and creating.

Tânia opened a creative workspace inside her house, something she had never imagined she could do, in order to bravely risk quitting her job to take care of Julie. She discovered a new skill and taste for artisanal work that led her to give birth to, develop, and assume a new profession. This was a clear result of her intense lived experiences and the transformations she had experienced during her trajectory of pregnancy, giving birth, and raising her daughter. Producing handicrafts seemed to translate the custom-made work Tânia had been doing in weaving the bonds of her relationship with Julie from the day she was born. She weaves as a mother. She does not weave Julie, but helps Julie weave herself as a person, little by little. It was beautiful to see the result of this project woven by the two. Tânia and Julie, side-by-side at their worktables, teach us how the birth of a child can foster mutual mother–baby growth.

As Julie developed, the mother increasingly demonstrated who she was: demanding, curious, independent, determined, creative, brave. Her authenticity allowed her to freely express her loving and aggressive feelings along with her values, limits, and mother–daughter hierarchy. Julie is clearly an intelligent little girl who is vivacious, creative, combative, very alert, and increasingly integrating with the free circulation of her affections, anxieties, love, and hate. This case exemplifies a living partnership that was connected, respectful, and interested in growth, which was also reflected in how the observer interacted with the mother–baby pair.

The daughter's premature situation was always very near the surface, which confirms the intense trauma the mother had experienced. Until she was three years old, Julie's development had to be physically and emotionally superior to that of other children born full term. It was clear how Tânia used her relationship with the observer to work through the trauma of lacking amniotic fluid, the possibility of death, and Julie's premature birth. A significant attitude that was repeated in every observation was the mother's constant need to keep the observer supplied with liquids—water, soda, juice, coffee, tea. In contrast with the scarcity of her pregnancy—of liquids, of affections—this period marks abundance—of milk, affection, and mutual mother–baby growth, despite all the instability and uncertainty that came with it.

CHAPTER SIX

Alice and her daughter, Valentina: a ferocious struggle to be born

Pregnancy

Our observations of Valentina's story began in the tenth week of pregnancy and progressed through eight monthly obstetric ultrasound observations, another one during the delivery, and fifty-three home observations until she was three years old.

The observer's first contact with Alice over the phone was as follows:

> The mother was nice, communicative, and very interested in participating in the research. She clearly stated her reasons and her desire to be involved in the observations. She was worried about the fact that she was pregnant at forty-one years of age; she had been pregnant once before, but had a miscarriage early on in the pregnancy and therefore thought it was a good idea to be observed during this new pregnancy. She also readily accepted the initial arrangements for the observations.

Alice's spontaneous and sincere attitude made the observer immediately want to get to know her. Her determination and decision to participate in the research and benefit from both the sonographer and the observer's presence seemed connected to this mother's determination and decision to keep this new pregnancy and keep the baby by reaching the balance or harmony she had been unable to achieve before. There was an immediate sense of empathy between the mother and the observer that was maintained until the end of the first phase—delivery.

The first meeting with Alice and Mário takes place at the first ultrasound scan. Alice is a simple, nice woman with pretty features. She is of average height, is slightly overweight, and has very short black hair. She is cheerful, strong, determined, and always prepared to mediate her husband's reactions and behaviour, as if to excuse him and rebalance the relationship. She is successful at her job with a small company where she has worked as an attendant for over ten years.

Mário is neither good nor bad looking. He is tall, bald, and seems much older than Alice. He is rather strange: he acts as if he is disabled and not very masculine; in other words, he is rather undefined. He is restless and sighs a lot, always moving and changing positions in his seat. He always leans his head to one side or the other, his mouth half open. He stutters when he starts to talk. He does not seem to know how to position himself and is uncomfortable, enervated, withdrawn, and frightened. He says he is a motorcycle mechanic: "The environment is really stressful, doctor . . . I get really worried, really nervous; when I get home I have to stay outside for a while until I calm down. I sit and play with the dogs until I calm down. And now she's like this [pregnant], I'm really worried, really anxious . . . my job is really stressful, I don't think I can come to the scans; I'm here today because I'm on sick leave."

Soon after the first scan, Alice explained parts of her story with Mário, which sheds light on the long and rigid construction of their relationship. They have been married twenty years. In the first ten years they did not think about having children because they spent all their time taking care of her mother in-law who was sick and, according to Alice, demanded a lot of attention. Alice took care of her mother in-law during one shift, and Mário slept regularly at his mother's house to take care of her during the night. In this way, they maintained a "brother–sister relationship" while taking care of his mother. As we will see in future observations, the Mário–Alice "fraternal relationship" had a great deal of rivalry, disputes, and polarisation, with Alice in an idealised position and Mário at the opposite extreme.

A significant factor in Alice's story might help us understand how this couple functioned. Alice had a twin sister who was idealised and valued by the family. Alice often extolled her sister's qualities as a mother in the observations, while she remained in the undervalued position: an "old mother", "clumsy", and "no one imagined a baby would come out of here". In her relationship with Mário, Alice found the chance to invert the original fraternal relationship by occupying the valued position that she so coveted, and, thus, maintaining the polarisation. Nevertheless, Valentina is the one used in her struggle to give birth to an Alice-mother who was capable and integrated.

Thus, after the mother-in-law died, Alice tried to get pregnant, "But I couldn't because I didn't want it very much." Three years ago, she had a miscarriage in her third month of pregnancy. At the time, Alice said she had felt "guilty", thinking, "I lost the baby because I was too anxious, I couldn't touch my belly, I wasn't affectionate, I didn't want the pregnancy; I wasn't prepared." Now, stroking her belly, she states with certainty, "I'm prepared and happy to be pregnant, I think it will work out, I'm always stroking my belly and being affectionate", and declares "It's a girl! Everyone wants a girl. Her grandfather would love a girl; he's only got grandsons and Mário wants a girl too . . ." Mário timidly adds, "It can be a girl. A girl would be good . . . I'm really worried, really anxious; I don't even want to think about it. The last time I was really worried too, really anxious, I didn't want to hear about it . . ." Alice cuts off her husband's conversation with a motif she maintains until the last scan: "Mário is like that, so worried, but he's a good man and was a very good son to his mother; I'm sure he'll be a very good dad too . . . We have to find the balance."

Alice used the word "balance" quite often during the ultrasound scans. From the beginning, it was clear that her strength and determination depended on Mário's anxiety, on him being undervalued, incompetent, aggressive, and lethargic. This kind of interaction between the couple became more defined and solidified throughout the ultrasound scans. It is a fundamental pattern for maintaining their fragile balance, which is now considerably threatened by the presence of a stranger, an uncontrollable outsider—the baby.

The second observation is an example of how the fragile balance of the Alice–Mário couple is maintained through disassociation and Alice's strong projection on to Mário. On one side, we see Alice smiling, firm, and paying close attention to the images, with her hands apart resting on her belly, but balled into fists as if she were cheering for something, willing the baby to work out. On the other side, we see Mário looking lost, distant, and needing the observer's instructions to sit down. The observer notices Mário's appearance and feels sorry for him, trying to help him by explaining what he might not understand. The relationship between the observer and Mário is, thus, defined and then repeated in the next scans:

> In this ultrasound scan, I had some trouble paying attention to the image of the baby and at times the image seemed less clear. I don't know if this was due to the fact that Mário was closer to me than in the previous scan and, as always, looked more at everything other than the baby. He looked at me, at the floor, at the ceiling, sighed . . . I noticed that I kept looking to see what he was doing, how he reacted, what he expressed; I had to control myself not to pay more attention to him than to the baby.

He was clearly behaving like a baby and strongly identified himself with the foetus.

In another description the observer stated,

> He moves his arms head a lot, he makes a lot of faces, sighs, and talks to himself. He sat on the edge of the chair and spent the entire scan with his face turned in my direction, looking at me . . . I felt watched the entire time and had the impression at times that he was watching me to figure out what I was looking at. It is as if he is looking at the baby through me. I noticed that he would look at me and smile or raise his eyebrows when I did, imitating me.

Mário seems terrified about breaking the rules and invading a sacred place: the mysterious interior of a woman's body.

The baby can be seen clearly and its movements are surprising. The doctor says, "Look at that, it's doing a headstand!" Alice is smiling and following the image closely, while Mário frowns, rubs his hands, squeezes his face, sighs, and quickly turns to the observer, looking at her. She asks, "Do you see it, Mário?" He laughs, "He-he . . ." and continues looking at the observer, unable to talk. Then he says, "I thought it was the dark part, oh my, oh my, oh my", rubbing his forehead and eyes. The doctor says, "The dark part? No . . . the baby is here, look! Do you see it?" Mário says, "No, yes . . . no . . . yes . . . no I see it, doctor", without taking his eyes off the observer. He continues, "Thank God, oh my, oh my, oh my", and sighs. Alice explains, "He's very anxious. We lost the baby the last time, now he's like this, always worried and really anxious."

The scan continues. Many details, measurements, and movements of the foetus emerge. The doctor comments on the foetus's beauty and gracefulness and says, "Look there, with its hand on its head!" and Alice answers, "Oh no! She's going to come out worried like her father!" The doctor asks, "Why? Is her father worried?" Alice replies, "Oh yeah . . . It's that he gets really anxious, and when he gets like that he gets aggressive."

Mário listens quietly to his wife's comments, and looks down. She continues, "I already told him we have to find a balance, you can't get anxious and aggressive." Mário listens silently and keeps his head down, looking at the floor. She firmly repeats the same sentence again, as if to make it penetrate her husband and stay in his head. It seems hard for Alice to accept any discrimination or differentiation between Mário and the foetus. They are both as she desires, thinks, and wants. To Alice, both her husband and the foetus rarely exist apart from her.

Next, the sonographer asks if they want to know the sex of the baby. The mother quickly says, "Yes", and states, "It's a girl, it's Valentina." The doctor directs herself to the father, wanting to know if he wants a girl. Mário answers, "No, doctor, only God knows; whatever comes is welcome, boy or girl, as long as it's healthy, oh my, oh my, oh my . . . the last time, you know doctor, it was terrible . . ." He sighs and turns red. His wife looks at the team and firmly says, "Yes, he was hoping for a girl", and takes Mário's hand. She keeps her right hand in a fist on her belly and the other one with him until the end of the scan. Mário seems to calm down, looking at Alice's fingers or at her wedding band. Once again, Mário acts like a child that is mistreated and then stroked in a sequence that leaves it confused and submissive to its tormentor.

This pattern seen in the couple's relationship continues as Valentina grows, develops, and exhibits her own movements, oblivious to what happens outside her intrauterine world. In this space, Valentina experiences maximum development and freedom. She seems competent and is undoubtedly progressing. The mother always seems tense and threatened by her daughter's freedom and singularity, and tries to erase her uniqueness. All Valentina's characteristics are invalidated by her mother, who thinks Valentina is rebellious for assuming her own control in a kind of power struggle. When the foetus puts her hand against her face, it is because she is embarrassed that her genitalia is showing, or it is because she is worried like her father. She will not have legs like her dad. Valentina's legs will be full like her mother's. The doctor says, "Look there, she's smiling", and Alice says, "She's smiling like her mother. I'm laughing and she's laughing too . . . she's imitating . . . Look, Mário, she's a carbon copy of you, look, she's just like you." The same happens when the baby yawns or sleeps.

There is only one observation where she is relaxed and satisfied, without needing to invalidate Valentina or impose her will. She is not afraid of the imbalance. She is lying in a way that seems very comfortable and without shame. Her legs are stretched apart, and her arms up high and open. She smiles a lot and looks attentively at everyone. The sonographer points to Valentina to show how she is swallowing liquid:

> She swallows liquid and moves her mouth and tongue, giving us the feeling that she is tasting something very good [twenty weeks]. There is silence as we watch the baby swallow. In that moment, when I look at the baby I have the feeling that I'm looking at Alice. They are resting in the same position, and look similar. The two relay a sense of satisfaction. The baby, with her open arms flung high and swallowing, and the mother lying back with her open arms above her head, smiling and looking at her baby. It is the first time that I feel this; that I have this impression . . .

> Depending on how Alice breathed, the baby would move her body in the same rhythm. She shifts to find a better position, making herself comfortable in the womb. She continues sleeping in the sway of her mother's breathing. It's beautiful to see [thirty-four weeks].

It is a rare moment in this observation, which also affects the father, who sighs, sweats, and wants to leave. When asked why he was in a hurry, he answers, "You know, doctor, I'm hungry, everybody is hungry, it's already noon, it's time to go, you know how it is, my stomach wants food . . . You fellows have to hurry it up over there. There has to be time for lunch, help me out, doctor, can't you hurry it up a bit, make time go a little faster?" The sonographer answers, "I can't control time, I can't do anything about it. Time moves on its own,

I can't do anything . . ." When the scan ends, Mário says, "Whew! Thank goodness, I'm starving, doctor."

At another scan, the baby sleeps the entire time and so does the father, his legs stretched out in front of him, his hands resting on his belly, and his head falling forward. The observer writes that at the same time that the baby opens her tiny mouth, Mário yawns. When the sonographer asks if he sees the baby, he wakes up, startled. The baby also wakes up and starts to swallow as she usually does—"tasting"—and then goes back to sleep. Everyone watches Valentina, admiring her beauty and gracefulness. After a time, she starts making rhythmic movements, pushing her body forward and backward as if she were on a little swing. It is beautiful to see.

To the mother, Valentina seems to exist only through similarities to, and comparisons with, adults. And the father, always perplexed, does not know how Valentina got in there, or how she will get out and wants to know why it takes so long for her to finish gestating: "Four or five weeks? No way! Why so long?" Alice says her husband is always in a hurry, and if it were up to him the baby would come sooner.

The strange, vague sense and compliance that Mário transmits is connected to the "straitjacket" Alice puts him in, which he accepts. Mário inhabits a skin that is not his, but it holds him together with some level of wholeness. Although he complains, he cannot imagine himself without this fake skin. Removing it would mean losing his packaging and safety and make him homeless. Alice is engaging and offers a relationship where she is a constant, determined, and possessive presence that guarantees Mário's life. He seems to see Alice as his salvation. The price he has to pay is automatic obedience and personal annulation. Mário shrinks away from Alice's threats as if afraid of the all-powerful mother who can give or take away life, like Medea, the mythological character of the mother who creates and then destroys.

The last scan was very intense and summarises the couple's relationship. The situation was brought on by the imminent delivery, the end of the first observation phase with the first observer, whose company they enjoyed immensely, the separation of the team, especially the sonographer, who had patiently answered the couple's questions about the baby, and the arrival of a new observer who would continue the observations in their home until Valentina's third year.

The couple is about to face a new stranger and all the challenges of a new phase.

As soon as she arrives, Alice says she met the paediatrician, whom she did not like. She is worried about breastfeeding; maybe she will not be able to do it because she has small breasts. She seems very nervous about the possibility of losing this opportunity—breastfeeding—of "putting something inside" the other, thus potentially losing a powerful instrument of control over Valentina. She might not have enough milk to assume control of her outside the uterus. Everything could fall apart. She "attacks" her husband for being late and for losing the house keys for the second time.

Mário arrives and peers in from the next room. He is frightened and seems about to explode. His face is serious and he keeps his face turned away, as if he did not have a friend in the room. He remains silent the entire time, tapping his fingers on his leg. He does not look at the new observer. The "dangerous" feelings and conflicts seem about to overflow. The dogs are threatening to invade the house. Alice's provocations overwhelm her husband and he sounds irritated when he answers her. He moves a lot, first fiddling with his cigarettes, and then his wallet. His eyes are distant and he makes faces and talks to himself.

It is interesting that Alice, after punishing her husband, tries to punish her daughter for moving in her womb. She complains about the enormous bumps she makes on her belly, saying, "Calm down, baby girl, calm down." Her belly expands and shifts to the other side. "Hey missy, you see this here? You're making a bump, look!" and she tells Valentina to move to the other side as if she were controlling/commanding her daughter. After several provocations and withering looks aimed at her husband, Alice says, "Smile, man, aren't you going to give your daughter a smile?"[18] He smiles slightly and looks at the monitor. Valentina's little face appears on the screen and shows her sleeping. Alice asks the doctor if it is normal for babies to sleep so much, she thinks it is too much. Alice seems worried, wanting in her omnipotence to dominate the baby by controlling the lumps she makes, her intrauterine movements, and her sleep and awake times, as she does with Mário.

Valentina is facing forward, once again moving rhythmically and calmly in accord to her mother's breathing. It looks as if she is on a swing or on an ocean wave that ebbs and flows. As before, it is pleasant to see how in tune Alice's breathing is with the baby's movements. Valentina keeps her eyes closed peacefully. Sometimes, she moves her lips and slightly opens and closes her mouth into a pucker. It is moving to see the freedom of the foetus's movements, "disobeying" the orders of the extrauterine world. She is protected by a contact barrier which blocks the demands and impingement of the outside environment.

Everyone is silent. The doctor reviews some aspects of the foetus, verifies the organs and measurements, and says that the ultrasound scans are coming to an end, and that, as far as can be seen in this scan, everything looks good for Valentina. Now they just have to wait for the delivery. Alice tearfully expresses her gratitude and says the time went by fast.

Mário exits the examination room without saying good-bye. Alice goes to the observer and apologises for her husband's behaviour. "So there you have it, doctor, he didn't have to get so upset. But he has a good heart. He's a very good man . . . I'm sure he'll be a good father to Valentina . . . he was a good son . . ." Mario's behaviour of slamming the door and leaving Alice alone with the baby portrays the family post-birth.

During her pregnancy, Alice demonstrated a strong need to express her omnipotence in controlling both the foetus's development and her husband's feelings and attitudes in order to maintain their "balance" as a couple. The approaching delivery will test and challenge this balance on many levels. During the pregnancy, the father withheld his intense doubts, fears, and angst regarding the mother's ability to generate a healthy baby and carry it in her womb until birth. Yet, he always expressed his fears and feelings of impotence and incompetence about parenting duties. The "beasts" inside Mário were threatening to escape, with no possibility of being controlled.

At the second to last observation, Alice told Mário, "Deal with it, man, the family is growing and after Valentina is born I won't be able to do everything I do now; you're going to have to help. Because now, doctor, everything is me. Not only do I have to make the dogs' food, I have to feed them, too. But later, with Valentina, I have already said there won't be enough time for everything."

The mother needs to relax, surrender, and trust, while, at the same time, collaborate and participate in the birth process, which requires a special kind of preparation and ability. The issue of not being able to control the process is important because, once started, it cannot be interrupted or reversed. The expectant mother's necessary surrender of domination to the forces of nature transforms her into a passive being, which renders her powerless in the face of her most primitive anxieties.

Valentina is positioned for delivery, seemingly having enough experience for the changes and transformations that are inherent to the delivery process, for going from unborn to born.

Delivery

Alice had come to trust and rely on the observer to the point that she wanted her at the birth. Silvia, Alice's sister in-law, called the observer to say that she was already at the hospital and she "wouldn't stop saying that you had to be informed; that's all she talked about". When the observer entered the obstetric centre, she meets Alice, who says, "Well, this little rascal decided she didn't want to stay in her mummy's belly any more. She wants everyone to know who Valentina is." Thus, Alice expresses how much Valentina challenges her and her command/control over what had, until now, been in her hands/uterus.

The observer stands at the foot of the bed. Alice has a series of contractions and complains a lot about the pain. The obstetrician instructs her patient, who is gripping the observer's hand. Alice is worried about the baby: she tries to keep her balance, as she always says, and at times almost loses it. The anaesthestist arrives and asks, "Where is the child's father?" Alice's face is a question mark. Mário is in the waiting room watching television, seemingly distracted. The familiar process of trying to get Mário to stay close to the action begins. It is interesting how everyone rallies around to help him enter the delivery room where Alice was calling for him.

> . . . He smiles, runs his hand over his head and face, sweating, sighing, saying oh my, oh my, oh my, and looking at me shaking his head no, no, and then nodding yes, yes. The doctor asks if he is afraid and he answers, "What if I faint? . . ." "We'll leave you there on the floor," she answers. We all laugh and she leaves. He says, "OK, I'll go." His sister cheers. After this ritual, Mário enters the delivery room smiling. He approaches Alice quickly, saying "You can do it, Alice Regina!" and makes a cheering gesture with his hands.

He chooses a place to sit, "I'm going to sit here!", which is next to the observer.

> He crosses his legs like me, tapping his fingers on the chair. He repeats the same behaviour he exhibited during the scans: he looks up, to the sides, and sometimes at me. When I look at him he glances away . . . He folds his hands and says something I can't hear. I get up and go to stand by the door. He comes and stands next to me.

He is like the observer's shadow.

The labour progresses quickly and then suddenly stops. The baby begins showing signs of distress and a caesarean is recommended.

It was clear how Alice and Mário again, and maybe this time more intensely, appreciated the support and protection of the observer, who talked to them, held the mother's hands and supported her back. She took the father to the delivery room and then introduced him to the hostile environment of the world he had so feared during the ultrasound scans. She told the father that he should stay on "this side" of the curtain, and he looks relieved, "I'm going to stay on this side of the curtain? Oh, that is a lot easier than I thought. Piece of cake!" The report continues,

> In the operating theatre, Mário sits by Alice's head and remains there the entire time, talking to her and lightly stroking her head. They speak quietly to each other, and I hear Mário say that the dogs, who Alice says are his children, are waiting for Valentina to play with them; they are going to love Valentina. Alice agreed with him.

Valentina comes out easily and is laid on her mother's legs. She cries loudly and seems very healthy. Still connected to the umbilical cord, she is calm and relaxed as the obstetrics assistant suctions out her little mouth, then cries a little more, as if irritated at being bothered. She is described as a "perfect little girl, pretty as a picture. She has a lot of hair, is chubby, and looks big". It must be noted that there is no observed report of her weight or size, similar to what happened in the ultrasound scans.

The paediatrician expertly cleans the baby and takes her to the mother to see. Alice kisses her baby and Mário throws up his arms, smiling and saying, "Oh my, oh my, oh my, oh my, oh my . . ." but does not want to take Valentina to the nursery. When the paediatrician asks Mário to give Valentina to her mother, he looks at his daughter and says he does not know how to hold her. After a few instructions, he quickly gives his daughter to Alice, who decides she wants to nurse the baby right there on the operating table.

> Because her arms were "tied up" with IVs and anaesthetic controls, the staff had to help put her daughter at her breast. Mário did not offer to help and seemed hesitant to touch the baby again; he only touched the tip of his finger to her tiny head and caressed her lightly. Alice talked to her daughter and didn't ask for Mário's help. Valentina, lying on her side with her face against her mother's breast, begins moving her mouth in the same way she did when she was in her mother's belly. I felt as if I was watching her through the ultrasound scan. She sticks out her tongue and licks her lips; then she swallows and seems to savour something, maintaining this non-stop movement with her mouth just as she did in the ultrasound scans. Because Alice had asked to nurse the baby, the anaesthetist helped to release Alice's arms and tried to position the baby's face next to the mother's nipple. The baby buries her face in her mother's breast, then, slowly, moves her head up and back, nosing the breast and looking for the nipple, opening her mouth, licking the nipple, and swallowing. She did this a few times until she was able to suck a little, smacking her lips so loud everyone in the room heard it. Then she laid her head on her mother's breast again and fell asleep.

Had she gone back to her intrauterine life to rest? It must be hard for a newborn infant with an extremely immature ego to confront an environment that contains someone who insists on being important and on requiring attention. There seems to be an inversion of needs and care.

The observer thought, "It's a victory! This baby will go after whatever she wants." Alice and Mário watch her sleep, stroking her face and head and kissing her. After a few minutes, Valentina wakes up, showing signs that she wants to nurse by nuzzling her mother, licking the nipple, swallowing, but unable to suck. Valentina demonstrates good capacity to come and go—sleep, wake up, nuzzle the breast. She is dealing capably with the rough interruption of continuity involved in the birth process and the changes it brings: starting to breathe, coming into contact with atmospheric pressure, and exchanging a water environment for air. She was obliged to react to the invasions of her weightless previous environment and go through a labour process that had initially been quick but then was impeded, necessitating a caesarean. Like the mothers, babies also experience post-birth imbalance. Additionally, babies are taken through a series of procedures and care that abruptly removes them from the state of cosy support of the intrauterine environment and are quickly launched into facing the challenges of the real world. Many need more time to recover their balance, but that is not easily done. There are the baths, the measurements, the weighing, aspiration, and the putting on of clothes. Besides all that, Valentina had to follow her mother's order to nurse while still on the operating table. Valentina responded, but did not satisfy Alice's high expectations. The next day, Alice said over the phone that

> She and her little gold nugget were fine . . . only Valentina hadn't been able to nurse. Her greatest fear was that everything she had truly strived for and achieved would come to naught.

The parents stayed a while longer watching the baby sleep, wake up, move her mouth, and lick the nipple, trying to nurse. It seemed as if Alice and Mário did not want the moment to end. They talked to the baby, telling her she was beautiful, they talked to each other about how the dogs were at home waiting for her, and they cried, albeit in a very calm, quiet, and intense manner. They seemed "enchanted", as if they were in a "state of grace". The observer pointed out the significance of the contrasts in the room, which seemed to express the trauma of birth:

> One side of the operating screen represents Valentina's intrauterine life: the almost silence, the respect, the tears and smiles, and all of us looking, looking, looking, looking . . . at her; on the other side, we see cutting, a lot of blood, suturing, the sound of metal clinking, instruments, needles, blood pressure devices beeping, doctors talking—the outside world.

The observer asks herself what Valentina's life will be like from now on.

The paediatrician had left long before the nurse came to get the baby and take her to the nursery for other procedures. The observer thinks it is time to say good-bye:

> I congratulate Alice, telling her she had done very well and had been very brave, and that Valentina is a beautiful baby. Alice says, "I know, right?

> It's hard to believe, isn't it, doctor?" I say that of course I do . . . "Congratulations, Alice! I'm leaving now, but I'll call you tomorrow for news." Alice says, "Thank you for everything, OK doctor? Thank you for your support. It really, really helped a lot." She grips my hand tightly. I say that I am also grateful to them for participating in the project and that it had been really great, and that now I will go to say good-bye to Mário.

The first three years

The first observation at the family home occurred after the second observer telephoned to find out how Alice and Valentina were doing. The baby was twenty-five days old. The house is in a neighbourhood far from the city centre in an industrial zone with many factories. The street is dirty and unwelcoming; there are always several parked trucks restricting cars from passing. The house, an old chalet, was built on a large plot of land with many trees. It is a very damp house situated just below street level. The rear part of the grounds is enclosed by a wooden fence that keeps the two family collies contained.

The observer arrives at the appointed time and rings the doorbell, but no one answers. She rings again, but still no answer. She notices the two big dogs in the back. She telephones Alice, who does not pick up. She decides to wait. Twenty minutes later, the mother and daughter arrive. The baby was sleeping because she had been fed some fennel tea so she could go with her mother to the bank. Soon after entering the house, Alice introduces the couple's dogs: "These are our beasts. Mário and I love our dogs. Before Valentina was born they were our children and stayed in the house with us." The inside of the house is simple and the furniture seems worn down by long use. The environment is dark, cold, and damp, even on sunny days. Every time the observer describes the house, she gives the impression that there is no one inside, even when there is. The physical and emotional environment did not seem welcoming or adapted for Valentina, but rather implied that she had to adapt herself to it. The house "didn't have a baby smell to it", says the observer. Chunks of dog hair covering the floor indicated that the dogs still shared the space with the couple and baby.

Alice places Valentina in her crib beside the couple's bed and the door is closed. The mother and observer go back to the living room. The observer notices through an open door that there is another bedroom with a bunk bed, with the bottom bed unmade.

Alice talks and shows her framed pictures, all photos of the dogs, saying that now they will have to get used to taking baby pictures. She said that a short time ago one of the female dogs, which had since died, used to sleep between the couple with her head on the pillow. Then her puppy took her place, and today he sleeps with Mário in the spare room. She added that another of their dogs had died tragically one week before Valentina was born. He had been badly startled by firecrackers and had run into the wall several times, leaving bloody marks until he jumped over and ran away. They found him locked up at a hotel. The couple took him to a veterinary clinic where he died from a haemorrhage a week later. Later, she says, "Everything changed when Valentina arrived; we'll teach her to like dogs, but because of their fur, they have to stay outside. Especially because everyone in the family has problems with bronchitis, so we have to be careful, right?"

Alice's need to be in control gradually became evident, especially in the feeding routine that was part of all the observations over the first three years of Valentina's life. Nursing time was extremely tense, indicating discord and misunderstanding between mother and baby. From the start, when the baby tried to latch on to her breast, Alice remained in a rigid and tense position, which visibly hampered Valentina from getting comfortable against her mother's body. She mentioned in several observations that the pain in her back kept her from holding her daughter, and that she had terrible pains in her breasts and head. Additionally, Alice worried about the quantity and quality of her milk, complaining that it was weak and insufficient. She referred to herself as incompetent, frequently telling her daughter that she was "clumsy" because she had no idea about temperatures, quantities, or Valentina's needs, asking the baby to forgive her and adapt to her. For example, when she noticed that Valentina was sweating and red from being dressed in too many clothes, she said: "Mummy is clumsy, isn't she, baby? But then, no one ever thought a child would come out of here."

During the observation at thirty-two days, Alice repeats the same refrain, telling the observer that the first time she gave her daughter a bottle, the milk was too hot and before she knew it the baby was all red and her eyes were full of tears. Later, when she started feeding Valentina eggs, she always prepared them hard-boiled, despite knowing the baby preferred them soft, saying, "Your mummy is clumsy, isn't she, baby?" She criticised herself frequently and did not allow the baby to show any kind of discomfort. Everything was organised and prepared ahead of time.

It is worth noting here that this pattern of preparing everything ahead of time was evident from the time of her meetings with the first observer, when Alice said she had miscarried her first pregnancy because she had not "prepared herself" enough as she had not stroked her belly. Everything was organised for the feedings so that the baby never showed signs of hunger, and balance could be maintained.

With Valentina only thirty-two days old, Alice is very stressed about which nursery school to choose, already thinking about when she would go back to work. This was a frequent topic during the observations, and a lot of practice was carried out in preparation for the occasion: she would leave Valentina alone in the house so that she would get used to the separation; she explained to her daughter in a threatening tone that the good life would stop when she went to day care. She would encourage the baby to smile at everyone, also in preparation for nursery school, and she started introducing soup to facilitate the transition.

Alice seems always to feel threatened with losing control over herself and over Valentina; therefore, she creates rituals to control everything. It is very clear how intensely she feels threatened and controlled by her daughter's gaze and presence: "Yesterday I had to look at her and say, sweetheart, it's time to go to sleep now. Then I turned over and didn't look at her any more. When I turned towards her again, she had fallen asleep. If we keep looking at her, she stays awake. It's as if she needs to look at us to stay awake. All I had to do was turn away, and she fell asleep. But then this morning we stayed in bed until late, didn't we Valentina, Mummy has to rest too, right? You know I can't even think about cleaning the house, she wants us to stay with her all the time. It's that during this phase they require a lot from us. Everything goes to them. And you won't believe it, but she doesn't like the pram, she just wants to be held, you know?"

Later, while she rocks the baby, she asks the observer, "It must be nice to observe twins, huh?" The observer answers yes, and Alice says, "Yeah, but it's not very nice having a twin sister."

Alice wanted very much to be seen and valued as a capable mother and frequently compared herself to other women. She especially competed with her sisters, particularly her twin sister. Since the first observation, every time she nurses Valentina she mentions her "weak and insufficient milk" and that she has already started giving the baby supplements. Yet, she intends to nurse her until at least six months. When Valentina was one month and twenty-four days old, the observer registered the following comment made by the mother: "This thing about all women wanting to have the same quantity of milk, it's like the doctor said . . . I don't believe it. Like, this week I had to go to the bank and to my workplace. My mum told me to wear nursing pads so I wouldn't leak on my clothes. In the end I left and said I didn't think my milk would leak. It was just as I said, not a drop. Some women think they can't go out without some kind of pad on their breast, or they'll have wet marks on their clothes. Not me. It's not worth it; I don't have enough milk. My sisters nursed their babies until they were a year old, but I don't think I can do that. There's no way! . . . I think this is happening because I decided to become a mum when I was already too old. Maybe if I were younger I wouldn't be going through this. But, I don't really know if age has anything to do with these things, right?"

At three and a half months, the observer reports,

> Alice says her daughter weighs five kilos and that a friend's son who is one month older than her daughter already weighs eight kilos. She complains that her friend had exclaimed, "That's all she weighs?" Alice does not see being fat as being synonymous with being healthy, which is why she thinks her daughter is doing super well.

In a provocative tone intended to stimulate rivalry between the observers, as she will continue to do in future observations, she talks about the first observer, praising her and saying how much she likes her and misses her, and that she is going to take a picture of Valentina and give it to her as a present, and how she will invite her to see her daughter. She says she has to put the first observer's telephone number next to her bed so she will not forget to call her. She also mentions how competent her sisters are and how they have healthy children, especially her twin sister, who breastfed her baby for one year, and about the scepticism that hovered over the family about her mothering skills, since she was too old for it. She asks the observer if she has children, and when the answer is negative, Alice "opens fire": "You'll see how it's not easy ... you don't know what pain is ... it makes me cry ... you can't imagine the desperation ... but she's a princess. A woman is only complete when she becomes a mother."

At two months and fifteen days, Valentina has been weaned because of Alice's insufficient milk coupled with her fear of not being able to give sustenance to her daughter. Valentina is not gaining weight and the mother attributes this to the fact that she is "an old mother". Alice is disorientated by the weaning process. The observer's description of how she was welcomed on this occasion is interesting:

> The dogs, which on other visits had been quiet, started barking.

Alice was losing her control over Valentina and over maintaining the ideal situation represented by breastfeeding—a closed and self-sufficient system that substitutes for the intrauterine placental complex. The observer describes,

> Alice holds her daughter in one hand and with the other she squeezes her breast to get milk to come out, which it doesn't, and this distresses her. The milk in that breast is drying up and she can't nurse from the other one ... because the nipple is still flat and makes Valentina angry. She squeezes her breast saying that this one with a flat nipple has a lot of milk. She doesn't know if her milk has dried up or if her daughter is abnormal and too demanding.

Alice says she feels a lot of pain when she breastfeeds, which translates her horror at not being able to nurse Valentina and confirms her fantasies of incompetence, being undervalued, failing as a woman, and dependence on her daughter. From the beginning, the baby does not meet the expectations of the mother and is blamed for being voracious and wanting to nurse too much; she regurgitates and burps from being "suffocated". Alice feels as if her daughter "drains" her, which is why she is unable to go about her business. She frequently repeats, "Motherhood is tiring; babies are really demanding. Prepare yourself."

When she had become pregnant, she weighed sixty-one kilos and now she weighs fifty-three. When she goes to the doctor for a follow-up scan, she hears, "My goodness, Valentina is sucking you dry!" She becomes desperate when the baby cries, always interpreting it as colic or constipation. She nervously says, "I don't know what goes in or what comes out from her. The juice will make her have a bowel movement, because all she knows how to do is pass wind and burp, right baby? She's a little farting machine." She attributes Valentina's insufficient weight gain to the supplement. She has the feeling that the baby holds something inside and only lets go when she feels like it and because she has a choice, thus manifesting a kind of autonomy and freedom that are threatening. Alice desperately begins trying to dominate her daughter using food, which ends up becoming synonymous with mashed fruit and evacuations that are supposed to be daily.

Even when her mother introduces new foods, Valentina's weight continues to be below average. Alice feels criticised by the paediatrician, her aunts, and her godmother. She stops going to the doctor. The baby, on the other hand, does not show signs of being hungry and seems synchronised with the maternal workings, a fact that concerned the observer, since it was possibly a sign of disturbances in her development and autonomy.

Several tense situations associated to feeding occur in the mother–daughter relationship that make the observations heavy and tiresome. The mother

> says from the kitchen that the mashed papaya is too cold, so she is heating it up a little in the microwave . . . Alice comes back to the living room with a bent plastic dessert bowl. There is steam coming from the papaya. Alice says she left it in the microwave too long and now Valentina will have to wait a little . . . Valentina sees the bowl with the papaya and starts to cry. The mother tells her that she has to wait because it's too hot . . . She gives her a spoonful and she turns red and starts to choke. Alice takes her out of the pram and pats her back. At first she thinks the papaya was still too hot, but after tasting it she realises that it's not. Then she notices that there are big chunks of papaya that weren't mashed enough for her daughter.

There are several moments of indiscrimination between who Alice is and who Valentina is, what Alice wants and what Valentina wants, what Alice likes and what Valentina likes, which had already been observed during the ultrasound scans when Alice repeatedly made references to their similarities. Because of Valentina's passivity, calmness, little appetite, and few protests, she contributed to the pattern of indiscrimination that had been established in their relationship. In the first home observation, Alice tells the observer that her daughter is very much like her: "She has slanted eyes just like her mum's. She really took after me, thank God, right baby?" Scenarios such as what follows became frequent:

> Alice says its time to eat an apple that she has already prepared; she feeds a piece to her daughter and eats the rest. She says the apple wasn't as good as it looked and asks her daughter if she wants to eat something else. Valentina says nothing, so Alice goes to the kitchen and comes back with a banana sliced in circles. She offers it to Valentina, who takes a slice, and then Alice takes two and eats them at once. She offers more to her daughter who refuses, and Alice eats the rest.

At four months and nine days, Alice says her daughter prefers fruit rather than savoury food. She proudly says that the baby is having daily bowel movements as she offers some previously prepared papaya to her daughter. The following Alice–Valentina interaction is described as follows:

> While Valentina eats, she plays with her bib and eventually pulls it askew. Alice tells her that it is time to eat, not play. Valentina puts her hand in her mouth, which makes Alice impatient and she yells at her daughter, saying she must not do that. She says she will not have it easy like this at nursery school, where they cannot pay attention to one individual child. Alice says her daughter now weighs over six kilos and measures over sixty centimetres. She comments about how the doctor told her she would be a model.

At five months, Alice says she took her daughter to the paediatrician, who said she had not gained any weight. According to the observer's report,

> The doctor said Alice was giving her too much fruit and not enough milk and savoury foods. One day, Alice arrived at home and Mário was angry because Valentina wouldn't stop crying. Alice says it was because she was hungry.

As time went by, a feeding routine was established for Valentina: nothing could be left over, nothing could be thrown out. Alice finished up everything, even when she gave the baby iron sulphate syrup with her fruit. She runs the spoon around Valentina's mouth and eats whatever is left over. Valentina swallows everything, and Alice swallows what Valentina leaves—fruit, egg, medicine, baby food—in a "closed circuit" of mutual retro-feeding, which is characteristic of how this family functions. Nothing could break the circuit. The father was rarely physically present at the observations, and this contributed to maintaining the "closed circuit" in the family. He featured mostly in the mother's criticisms: "The lesions on the skin of her elbow come from her father; Valentina didn't gain weight this month [father's holidays] because he only knows how to give her a bottle; leaving you with your father doesn't work, he's too dumb and disorganised, right baby? He let Valentina fall from the car seat; he doesn't even know how to choose fruit, he always buys small ones that are bad quality . . . but he's a good man, a good father."

When Valentina is five months old, Mário greets the observer at the door, saying that she was punctual, a very important fact, and nervously added, "Since you're a psychologist, you'll understand what I want to say. What can people do to control anxiety? For example, I have a bunch of problems at work, then I come home with a lot on my mind and she comes at me and attacks me." Alice tries to ameliorate: "OK, daddy . . ." He continues by repeating his question and she answers, "Balance! We have to be balanced." He answers, "Yeah, right . . ." and finishes his coffee in silence, then goes to the kitchen and disappears. Alice continues, "He's very clumsy and anxious, but he's a good man."

Thus, Alice "shuts Mário's mouth" easily, preventing any type of revenge, objection, or retaliation. She tries to do the same with Valentina. Mário continues to be submissive, a repository for Alice's negative and fragile characteristics, sleeping with the dog in the guest room until the end of the observations when Valentina was three years old. He was not capable of changing this familiar conformity that had developed and been maintained over many years.

Later on, when Valentina is bigger, she is looking out of the window trying to communicate with the neighbours. Alice tries to stop her from looking out of the window to outside the house. An important aspect that must be pointed out is that all the observations throughout Valentina's first three years were conducted inside the house, regardless of the weather or time of year. In one observation,

Alice said she would take advantage of the beautiful day to do some cleaning inside the house. There was never any mention of going for walks with the baby. When the baby started interacting with the observer, Alice frequently interfered, whether by interrupting with games or by stopping her daughter from touching the observer's bag:

> Valentina is placed on the floor and she goes to my bag. Alice says to her daughter that my bag is very pretty. Valentina crouches down, because my bag is on the floor, and tries to grab the handle. Alice says the bag is too heavy for her. Even so, Valentina tried to pick it up, but Alice moves her away from the bag and takes her to another corner of the room. Valentina whines and Alice says it's not time to sleep yet, so don't even try complaining.

Valentina was constantly encouraged by her mother to smile, to which she corresponded. In the first observation, the mother calls the observer's attention to Valentina's smiles while she nursed: "Look at that, she's smiling." A ritual was created where Valentina always had to greet the observer with a smile. Even when she was woken up and taken from her bed, she had to "be nice and smile". She was threatened with punishments if she did not comply with her mother's command. Her daughter's smiles made Alice feel satisfied and proud. She reaffirms how she sees herself in her smiling daughter and that she takes after her mother. "All the mother has to do is speak and the baby breaks into a big smile." As we saw in the beginning of the pregnancy, Alice was already saying that Valentina would smile a lot, just like her, and that when she smiled, her daughter smiled, too. At two months, Valentina impressed a photographer with her smile, nice personality, and willingness to be photographed. At three months, the doctor was surprised at how friendly Valentina was. At around four months, she went to a day care centre and, according to the mother, adapted quickly and completely, earning the nickname of "smiley girl" and later "smiley bird", because of how she moved her little arms and legs trying to stand up. Alice believes Valentina is under her control and is satisfied by her daughter's behaviour in this respect, which is proof of her competence as a mother and of her daughter's love for her.

Also constantly present in the observer's reports were descriptions of Valentina's ability to observe and pay attention from the very beginning of her life. Valentina was an alert baby, connected to the world around her, probably because of the frequent impingements on her environment:

> At one month and twenty-four days, Valentina gazes firmly at her mother, listening attentively to what she is saying . . . Valentina watches everything, her eyes don't stop . . . she listens quietly and explores the environment . . . she stares out of the half-opened curtains at the window . . . gazes firmly at her mother and follows her movements . . . she notices the presence of the observer and looks her in the eyes . . . she is alert to sounds of her father in the yard and the mother says she watches the door where he comes in.

Alice proudly shows how fast her daughter is growing and how she would be Gisele Bündchen [a model]. She forcefully and continuously expressed patterns of control and invasion that hampered Valentina's development. In this setting, the father helped Valentina very little in confronting Alice's invasion patterns or in the process of differentiation and separation from the mother.

Between three and four months of age, Valentina played with her hands, pulled at her feet, and played with her dummy and tried to put it in her mouth. At around four months, Valentina began going to the day care centre. Interestingly, the observer's reports say nothing about Alice or Valentina experiencing any anxiety over their separation. At five months, Alice goes back to work, but the only comment in that period was that on the first day "she felt bad and went home crying". There was no other reaction to the separation. At the same time, the intense Alice–Valentina connection and indiscrimination is constantly visible. When Valentina is five months and twenty-one days, Alice says her daughter is everything to her. Her eyes fill with tears. She says that when she says that she chokes up. She tells how Valentina was very much desired and expected: "She is my life. I come home and ask, 'Where is my life?'"

At around six months, Valentina was already able to sit "like a young lady", according to Alice. Valentina smiles and listens to her mother: "It's time to crawl. I want her to let loose . . .!" She says she is satisfied with the day care centre. At around seven months, she is more stable and nimble. She crawls everywhere. Alice thinks she will be walking soon. At nine months, she measures seventy centimetres and, according to Alice, will be a model. Although they still think the baby is thin, Alice says that it is her destiny to be like Gisele Bündchen, and, holding Valentina by her hands, shows how she can take steps. It is as if she were already leading her down the catwalk. At six months and four days, the observer says it seems the dogs had been in the house because it was only after Alice saw her that the dogs were taken out. Mário is the one who opens the gate and says Alice was expecting her the next week. The observer can smell the dogs and sees their fur all over the house. This is how she described an Alice–Valentina sequence of interaction:

> Valentina is smiling a lot. She plays with her dummy, taking it out of her mouth, but her mother puts it back in, interrupting her daughter's exploration. Valentina tries to put the dummy pin into her mouth and Alice says no, it's metal and can hurt her gums. Alice forcefully opens her daughter's mouth to see if there are any teeth coming in. Valentina starts crying and Alice says she's being mean to her daughter. She says it's time to eat an apple. Mário comes into the room and asks if it's time for Valentina to nap. Alice replies that now it's time to eat an apple, which is already prepared. She says Valentina will be a model because everyone in her family is thin. She tells about how she stopped going to the paediatrician because she felt she was being criticised. "Eat the rest of your apple, honey".

The first filming is done at six months and eleven days, and the observer thinks the dog smell is stronger that day. Her report states,

> Alice places her daughter in the pram and tries to get her to smile the entire time. She tells her daughter many times that she loves her. Valentina responds to her mother's wishes and smiles. She is much more vocal than in other observations. The filming ends and Alice brings Valentina a teething toy, which she puts in her mouth and makes chewing movements. Alice says she has some papaya for her daughter already mashed and in a container, and goes to get it.

At eleven months, Valentina was already walking, and the father was still as perplexed about the baby as he was during the pregnancy. Alice says, "Mário doesn't believe he has a baby." During Alice's pregnancy, he frequently expressed his perplexity when looking at the ultrasound images: "How can it be? Oh my, oh my, oh my . . ."

At the one year filming, the observer gives Valentina a doll as a present:

> Alice says she had already got one. She says her daughter has a lot of clothing and will have to do a modelling show. During the filming, Alice places herself behind the camera and spends the entire time encouraging her to show everything she has learnt: clap her hands, blow kisses, say daddy, mummy, baby, walk. Alice asks Valentina to look at the camera because she is being filmed. Valentina grabs the balloon and Alice asks her to throw it up. She does everything her mother asks. At one point when she looks at the camera, Alice asks her to blow kisses and say thank you for the present. Valentina does what her mother asks. She is very active crawling, walking, clapping her hands, blowing kisses, and doing practically everything her mother asks from behind the scenes. The filming ends and Alice offers her daughter some papaya that she has prepared ahead of time. She says a papaya tree is going to grow in her stomach. Valentina eats everything, grabs the doll I gave her and drops it on the floor. Alice tells her not to be a bad mother.

The mother's greatest fear began emerging after her daughter's first year of life. At around twelve or thirteen months there are specific moments when Valentina does not comply with her mother's command. Alice reacts with a firm reprimand:

> Alice harshly reproaches her daughter and says, "Smile at your aunt, don't look at her like you're showing off, point that nose down."

Valentina is no longer the "smiley girl" of her first year who made her mother so proud. Alice says, when her daughter is two years old, "Valentina used to smile more when she was smaller."

The confrontations between mother and daughter begin when Valentina starts challenging her mother by not obeying all her orders. She resists putting on her coat, her shoes, taking medicine, and in general reacting to her mother's invasions. On one occasion, Alice wants Valentina to take some syrup, which she refuses; the ensuing fight is solved by Alice taking the medicine herself. Also in that period, Valentina began showing aggressiveness in school. Alice said Valentina had been biting a classmate at the day care centre and pulling his hair. One day she came home with a red chin because a different classmate had bitten her for pulling his hair. Valentina's teeth become a frequent source of worry for the mother. The observer writes,

> Alice says Valentina's teeth came out later, that's why they're stronger. She added, "Valentina only has two lower teeth, but they are enough to bite because the other day she bit my nose and it hurt."

The dogs gradually invade the house. The observer reported the invasion as a crescendo, first it was just the dog smell, then they began reacting to her arrival with loud barking and by sticking their noses through the opening of the door, demonstrating a clear escalation of aggressiveness in the family environment. As Valentina grows, Alice fears losing control over her daughter, and losing her love. She asks, "When are you going to tell me that you love me? I'm the only one that says I love you."

Alice tells her to blow kisses and becomes very irritated by what she considers her daughter's "disobedience", saying, "Blow kisses or I will lock you in there!" Valentina immediately blows kisses. The "in there" used as a threat is the dark room where her father slept with the dog. As Valentina's "disobedience" continues, Alice's threats increase. When Valentina does not repeat what is asked of her, she says, "If you don't talk now, I'll shut your mouth later."

At one year, four months, and one day, the observer reports a sequence of strong mother–daughter conflicts:

> Alice told me that Valentina has been awake since seven in the morning, and that it's been like that every day. Alice also says Valentina had bronchiolitis again and had to take medicine and use a nebuliser. She said she hates using the nebuliser and that she throws a fit, as if we were trying to kill her. Alice offers her daughter an apple and settles her in her new highchair. Valentina starts showing signs of agitation. She slides down in the chair and gets stuck between the seat and the tray-top. I see that Alice gets flustered and doesn't know if she should hold the apple or help her daughter. She ends up helping her daughter and gets her out of the chair. She shows signs of anxiety and fear and yells at her daughter, saying that if she keeps that up she'll have to put a safety belt on her since she won't sit still! Alice says she was frightened. I am very upset in this situation. I had to control myself to not get up and help Alice. She put her daughter back in the chair, but this time keeps an eye on her. She starts to feed her the apple by scraping the fruit with a spoon. While she does

that she says her husband can't buy apples any more because he always buys the small ones that are hard to scrape. Alice says the best ones are the big ones. She has trouble scraping the apple, and meanwhile Valentina is impatient to eat it. So she starts cutting it into small pieces and feeding them to her daughter. It doesn't take long for Valentina to choke. Alice once again yells at her that now she would have to wait until she scraped an apple. Valentina looks frightened!

Alice goes to the kitchen and gets the other half of the apple, saying it will be better to scrape that way. She eats a piece of the apple herself and says it isn't any good, too acidic. She finishes feeding the apple to her daughter and leaves the spoon and knife on the highchair tabletop. Valentina grabs the knife and spoon and bangs them hard on the tabletop. At first Alice lets her do it. I feel a little apprehensive since I can see that Valentina could hurt herself. Alice asks her to stop, but she doesn't. Alice seems bothered only by the noise, not by that fact that her daughter is playing with dangerous objects. Valentina does not stop the banging. Then Alice yanks the objects from her hand and puts them where her daughter can't reach. Alice looks at me and says that now she has to be that way or else she won't obey. Then she looks at her daughter and asks for a kiss, and Valentina obliges. Alice asks her to say "I love you" and to throw her a kiss, but this time Valentina does not respond to her mother's commands. Affecting an air of disappointment, Alice imitates her daughter's voice, saying, "I don't love you?"

Alice takes Valentina out of the highchair and she goes into the kitchen and comes back to the living room with a plastic phone. Alice says Mário calls every day to talk to his daughter. Valentina comes in my direction with the phone pressed to her ear as if she were talking to someone. She hands me the phone. I take it and say hello. Valentina smiles. I start giving the telephone back to Valentina, but Alice takes the phone from my hand. Valentina tries to take her boots off and Alice gets very angry. She says she can't take them off because if she does she'll get sick and have to go to the doctor to take medicine and use the nebuliser. Even so, Valentina takes off her boots, which makes Alice even angrier. Alice sits Valentina in her lap and tries to force the boots back on, but can't. She pins down her daughter in her lap and is finally able to put them back on. Alice opens her daughter's mouth to show she already has five teeth, saying she has five teeth to bite her mummy with. Then she corrects herself and says that she kisses her mummy, because dogs are the ones that bite. Valentina once again takes her boots off and Alice puts them back on. Valentina, angry at her mother's attitude, starts whining, on the verge of tears.

In almost all the next observations, Valentina stays on her mother's lap. When Valentina is about one and a half years old the observer assumes that the filming will be done outside because there is a very strong dog smell in the house. However, Alice takes them inside the house. Valentina wants to stay on her mother's lap with a dummy in her mouth. She asks for another dummy and Alice says no because she only has one mouth. The atmosphere becomes tense and the dogs do not stop barking. The observer writes,

> As usual, Alice asks her daughter to smile and blow kisses, saying she adores her daughter. But Valentina is more frightened than usual and does not respond to her mother's requests. Alice tries taking away Valentina's dummy, but every time she does, she starts crying.

Things are not going according to the mother's satisfaction, and she talks about her daughter's misbehaviour and that she cannot be left alone any more "because she climbs on to the back of the sofa next to the window and talks to the neighbours". She says proudly that Valentina likes to draw, showing some of her drawings. Valentina gets off her mother's lap and takes a pen and paper from her mother and quickly scribbles on it. The mother tells her to stop using her left hand (she is left-handed) and to use her right hand. She offers her daughter cookies, but Valentina ignores her and the mother eats them all.

As has become the routine, when Valentina is one year and eight months old, Alice wakes Valentina up saying, "Your friend is here", and makes the girl smile at the observer:

> Valentina looks at me with a serious look on her face and does not do what her mother asks. Alice tries to take away her dummy, but Valentina doesn't let her, pushing her mother's hand away with her own. Alice tries to put her daughter on the floor, but she wants to stay in her mother's arms.

Then there is the following sequence of Alice–Valentina interaction:

> Alice tries to feed a chopped egg in a cup to her daughter, who doesn't want it. Alice gives her daughter the cup and she takes the spoon that is inside and eats a little bit of egg, but soon gives up and gives the cup back to her mother. Alice tries to feed her again, but Valentina shows that she does not want to eat by spitting out part of the egg that Alice had

> "shoved" into her mouth. Alice wipes her finger around Valentina's mouth, takes the part she spit out and eats it. She is impatient with the fact that Valentina didn't want to eat the egg and offers some fruit, to which the girl says no. Valentina goes to the coffee table and takes a box of Lego. She pulls the box on to the floor. Alice reprimands her, saying she should not do that with the box. Valentina looks at her and throws the box on the floor again. Alice gets up and looks firmly at her daughter. She offers half an apple to her, which she refuses by shaking her head. "Sod it!" says Alice in an aggressive tone. Alice eats some of the apple her daughter didn't want. She offers her a cookie and this time Valentina eats a small piece and puts the rest on top of the coffee table. Alice takes what is left of the cookie and eats it. Valentina gets some dolls and brings them to me. She gives me the dolls one at a time and I hold them on my lap. Then she takes them back again. She repeats this scenario several times until Alice sits beside me and Valentina gives her the dolls too.

Valentina is about two years old at the fourth filming and the observer gives her a present. She becomes serious and shows no reaction to it. Alice holds Valentina on her lap and the dogs bark a lot, to the point of slamming into the kitchen door. It is hell. Alice asks Valentina to give the observer a smile, but she is serious and quiet. The mother opens the present—a puzzle—and starts a sequence of stimuli to try to demonstrate her daughter's development, which creates an uncomfortable atmosphere. The more Valentina frustrates the mother by not complying with her, the more agitated and desperate she becomes. The daughter refuses to obey orders. "Who knows", says Alice, "maybe she's slow because she slept late and still has to wake up." They are on completely different wavelengths. Alice asks Valentina to show Grumpy and the other dwarves, but she wants the puzzle box. The mother insists that she show Minnie, but she wants another doll. The mother moves to go back to the puzzle and Valentina pulls on her hand to keep her playing by her side. Alice does not leave her daughter in peace, constantly asking her to show something or say something. When Valentina does not respond, Alice says in a challenging tone, "You don't want to talk now? I'll shut your mouth later." She then says, "You have to count (she already knows how) for the doctor to see", and she cannot do it. She insists that Valentina imitate a rooster or a dog. Then she offers some fruit, which the daughter refuses, and Alice eats all of it.

At two years and three months, Valentina sits on her mother's lap and gazes seriously at the observer. As usual, Alice asks her to give a good morning smile, but Valentina does not respond. Alice says she cooked an egg but she cannot seem to get the cooking time right, which is an "old mother" thing. She tells about how the first time she made soup, Valentina rejected it. She starts a confrontation with her daughter because she wants her to put on a jumper and Valentina refuses. She tries again, but Valentina takes it off. Alice yells at her and shoves the jumper on her, not caring that she has a spoon in her mouth. Valentina cries and Alice puts her on her lap.

Alice is projecting on to Valentina the rivalry and jealousy she has towards her sister. She says Valentina is very jealous of her cousin who is five months old. She says her niece weighs "seven kilos against her twelve kilos". She adds that she is being breastfed and is very chubby, and that the paediatrician said her sister has to reduce the breastfeeding. She finishes by saying in a critical tone that even though her sister was breastfeeding, her niece had already become sick. Once again the intense fraternal rivalry that stalks Alice emerges. She really wants to win this competition and finally be able to show that she is competent and, through Valentina, wants to be reborn as more integrated, admired, and valued.

At two and a half years, the fifth filming is conducted, which is also stressful. The dogs bark a lot and Valentina stays on Alice's lap. Alice shows the observer some scars on Valentina's face left by a dog bite: she has several stitches on her cheek and others on what looks like a tear near her mouth. The bite was very deep and required suturing at the hospital. The heartless way Alice relates this episode is startling. She says her daughter went to play with the dog and he bit her to defend himself. The next thing she knew, Valentina had both hands to her face and was bleeding. She tells about another time when the dog almost bit Valentina, but because they were together, she was able to prevent it. This time Valentina was alone. She repeats several times that the dog and her daughter have become friends again.

Alice says Valentina had been waiting for the doctor by the window. They move into the usual pattern where Valentina has to do what her mother wants and show what she knows: new sofa, Minnie, Mickey, smile, speak. After some resistance to leaving her mother's lap, Valentina goes to play on the rocking horse. The observer notices that she is more relaxed and active, seems to recognise her, and be comfortable around her. Valentina wants to use the bathroom for a bowel movement, so the mother brings toilet paper and leaves the room. The girl gets her potty and then wipes herself when she has finished. She puts her panties and skirt back on, which are crooked. Alice comments on her "big poop" and tells the observer that she "is very regular". She gives Valentina a piece of apple and then asks her for a hug, to which her daughter complies. Alice also asks her to give the observer a kiss, which she does.

At the next observation, the mother has the schedule mixed up and thought there would be filming that day. She has her daughter all dressed up in a matching outfit: orange shorts and a T-shirt with orange tones. She is wearing pink Havaiana flip-flops and an orange Hello Kitty tiara. She is also wearing lipstick and keeps her mouth open so her lips do not touch. Alice says her daughter is afraid the lipstick will come off. She says Valentina's new nickname is Penelope Pitstop because she always wears pink. Alice comments about how Valentina has grown, as if wanting the observer's confirmation. The observer reported the following sequence:

> Valentina shows her Powerpuff dolls and another one that she calls a witch, placing them in the observer's lap. Alice says the observer will take them home. Valentina quickly takes the dolls from her lap and places them on the sofa. Alice asks her daughter to talk, but she says nothing, just passively participates in the dialogue. Alice keeps talking about how Valentina has slept early and woken up early. That way she can eat more fruit in the morning. Alice praises her daughter, saying she has been eating a lot of fruit. She tells about how they were watching television one day and they saw the model, Gisele Bündchen. When Valentina saw her, she said she was beautiful, and Alice promptly told her that she was beautiful because she ate a lot of fruit and vegetables. Alice now always offers "Gisele Bündchen" fruit so that Valentina will eat it and become like a model. Next, Valentina plays with some Lego pieces and Alice interferes in her playing. Valentina becomes aggressive and throws Lego pieces in her mother's direction, on the floor, and in my direction until Alice calls her to eat half of "Gisele's apple".

At the last observation and filming, Valentina is three years old and the same pattern continues. The dogs bark non-stop. Valentina smiles and takes the present the observer brings her for her birthday. She is big. Alice insists that Valentina say thank you for the present, smile, and give kisses. She tells Valentina she will be on television. She insists that her daughter say what is written on her jumper and that she should talk more. The mother comments, "She's grown, huh? She's just like Gisele Bündchen, thin and tall." This dialogue stands out because the mother is enunciating her words as if she were a child. She needs to show her daughter's skills and growth, to show that Valentina is capable of eating cookies and of offering them to others, and that she can draw the Powerpuff Girls. Valentina throws a pen at her mother, who asks her once again to draw the doll. Valentina says she does not know how and that Barbie will bite mummy, and a battle ensues to "shove" on her clothes, shoes, and boots.

Through Valentina and the much dreamed about and admired Gisele Bündchen, Alice demonstrates how much she wanted to be born as a daughter/mother that is admired and valued. But Valentina resists her, in her fierce struggle to be born as herself.

Final considerations

Valentina's development from pregnancy to her third year of life teaches us about the tenacity of babies and about their struggle to be born in an environment ruled by the rigid defence structures of control, invasion, and ambivalence that impair growth, creative living, and the free circulation of affection. Valentina is born after years of marriage without children to a couple who have managed to live symbiotically because of a perverse pattern of relating that is supported by primitive defence mechanisms of, primarily, discord, projection, and projective identification. Alice is strong, powerful, authoritarian, and capable. She maintains these characteristics at the expense of Mário, who is threatened into submission and carries the fragility, aggressiveness, and inability of both of them. Their relationship is heavily charged with a fraternal rivalry that Alice brings from her family history with her twin sister. When Valentina arrives, Alice shifts this undifferentiated relational pattern to her daughter, and increasingly demands her submission as their mother–daughter confrontations escalate and Valentina struggles to differentiate and become herself.

Beginning with the first ultrasound scans, Alice spontaneously and sincerely shows who she really is and displays her grandiose desire to be recognised as the creating divinity of an exceptional and unique girl she had idealised for so long. She believes in the power of her "hands"[19] and, thus, got down to the business of sculpting her girl—Valentina–Gisele Bündchen.

During pregnancy, Alice demonstrated a strong need for omnipotent control over both the development of the foetus[20] and her husband's feelings and attitudes in order to maintain the couple's "balance". She fully benefited from the holding, containment, patience, and support given by the observer during pregnancy and her transition to the motherhood she so desired and feared. The father benefited from the observer in a more private way, in that she permitted his gaze to invade, siphon, and follow her, and allowed herself to be used as an emotional drain or receptacle to alleviate the fears, aggressiveness, and angst deposited in him.[21] In keeping with her function, the observer enabled Mário to be more present during the observations. At the end of the scans, he exclaimed, "Thank God! Well, now let's have our 'little speech'", which was a short meeting between the couple and the observer to talk about issues, clarify any doubts, and plan the next scan. Mário liked and benefited from that space. The observer's live personal presence helped circulate affections and detoxify him. Alice sought relief from Mário, who sought relief from the observer, who sought relief from the supervision group. Every human being needs another human being in which to deposit and elaborate his or her angst. Therefore, by maintaining her availability, the observer helped facilitate the couple's entry into, and exit from, the intrauterine space that haunted especially the father.

The sonographer's clear and objective explanations also contributed to easing the tension and attenuating the mother's insecurities during pregnancy; more realistic boundaries were slowly created as to the development of the foetus. Mário seemed not to believe or understand how the foetus got there and that it was his child.[22]

As Valentina grows, her parents, surprisingly, do not see her changes and measurement transformations; they seem inattentive and show no interest in her development, which is communicated nonverbally to the sonographer, who, strangely, never mentions the baby's measurements or weight during the scans.[23] The first reference to weight only appears in the seventh observation, when the pregnancy was thirty-seven weeks along and the mother said she had had a Doppler examination at the hospital because her glucose was high and she was gaining a lot of weight. At the time, Valentina weighed 2.160 kilos. Later, the doctor measures the baby who was then weighing 2.410 kilos, which showed how she had grown. The baby's complete intrauterine growth certainly challenged Alice because it was out of her control.

The end of the pregnancy was a preview of the turmoil that was to come with Valentina's birth and the loss of control and "balance"—hormonal, physical, and psychological—that Alice so feared. Valentina threatened Alice's psychological integrity as well as her command and control. This plays out intensely at the last scan when Mário arrives, fearful about having lost the house keys for the second time. Alice gives him a strong reprimand, leading us to think that she felt threatened by the serious risk of losing what she had deposited in him. He was at the point of exploding and physically attacking Alice. He leaves without saying good-bye at the last observation session, thus expressing the threat of rupture—"losing the keys"—that surrounded this pregnancy, and the escalating violence that repeats itself in the Alice–Valentina relationship. The "beasts" start circulating more freely without the containment provided by the first phase of pregnancy, which culminates when Valentina is attacked and bitten in the face by one of the family dogs when she is two years old.

Having surmounted the pregnancy phase with its inaccessibility to maternal control, and despite her inherent doubts and uncertainties, Alice celebrates the fact that her girl is now within reach of her "hands" and announces that everyone will now meet "her Valentina": "Well, this little rascal decided she didn't want to stay in her mother's belly any more. She wants everyone to know who Valentina is." Thus begins the first face-to-face battle of many wars to come. It is interesting to notice the contrast between the observer, who recognised Valentina as the same being that was in her mother's belly—lively, graceful, active, healthy, with her habit of tasting and swallowing, and experiencing pleasure—and the mother, who not only did not recognise her, but announced that the real Valentina was yet to be born from her own hands. In this way, the moment of birth represents a significant rupture in the life of this baby.

Alice was the only mother in our research who demanded that she be able to nurse her baby while still on the operating table with her arms still attached to IVs. Valentina fulfilled her mother's demands that she nurse when placed on her breast. Yet, this was still not enough for Alice, who, the next day, said her daughter still had not nursed. Nothing Valentina did was enough to please her mother, which created a pattern: Valentina had to adapt to this environment from early on; if she did not, her mother would "act hurt" in the sense of rupture, abandonment, and revenge.

After Valentina's birth, a mother–baby pattern developed where the baby nurses and sleeps because the mother wants her to, and then later eats when and what the mother decides. The baby behaves in accordance to her mother's commands. In her first year, she becomes "smiley girl", which makes Alice very proud. In the second half of her first year, Valentina transforms into the "smiley bird". She begins flapping her wings and practising to fly, which certainly threatened the mother significantly.

Alice suffered from a lot of pain, irritability, migraines, and problems breastfeeding. There is a clear mother–baby "derailment of dialogue" (Spitz, 1964). We followed the discords, non-conformities, and clashes between Alice and Valentina, which accentuated as she grew. The mother feels drained by the baby and is afraid of not having enough milk, of coming up empty in the relationship, and of losing herself and her "balance". The responsibility for weaning falls on Valentina: "There's nothing left there, you didn't want to nurse."

Valentina starts having problems with constipation, which Alice attributes to the supplements, thus giving more value to her own milk: "When she has my milk, her bowel movements are just fine." The mother tries to regain control of what goes in and what comes out of her daughter, which became synonymous with mashed fruit and evacuations that must happen daily. In the period when she was introducing other foods, the mother reveals her control: she offers food without considering her daughter's rhythm, without waiting for her to announce that she was hungry. The mother says she's "clumsy" and never knows if she should heat the fruit, mash it, or cut it into pieces, but Valentina has to swallow it. Several stressful incidents took place that had a strong impact on the observer.

Alice was satisfied that her daughter would be a model like Gisele Bündchen: she is thin and only eats fruit. This was another motif about Valentina: her destiny had been predetermined. Alice develops a distorted image of her daughter without ever recognising her responsibility for her state: "There is no reason for her to be thin, she eats everything."

By the beginning of the fourth month. Alice has calmed down because, through feeding her daughter papaya and using suppositories, "she has a bowel movement every day". Alice systematically prepares fruit ahead of time and offers it before the baby shows signs of being hungry. Alice fought hard to maintain her control over Valentina. She was especially concerned about what stayed inside her daughter and was able to reach the "right measure", an infallible recipe to maintain the lack of differentiation that guaranteed Valentina would remain an extension of herself, the wonderful and valued daughter/twin sister that she so wanted to be. The mother needs her daughter and struggles to maintain the indiscrimination.

Valentina gradually distances herself from her intrauterine experiences, and her spontaneity and freedom allow her to savour it in accordance with her own rhythm and timing.

We thought of how difficult it must be for a baby with an immature ego to face an environment with someone that insists on being the most important and that requires care. In this case, the conditions necessary for the maternal function of mirroring, which is fundamental for the baby to begin existing, fails. Winnicott (1971a, p. 103) asks, "What does the baby see when he or she looks at the mother's face?" and answers, "I am suggesting that, ordinarily, what the baby sees is himself or herself". However, in order for that to be possible, it is important that the mother makes herself available, stripped of herself and devoted to the baby, thus empathising with him or her. This position is similar to that of the observer/analyst, who abstains from action in order to be receptive and have an attitude of waiting, tolerance, and patience with the other, the stranger. If not, when the baby—or the patient in analysis—gazes at the mother's face, he or she does not see himself or herself, but the mother/analyst with her moods and the rigidity of her defence structures.

The competitive and destructive relationship with the twin sister is remade, which is increasingly played out by Alice and her daughter. Valentina's attempt to differentiate provokes in Alice more than an experience of abandonment; the baby threatens her with losing a part of herself that was struggling to be born. Valentina has to put up a fierce struggle to differentiate herself. Thus, after the first year, we watched the baby fight numerous battles in the war declared by Alice against Valentina's discrimination: "She is my life." Valentina reacts to environmental impingements and begins disobeying her mother. She stops being the "smiley girl" that she was in her first year. Although she remains enclosed in a dark house, Valentina insists on seeking the light.[24] Alice did not tolerate her daughter's movements toward separation. Valentina could count on neither her father's nor her mother's partnership in this process. The mother had no space for the frustrations the baby was beginning to provoke as she grew. She frequently used retaliation, threats, bribery, and tongue-lashings to imprison Valentina, repeating the pattern observed in the Alice–Mário relationship since pregnancy. After the first half of the second year, Valentina stays in her mother's lap during the observations, which was also not tolerated by Alice because it contradicted her to desire to show off her daughter's accelerated growth. Actually, Alice communicated with Valentina through contradictory messages, which left her at a dead end: at the same time that the mother said, "grow", she non-verbally communicated the exact opposite, "don't grow, don't abandon me".

After the first year, Valentina experienced numerous close calls and negligence that put her at risk. The dogs—their smell and barking—progressively invade the house and reach Valentina. As was described, when she was two and a half, one of the family dogs bit her face. Valentina had no choice other than to adapt to the dogs.

At the last observation and filming, Valentina is three years old and the same pattern persists. The dogs bark incessantly. Valentina throws a pen at her mother, who says nothing. Later, she asks her daughter once again to draw a doll and she answers that she does not know how and adds that Barbie is going to bite her mother. This is followed by a struggle to put on clothes, shoes, and boots.

Valentina demonstrates an irritability that is typical of infants who react to environmental impingement. She has no space that welcomes her spontaneous gestures, which are frequently substituted by the mother's gestures. Without being able to have her aggressiveness contained and integrated in a healthy way, Valentina starts biting her little friends at the day care centre.

Six years after the observations ended and Valentina was nine years old, the observer contacted Alice about giving her a recording and goes to her house. Everything was still the same; no changes had been made to the environment. Alice was still impenetrable and demonstrates no critical thinking. She works at the same job, where she says she is highly respected as a "model employee", a fact that she is very proud of. The observer thought Valentina had become rather antisocial. The house was still closed, damp, and inhabited by the dogs and their smell.

Environmental impingement can atrophy creative capabilities and be fertile ground for developing a false self. However, it is not easy to destroy the creative potential of human beings, their true self. Valentina's withdrawal protects her from environmental impingements and safeguards a wealth of potential inside her. We are hopeful that it can be reached at the right time and in more facilitating environmental circumstances. In the words of Winnicott (1971c, p. 91):

> As I have already indicated, one has to allow for the possibility that there cannot be a complete destruction of a human individual's capacity for creative living and that, even in the most extreme case of compliance and the establishment of a false personality, hidden away somewhere there exists a secret life that is satisfactory because of its being creative or original to that human being. Its unsatisfactoriness must be measured in terms of its being hidden, its lack of enrichment through living experience.

CHAPTER SEVEN

Philomena: an inner journey back to the beginning

Philomena is a polished-up true story[24] about a woman who kept a carefully guarded secret: fifty years ago she had given birth to a son who had been ripped away from her when he was three years old, and when she had been living in forced confinement at a Catholic convent in Ireland—the Roscrea Abbey. There, teenage girls that had become pregnant out of wedlock were abandoned and forgotten by parents and society. In order to atone for their "sins" and pay the "debt" they owed to the nuns who "sheltered" and exploited them and their babies, they had to work as slaves for around four years. They were only allowed to see their babies for one hour a day.

Philomena's story allows us to share in the experience of a biological mother who, despite the limitations imposed by the environment, had an intense relationship with her son that was prematurely ruptured when he was given to another family for adoption. All that the mother and son had left to hold on to from their story were predominantly wordless memories of powerful and unforgettable experiences that led them to search in vain for each other. The intensity of their connection, which endured despite never seeing each other again, is proof of the importance of the predominantly non-verbal phase of babies (*infans*) in human development. We see that the relationship was able to continue in the interior worlds of each of them, which facilitated satisfactory and creative personal growth for both.

It can be said that Philomena is an exemplary case that brings together many important aspects that the "descent to the realm of the mothers" can contribute to understanding human nature and analytic techniques. We see the effects of a transforming partnership, similar to the mother–baby–observer and patient–analyst alliances, and can follow the progression of a true "analytic process" where integration is the main outcome. For this reason, the "Philomena case", based on the screenplay entitled *Philomena* (Coogan & Pope, 2013),[25] which won nine awards at the Venice film festival in 2013 and was nominated for an Oscar in 2014, concludes the cases presented in this book.

Philomena was a religious woman of unshakeable faith, which she maintained even after the terrible experience she had at the convent. Part of her inner journey is her search for reconciliation with religion and an attempt to be free from the guilt it had burdened her with. She also sought reconciliation with her parents. During the time she was confined in the convent, she could not count on her mother, who had died when she was a child, or her father, who had disowned her. Neither could she count on substitute mothers or fathers. On the contrary, the nuns and priests never stopped accusing, punishing, perverting the facts, and heaping guilt and repression on Philomena. This environment weighed heavily in its effect on her fears and struggles. We could say that she was unlucky, that she did not find solidarity, receptivity, or shelter.

In the second scene of the film[26] we are suddenly in an empty church with Philomena, aged seventy, and witness this brief dialogue with a priest:

> "Hello Philomena, how's the new hip?"
>
> "It's very good. It's titanium."
>
> "Haven't seen you for a while."
>
> "I just came to light a candle."
>
> "Someone special?"
>
> "Yes" [she does not elaborate any further].

A flashback cuts to Philomena as a young woman, petrified and ashamed, standing before Mother Superior Barbara and Sister

Hildegard, who questioned her about the circumstances of her pregnancy and blame her for her indecency.

> [Trying to defend herself, Philomena argues] "Oh Reverend Mother, the sisters at school never told us anything about babies or . . . the thing."
>
> "Did your mother not tell you?" [asks Mother Barbara]
>
> "Her mother died ten years ago." [answers Sister Hildegard]
>
> "But don't dare to blame the sisters! [The nuns who taught Philomena at school.] You are the cause of this shame. You and your indecency! (says Mother Barbara)

The scene depicts a violent repression of the teenager's aspects of love and sex, which are buried in indecency and bad things. The nuns, thus, seal the fate of Philomena's pleasure and sexuality.

A series of flashbacks follow, showing Philomena meeting John at a funfair. He is the young man who charms her, gets her pregnant, and changes her life forever, even though she never sees him again.

Philomena heads to her daughter Jane's house, lost in thought, reliving vivid flashes of herself agonising in childbirth at the convent. A young nun—Anunciata—decides she will not follow Mother Barbara's precept that the delivery was "in God's hands" and delivers the baby herself with forceps,[27] saving the lives of both mother and baby.

Philomena is distant, absorbed in terrible memories and images when her daughter arrives. She asks if she is all right, and whose picture[28] that is in her hands.

> "It's his birthday. He would have been fifty today . . ."
>
> "Who?"

We do not know for sure what made Philomena reveal her secret at that particular moment, but it is clear that for those years she never lost hope of finding her son. Some kind of inner transformation, and certainly her own seventy years, led her to "light a candle" for her son on his fiftieth birthday, thus illuminating and making real all that had been annulled and erased from the period when she had been abandoned and confined without any contact with the outside world for so many years.

Determining factors that gave Philomena's revelation a destination and imbued it with a transforming power were her daughter, who listened to her, and the improbable chance meeting with political journalist and atheist (the opposite of Philomena), Martin Sixsmith, precisely at a time of transition in his career due to having been unfairly dismissed from a position in the Blair government. Philomena's daughter meets him the same night that her mother reveals her secret, at a party where she was working as a receptionist. She overhears a conversation between him and some friends and learns that he has just been fired. Feeling sorry for him, she suggests that he write a story about her mother. Martin, who had coincidentally just turned fifty himself, immediately refused her proposal, saying that what she was suggesting was a "human interest" story, which he did not do because they are "stories about vulnerable, weak-minded, ignorant, people to fill up the pages of newspapers read by vulnerable, weak-minded, ignorant people". He was actually planning on writing a book about Russia.

Here, we see Martin's natural resistance to embarking on this journey with Philomena, on this story of "human interest". An analogy can be made here with the not readily recognised natural resistance felt by analysts when making contact with new patients and the typical vulnerabilities of the beginning of life, the resistance an observer feels when entering an infant's house and beginning the infant observations, and the resistance mothers feel when making themselves available to their babies.

> "I don't believe in God. And I don't know when I stopped. [Martin's wife is beside him and he continues] And I don't know why it bothers me . . . Should I do a human interest story?"

After much resistance, Martin decides to meet Philomena and her daughter at a restaurant. Philomena draws attention because of her natural, simple, strong, firm, and authentic personality; a common example of a mother who connects and communicates very genuinely through her gestures, her gaze, and the active silence of someone who is involved. She tells Martin about her time in confinement at the convent: "I disappeared from the world. My family didn't visit me, and out of shame my father told everyone that I was dead". She had been a typical "Magdalen girl", as the girls in those conditions were called. Martin listens to her shocking and moving story and decides to join her on this journey of revelations that will both bring them together and force them to face their differences, but will produce profound transformations in both as they discover each other and themselves.

> "So, can we go and talk to these nuns?" [asks Martin, stepping into his role and determined to investigate reality]
>
> "You can try; maybe you'll have more luck than mum's had."
>
> "Can you help me find him, Martin?" [asks Philomena, looking firmly at him]
>
> "Well, it's certainly an interesting story." [answers Martin in his role as "journalist" and still not sure where Philomena will take him]

Martin and Philomena head to Ireland and go to the Roscrea Abbey together. Philomena has told her daughter that it is not necessary for her to go along. Martin is somewhat apprehensive at the idea of being alone with her. Once again, we see his resistance to being in a position other than writing a story, rather than sharing this experience and intimacy with Philomena. As the story unfolds, we will see that he inevitably becomes less of a journalist and more of a partner.

When they arrive at the Roscrea Abbey, they look around the place, which is still oppressive and haunted, full of secrets. Martin, who is learning from Philomena to be more connected to people, asks,

> "You all right?"
>
> "I'm fine."

Philomena leads the way and, before knocking on the door, pauses to say, "I'm one of the lucky ones, Martin. Some of the mothers and babies didn't even survive childbirth."

A subtle interaction, empathy, approximation, and concern with the other, characteristic of a connected and respectful duo, begins to emerge and grow. They take turns, first one taking the lead, then the other, sharing the roles. The journalist in Martin helps him take on the role that is so difficult for Philomena, of investigating reality, confronting her past, and setting things right. Philomena, on the other hand, can begin to exist, her feelings can be revealed and respected, and she can begin her explorations "back to the beginning". She has a true friend helping her confront a story that had been too violent to reveal for fifty long years. As their explorations begin taking them towards their objectives, Martin is able to see more and shares a very human experience with his friend, while being less resistant.

Philomena rings the doorbell and a young African nun opens the door:

> "Can I help you?"
>
> "I'm Philomena Lee. I made an appointment."
>
> "Oh yes, come in Philomena."
>
> "And this is my friend, Martin Sixsmith, *News At Ten*."
>
> "*BBC News*, actually, but not any more."

The two are led to a room reserved for official meetings. There are several framed pictures of the Madonna and a crucifix with Jesus bleeding on the cross. The young nun says Sister Claire will be with them in a few minutes and asks if they would like some tea.

> "Can I use the bathroom?"
>
> "It's downstairs on . . ."
>
> "I know where it is."

Philomena retraces the steps she took so many years ago, climbing some stairs to the window where she saw her child for the last time. She looks down at the courtyard and the gate where she saw Anthony disappear into the car of his "adoptive" parents. Because she had always paid attention to everything that went on in Roscrea, Philomena had known that Mary, a little girl the same age as Anthony and raised with him, whose mother was her friend and confidante, was being given away for adoption and that the adoptive parents had arrived at the abbey. However, she had no idea that Anthony would be going with Mary. Through this window she had seen Sister Hildegard taking her son to the car; according to the nuns, he went with them because he did not want to be separated from his little friend, Mary. Philomena was told nothing further on the matter. The nuns, who were also jealous of Philomena, said that whoever did what she had done deserved to be treated with disrespect and aversion and have their motherhood interrupted. Deep inside herself, Philomena keeps vivid images and emotions, exactly as they happened fifty years ago.

Meanwhile, in discreet and subtle harmony with Philomena, Martin takes on the role of facing the facts head on and at face value, pressing for answers and trying to understand. He begins his exploring looking around the room at the then and now pictures and sees photos of Sister Hildegard and Sister Barbara, both young in the 1960s with crucifixes around their necks; of a nun holding a baby; two nuns standing between rows of cots. Then he sees a seemingly out of place photo of a glamorous, busty Hollywood actress—Jane Russell—signed "with much love". Martin is puzzled. Being nosy, he stands at the bay window and sees a very old nun leaning on two sticks, staring at him.[29] He is startled by Sister Claire, a nun in her mid-forties, who greets him cheerfully. He asks about the photo, thinking it was Jayne Mansfield. The sister corrects him and says it is Jane Russell.

> "Why is she on the wall?"
>
> [Changing the subject] "Sorry, I didn't catch your name?"

Philomena enters the room and brightly introduces her friend to Sister Claire the same way she introduced him to the other Sister at the front door, evidently proud of her partnership with a successful journalist from *News At Ten*. He again corrects her:

> "*BBC News*, actually. But I'm not with them any more."

Philomena seems happier and more upbeat now that she can count on a partner–friend qualified to help her go back to the beginning, to "know the place for the first time" and take ownership of the story she had experienced so passively and in utter aloneness. For the first time, she relies on someone she can trust, who is developing a genuine interest and appreciation for her person and story, an ally to defend her.

Winnicott, when referring to whether an infant's ego is strong or weak, states that it depends on the actual mother acting as an auxiliary ego; the tendency towards early integration depends on the support and protection given by a mother's ego. Therefore, the mother–baby, patient–analyst partnerships are important in accomplishing the mission. The partners must be in tune with each other and be brave enough to move forward, like Philomena and Martin. They change and exchange roles, sometimes she is the locomotive and at other times the carriage, and *vice versa*. The relationship is not based on authoritarianism, control, and submission, but, rather, on respect and a genuine desire to be together and help each other, respecting differences and limits. The spectator is involved in the duo's experience, similar to the observer in the infant observations. The harmony that develops between Philomena and Martin transmits to the spectator. The film clearly and movingly expresses the transformation and growth experienced by both protagonists when this happens.

Sister Claire welcomes them with "tea and cake" as usual, and says she does not know if Philomena has been told, but, since the last time she had been there, most of their records had been destroyed in a big fire. After an extended silence—fifty years—Philomena starts talking, and Martin watches her:

> "I still go to Mass . . . I don't want to cause any fuss or point the finger at anyone, or blame the church in any way. I just want to know that he's all right—I don't even have to see him. Sometimes I have visions of him and he's homeless and nobody loves him . . ."

Martin, who at this point has already "adopted" Philomena, takes over the confrontation without criticising her. He asks if they could talk to one of the older nuns. Concerned about the intentions of the journalist's line of questioning, Sister Claire says no and asks to speak privately with Philomena. She certainly realised that she could not mislead him as she had always done with his partner.

Martin leaves the room, but does not give up. He walks towards some double glass doors and, peering through them, once again sees Sister Hildegard and her sticks; her eyes meet his and her expression is inscrutable. When he reaches to open the door, he hears a voice emanating from someone coming down the staircase. It is the young nun who had opened the front door for them, saying those are private quarters.

He decides to wait outside the house. He finds an old graveyard, hidden by overgrown weeds, bushes, and brambles, where mothers and babies are buried. One of the girls was only fourteen years old and many of the headstone inscriptions read that mother and child had died in childbirth.

Philomena comes out of the front door pale-faced and clutching an envelope. When Martin sees the expression on her face he asks her if she is all right. She does not answer; she just wants to get into the car as quickly as possible.

> "What did she say to you?"
>
> "She said you were a journalist and that you were trying to manipulate me and I should be careful what I say to you. And she gave me this" [takes the envelope from her purse].
>
> "Do you want me to open it? [She does not reply and he continues] It's a contract . . . signed by you, in 1955." [He reads the contract and tells her she had relinquished all claims to Anthony Lee forever.]
>
> "I'll never find him."
>
> "If they coerced you in any way to sign that piece of paper, we can challenge them legally."
>
> "No one forced me, Martin. I signed of my own free will."

We see Martin and Philomena talking in a field outside the parked car.

> "Funny isn't it, how every piece of paper that might be able to help you has been destroyed. But guess what? The one piece of paper designed to stop you from finding him has been lovingly preserved. God in His infinite wisdom decided to spare that from the flames."
>
> "I signed it because I believed I'd committed a terrible sin, Martin, and I had to be punished. And . . . what made it so much worse, was that I enjoyed it."
>
> "What?"
>
> "The sex. Oh, it was wonderful. I thought I was floating on air. He was so handsome and the way he held me in his arms and—well, I didn't even know I had a clitoris, Martin."
>
> "Really?"
>
> "And after I had the sex, I thought anything that feels so lovely must be wrong."

"Fucking Catholics . . . Sorry."

[She smiles] "I spent thirty years as a nurse, I've heard worse than that."

Philomena begins to exist; her suffering, which had been frozen in time, can now be brought out and shared, along with her lost hope and disbelief that she could ever recover what life had so brutally taken away from her. Her pleasure and satisfaction with life—aspects that are especially repressed and coveted by the nuns—that had been tucked away inside for all those years could also be recognised. Martin was a good container; she could trust him.

As these feelings are released within the vivid and true partnership offered by her friend Martin, Anthony also begins to exist and grow into reality. A "silent film" appears of Anthony at the age of eight on a sunny day, playing baseball. He has a family and two older brothers. This reveals what Philomena has feared: he is no longer her little boy.

It is very moving how the film subtly and non-verbally communicates the intensity of a story that had been lived in silence and in pieces, inaccessible and unintegrated, by using flashes of silent film. We are surprised by silent images of Anthony as he grows: eight, fourteen, twenty years old. The director's strategy brilliantly shows Anthony beginning to exist and taking on life in Philomena as she integrates him into herself with Martin's help.

Philomena and Martin leave the Abbey and head to their hotel. They are sitting at the bar having drinks when Philomena's daughter walks in.

"How did it go?"

"What, from the Sisters of Little Mercy?" [asks Martin]

"Just 'tea and cake' then. That's all they've ever given mum."

Philomena and her daughter leave, and Martin talks to the barman, who asks if he had gone to the Abbey. He says that a lot of women—"ex-Magdalen girls"—stayed there while trying to find their children. He says he thinks the nuns set fire to all the records because they were probably embarrassed about selling babies to Americans for a thousand pounds each. Martin discovers that Jane Russell was one of those who bought a baby.

Like a father opening up opportunities for growth and confronting reality, Martin proposes that they go to the USA together. Philomena accepts after a brief silence, and again demonstrates her usual courage, discrimination, and determination when she tells her daughter that it is not necessary for her to come along because she has her work to worry about. Philomena reveals her prime objective, her mission. Something she had always wanted but had kept hidden from herself because it terrified her. During all those years, she had kept going back to a place where she knew she would not get any answers. Martin shows her a way out of that dead-end street that only served "tea and cake". Philomena decides to live and face reality, despite all her fears of disappointment: "I'd like to go. I want to know if he's ever thought about me, 'cos I've thought about him every day . . ."

Anthony keeps growing and his reality becomes increasingly more vivid. Another "silent film" image shows Anthony's tenth birthday celebration with cake and candles. There is something sad about his expression.

At their hotel, Martin and Philomena talk and Martin invites her to visit the Lincoln Memorial, which she has always wanted to see.

> "Isn't he wonderful? I've always wanted to see him in his big chair" [says Philomena].
>
> "Well, he was a big man. Literally. Tallest American president."
>
> Martin asks if he can take a picture of her.
>
> "Is it for the article?"
>
> "Erm, yeah."
>
> "Only I'm a little bit worried you see, because if I find him he might be very disapproving of talking to the papers. Families are very private things."
>
> "I won't write anything you're unhappy with. Just the truth."
>
> "That's the thing I'm worried about."

Philomena is terrified about being so close to the truth that she had kept hidden her whole life; scared of what she might find. She is especially afraid of Anthony not returning her love, a connection that for her has been unbreakable for fifty years.

Another flash of film, this time with sound, stages Anthony's approaching reality. He is twenty-something years old at a party full of young, beautiful people. He calls out to someone behind the camera, "Hi Pete . . ."

Martin is asleep when Philomena knocks on his door to tell him how lucky and grateful she is for having found him, leaving him momentarily stunned.

> "Martin, I wanted to tell you something earlier but it slipped my mind, and I was going to tell you on the phone but I forgot the number, so I thought I'd come and tell you in person . . . What I wanted to say was, thank you Martin, for helping me to look for my son. I know you got the sack from your job—not *News At Ten*—the other one. And I just want to say, that their loss is my gain. Good night, Martin."

The next day at breakfast, a determined Martin is working at his laptop in a room full of guests. He is impatiently searching names and photos for Anthony Lee while Philomena happily investigates the buffet and talks to the Mexican chef. They are on completely different wavelengths.

They are both tense as they come closer to the truth and its inherent uncertainties: she both wants and does not want to come face-to-face with Anthony's reality. Martin had started the day armed with his work tools and ready to begin the mission of finding Anthony. He is concentrated, with his head bent, oblivious to all the movement around him. He energetically works through all the Anthonies that parade across his computer screen. Impatient that his searches have produced nothing about Anthony Lee, he calls his friend Caroline, who sends him the link to the immigration files. As he connects, he is interrupted by Philomena who wants to tell him about the results of her research at the buffet. He tries to demonstrate that he already knows everything about the buffet and that he is trying to stay focused on their search. She feels they are not connecting.

> [After Martin's unenthusiastic reaction to Philomena's report, she asks] "The breakfast is included, isn't it?"
>
> "Yes, yes —I'm just not hungry. My stomach hasn't woken up yet."
>
> "Mine wakes up before I do."

Martin tries to bring Philomena back to reality and reminds her why they are there: "I'm trying to help you find your son, OK? So please, could I have some quiet time?"

Philomena looks at him, her nose defiantly up in the air. She goes to say something but gives up and goes back to talk to the chef. Martin returns to his laptop and sees he has received an email entitled "Anthony Lee". The image downloads line by line and eventually shows a picture of little Anthony in a newspaper photo, clutching a tin toy aeroplane on his way down the aeroplane steps upon his arrival in the USA with Mary. Stunned, he recognises Anthony and reads the headline above the cutting: "New Life for Irish Orphans". The article uses Anthony's new name: Michael Hess. Martin finds a photo of him as an adult, age thirty, smiling at a party. Then, at the top of the page, he reads: Michael Hess, born on May 7, 1952, died August 15, 1995. He can't believe it: "Oh God, he's dead . . ."

Philomena comes back to the table and glances towards the photo, which Martin quickly makes disappear. He stares at her, his face frozen, and she knows something terrible is happening. She looks at the screen that now shows Michael as an adult in a formal pose and exclaims, "That's my Anthony!" She looks at Martin, but he does not answer. His eyes not only confirm this, they tell her something else. She says, "He's dead, isn't he?" Martin chokes: "Yes. I'm sorry." A silence descends on them and remains as they head to the airport to go home. Philomena is numb, disengaged from everything around her. She cannot understand how life can go on when her Anthony is gone. Martin looks over at her and does not know what to say.

Their plans disintegrate and they decide to return home. At the airport, Philomena continues to be lost in her thoughts. Martin tells Sally, his editor, about Anthony's death. She asks how he died and about the book. She thinks that, dead or alive, he should find a story and suggests that he stay there and keep Philomena with him. She reminds him of the contract he signed.

Very carefully and respectfully, Martin sits next to Philomena, who is broken and silent. The connection between them is so strong he does not need to say anything; she asks if it is possible to change their tickets to another day and stay there for a while longer.[30] That way they could get to know Anthony through some of the people who knew him and find out what had happened to him during all this time. It is a crucial moment that takes Philomena's inner journey to a deeper level. Martin agrees to accompany her in this "descent" that enables her to find her son and herself.

Martin and Philomena go back to the hotel. He asks if she wants to see the photo that Marcia sent him. Marcia is one of Anthony's colleagues whom they are scheduled to meet the next day. To their surprise, Philomena recognises Martin in the photo—he was one of the photographers covering the event where Anthony appears shaking President Reagan's hand. She is excited and asks him to tell her about what it was like to meet Anthony/Michael, eagerly trying to compose an image of her son:

> "What was he like?"
>
> "Erm . . . I can't remember too much . . . It was a Republican thing . . ."
>
> "You must remember something."
>
> "I shook hands with him."
>
> "What was his handshake like? Was it strong?"
>
> "Yes . . ."
>
> "Well that's something . . . What else?"
>
> "He looked very smart."
>
> "Oh, I always dressed him smart."
>
> "I said 'hello'."
>
> [Repeating the word, as if it were significant.] "'Hello'. So, he was smart and he had a firm handshake" [says Philomena, trying to convince herself that this information about her son is enough].

They meet Marcia, Anthony's colleague, in Washington. There is a table covered with photos of Anthony/Michael taken in places unknown to Philomena. Marcia explains that he was senior legal counsel for both the Reagan and Bush administrations. Philomena says he never would have obtained a job like that if he had stayed with her. She asks Marcia if he ever mentioned Ireland. She says no, but gives her the telephone number for Mary, the little girl who had immigrated to the USA with Anthony and had been raised as his sister. Philomena finds a picture of him with a tall, handsome, bearded man. Marcia says it is a friend of Anthony's, Peter. In another photo, he is with Marcia. Philomena asks if he was her boyfriend. She says no, that he was gay. She would accompany him when he went to official functions because being gay was frowned upon in the Republican Party. Martin seems to freeze at the news, but Philomena hardly reacts at all.

> "Did Peter love him?" [asks Philomena]
>
> "Yes, he loved him." [answers Marcia]

Martin and Philomena continue in their investigations and head towards Mary's house. She is in her fifties and is rather strange, with a hard and tired-looking appearance. She does not show any reaction to Philomena's arrival, even when she says Mary looks just like her mother. As they look at some childhood photos taken with their adoptive family, Philomena asks if her adoptive mother was a nice person.

> "I won't lie to you, Philomena; we didn't have the happiest childhood. Marge was OK, but our father could be a very hard man." [She looks behind her and yells at the children playing outside.]
>
> [Philomena sees another photo of Anthony/Michael looking thin and ill, and digests this information.] "It must have been terrible, keeping it a secret his whole life [she speaks of Anthony, but also of herself]. I assume he died from Aids."

Just as she had kept her son's existence a secret for fifty years, he had also kept it a secret, along with his homosexuality and illness because it was not accepted. All the new information and the feelings, memories, and discoveries had a strong impact on Philomena and gave her a lot to digest. To think the nuns had been denying his existence this entire time.

> "Yes. He did. He wasn't too happy with himself, last couple of years of his life . . . working for the Republicans." (says Mary)
>
> [Philomena looks up from a photo she had been studying, puzzled. Martin explains.] "The Republicans cut funding into Aids research because they blamed the epidemic on gay lifestyles."
>
> "Where's he buried, Mary?"
>
> "You know, I think it's out in West Virginia near where he lived. Dad wanted him buried in the family plot in St Louis, but Pete wouldn't allow it. They had a big row . . . You should talk to Pete about it."

> [A silence. The unfolding soap opera of Anthony's life is alien to Philomena. She feels disconnected, unable to relate to it. Martin steps in.] "We got his number from Marcia—we'll go and see him, won't we Philomena."
>
> "Hmm . . . [after a pause] Mary, can I just ask, there's one thing I'd like to know. Did Anthony ever mention Ireland, or where he'd come from?"
>
> "Not really. Neither of us really talked about that."

A flashback appears of a dialogue between Peter and Michael, who is already ill and thin, his clothes too big.

Philomena asks if it is possible for Martin not to use her real name in the book. She was anxious about the reality that was coming out. Martin reminds her that, as a journalist, he deals with real names, with reality. Philomena asks him to stop at a church along the way so she can confess. Martin says it is the Catholic Church that should confess, and they discuss religion. Philomena's retreat to the shelter of religion as she gets closer to reality is interesting. Philomena grabs on to her old defences, to her contract with the church to remain in silence and be invisible.

The two have an explosive argument about religion and she ends up swearing at him in the end, before going into the church. The effect of the argument continues inside the church. Philomena kneels in the confession box before the priest, and then leaves without saying anything. She was coming to terms with the drama she had silently lived her whole life in a final dialogue with the church before completing her mission of integrating Anthony's reality, this time with the help of his partner, Peter.

Philomena is purposeful as she leaves the church; worried about the point they had come to. She speaks firmly to Martin, saying she will pay him for all the expenses he has incurred because of her, and that she wanted to give up and end her contract with him.

> "You heard what Mary said—she said he never gave me a second thought. He wasn't my Anthony—he was someone else's Michael. He probably hated the thought of me."
>
> "We need to talk to Pete Olsson. He lived with him. He knew him better than anyone . . . People need to know about what happened to you. This is an injustice that needs to be exposed."

Philomena's uncertainty about continuing the investigation and "publishing", that is, publicly exposing her intimate story, intensifies. Additionally, if she continues, she will break the contract she has with the church that requires her to never look for her son. Her contract with Martin, on the other hand, cannot be broken either. Philomena's conflict between two contracts is exacerbated: the one with the church, and the one with Martin, at the exact moment the story is becoming reality. She proposes to break her contract with Martin, which is her easiest option. However, Martin refuses to accept. At the hotel, Philomena cannot get her key to work, and he helps her.

> "You need to put it with the arrows pointing down."
>
> [Philomena, still angry] "I know how to do it."

He wants her to know that he can continue opening the doors that she is not able to herself. After their confrontation, Martin goes for a run in the park and tries to contact Peter by phone, but gets no answer. When he gets back to the hotel he knocks on Philomena's door and she does not answer either. He calls out, "Phil?" showing their level of intimacy. There are many closed doors. Martin asks the hotel for help in opening Philomena's door. They ask him if she is a relative, and he says, "She's my mother." The bellboy opens the door to Philomena's room, which is empty. They look everywhere and Martin starts to panic until he sees her out on the balcony, crouched in a corner: "There you are!" Embarrassed, Martin tells Philomena that he had to say she was his mother to get them to let him in. She says, "I was just out here having a little cry, that's all . . . I hope you didn't think I was going to jump off the balcony?" Martin says he had not thought that. She says she just wanted some quiet time.[31]

Martin goes down to the bar to continue investigating. The trademark of Guinness, a Celtic harp, reminds him of the symbol he saw on Anthony's jacket. Philomena comes down and firmly tells him that she wants to take a plane back to England, full stop. She tells him not to try to change her mind.

> "I think we should visit Peter Olsson tomorrow."
>
> "Go on your own! I'm not going all that way just to hear another person say Anthony didn't give two hoots about me, and that I abandoned him . . ."

> [Martin points to the Harp symbol] "What's that?"
>
> "All I want to do is go home."

Martin insists about the symbol, and Philomena says it is a Celtic harp. He remembers the photo of Anthony with President Reagan that they had seen. He zooms in on Anthony's jacket lapel where there is a gold Celtic harp badge. If he cared so little about where he came from, why would he wear something so Irish?

> "Perhaps he played the harp? He was gay . . ."
>
> "He didn't play the harp."

Philomena's resistance and uncertainties are clearly seen in both her terror and desire to find her son. Martin, like a good analyst, is lucid and strong and makes Philomena think by suggesting an interpretation that could bring something new to the case.

There is a short flash of Peter and Anthony that adds one more facet to the Anthony who is being pieced together. He is very sick. While in the flashes we see Anthony dying, to Philomena he is about to be born. It is a sad disharmony that can also happen in mother–baby relationships.

They arrive at Peter's house and study it from outside. Philomena repeats that Anthony had been able to achieve much more than she could have given him. They see Peter enter the house after saying goodbye to his new boyfriend. Martin takes the lead and decides to doorstep him, something journalists do. Philomena does not think he will want to speak to her and will slam the door in their faces. Martin rings the doorbell. Peter opens the door. Martin introduces himself and Peter immediately closes the door. After this first failed attempt, Philomena decides to leave the car and knock on the door herself. Peter opens the door and she says firmly,

> "I just want to talk about my son. He was taken from me. And I've been looking for him ever since."

Peter sees the honesty in her eyes and opens the door. Philomena's face is bright as the three watch a film of Anthony that brings together the various short and isolated flashes into a story. Philomena puts the pieces together and finally finds her son; their two stories finally meet.

The camera moves between Philomena's face and the film about Anthony playing on the screen. A shocking moment occurs when Michael is seen in front of the Roscrea Abbey, standing beside Sister Hildegard.

> "He went to Ireland? He went to Roscrea?" [asks Martin]
>
> "I took him. He was looking for you, Philomena."
>
> "He came to look for me?"
>
> [Pointing to Hildegarde, Martin says] That nun . . . I saw her at Roscrea on our last trip."
>
> "They always told me they didn't know where Anthony was." [says Philomena]
>
> "But they told us that they couldn't find you. They said you'd abandoned him as a baby."
>
> "I did not abandon my child."
>
> [Martin angrily defends her] "She was looking for him! She's spent her whole life trying to find him."
>
> "He's there now."
>
> "What do you mean?"
>
> "I had this huge standoff with his father. He wanted him buried in the US, but it was your son's dying wish. He said he wanted to go home. He's buried at Roscrea."

Anthony had come that close to Philomena and she did not know it. Both mother and son had arrived where they wanted and had partners to help them. Anthony arrived first. Martin accompanies Philomena on her journey back to the beginning as they go back to Roscrea.

> "We've come full circle." [says Philomena]
>
> "'The end of all our exploring will be to arrive where we started, and know the place for the first time'."
>
> "Oh Martin, that's lovely, did you just think of that?"
>
> "No, it's T. S. Eliot."

They arrive and Martin angrily says, "No more tea and no more cake." Everything is like before. The nuns continue their denials, but what Martin wants is a clear "settling of accounts"—something also accomplished in analysis—but which Philomena cannot face. He barges into the nuns' private living quarters without asking for permission and goes into Sister Hildegard's room.

> "I'm not here to hurt you; I've just come to ask you a question. I'm a friend of Philomena Lee . . . [he pulls up a chair to sit in front of her]. Why did you do it? [Silence] When a mother and son are looking for each other, why did you keep them apart?"

The priest tries to convince Martin to leave and threatens to call the police.

> "I'm not leaving without an answer."
>
> "I'm sorry, I think your whole manner, coming into a holy place like this and behaving the way you have, is absolutely disgusting." [says the priest]
>
> "I'll tell you what's disgusting, lying to a dying man." [answers to the priest and then speaks directly to Hildegard]
>
> "You could have given him a few precious moments with his mother before he passed away—but you chose to lie. *That's* disgusting."
>
> "Not very Christian, is it? [says Hildegard] Let me tell you something—I have kept my vow of chastity my whole life. Self-denial and mortification of the flesh, that's what brings me closer to God. Those girls have nobody to blame but themselves, and their carnal incontinence."
>
> "You mean they had sex?"
>
> "What's done is done—what do you expect us to do about it now?"
>
> [Philomena enters and answers] "Nothing. There's nothing to be said. I've found my son, that's what I came here for."
>
> "Hang on, hang on [says Martin, turning back to Hildegard]. What you can do is say sorry!
>
> "That's enough Martin!" (Philomena apologises to them).
>
> "Why are you apologising to them? Anthony was dying of Aids and she still wouldn't tell him about you."
>
> "I know! But it happened to me. Not you . . . Sister Hildegard, I want you to know that I forgive you."

Philomena is able to add this to her victories. Although she likes Martin and enjoys his company, she maintains her distinction from him. She is an exemplary woman. Martin cannot believe what he has just witnessed and as he leaves he says that she can forgive Sister Hildegard, but he will not. Philomena is taken to her son's grave, and the inscription on the headstone reads, "A Man of Two Nations and Many Talents". Philomena travelled to the other side of the world while the answer to all her questions was right here where her their story had begun: "He knew I would find him here."

After an intense journey of shared experiences and personal transformations that made him more malleable, observant, and sensitive to "human interest" matters, Martin decides he will not publish Philomena's intimate story. "It's just between you and him." But Philomena tells him to go ahead and make her story known.

Final considerations

Philomena is the story of a mother–baby relationship that was kept from developing. It was violently severed, causing an abrupt "stop in development". However, mother and son remained as connected as they were in the first three years of life, despite the external environmental circumstances that restricted mother–baby contact to one hour a day. She had permission to exercise her motherhood even though she was criticised and threatened with "losing" it, in that her son could be sold at any moment. We see this mother's "descent" into "confinement" in all mothers who live with their children in the first three years of life.

It is a story filled with human material that allows us to reflect once again on how human beings depend on other human beings to be born and to become real, something that is unmistakably established in mother–baby and analyst–patient relationships. This is a story that "is born" from an intimate dialogue between the two main characters, Philomena and a journalist who becomes interested in her. By sharing and participating in Philomena's inner journey, Martin Sixsmith—a journalist accustomed to investigating reality—helps her find the truth in a story that refused to disappear. By making the story public, Martin goes a step further and breaks the silence, invisibility, and confinement of an intimate story experienced by a mother–baby duo in the baby's first three years of life which left indelible marks on both.

In terms of analysis, we can think of the observation cases related in the previous chapters, which were also "born" from the intimate dialogue between two main characters—the mother–baby duo and the observer, and how we helped take their private stories out of confinement and make them visible, shareable, and public through our writing. These stories are results of the intense experience of intimate sharing from which all of us emerge enriched.

When her son turns fifty, Philomena decides to "talk" and give continuity to a story that had been interrupted when Anthony was three years old. The trauma had been so great it took fifty years to mitigate its intensity, during which time Philomena remained forced into "confinement". Yet, now, she decides to take back her emotional life where it had been cut off, propelled by some kind of internal transformation and by where she was in life. She was no longer ashamed or dead. She needed the continuity of Anthony inside her in order to keep existing. All that had been left for Philomena from the time they were together was a photograph taken shortly before he was wrenched away from her. An emptiness was left behind, a fifty-year gash that had to be sewn back together. She had no idea what had happened to Anthony, who he had become, or even if he was dead or alive. With Martin's help, she began sewing delicate stitches and pulling together the pieces—Anthony's toy plane, the Celtic harp, his grave at Roscrea—to discover a truth that neither she nor her son had forgotten. The "flashes of silent film" depicting a story that could not be shown were integrated into a continuous story that gave Philomena the possibility of finding her son and herself.

She obtained the courage to speak and overcame her fear of breaking the internal contracts that kept the story annulled and silent. She journeyed deep inside to find not only her son, but also the parents that had abandoned her, and herself. She "settled her accounts", especially with her parents. She forgives the nun/mother that had mistreated her. Philomena also forgives her father, who had rejected her, and creatively benefited from the relationships with all the men who helped her along her journey to rebirth: Martin, who defends and protects her, actor Steve Coogan, who wrote the screenplay, played the part of Martin, and with whom she developed a close friendship, and the director, Stephen Frears. They all valued her and were interested in her story, thus helping her deal with her relationship with her parents and the damages life had imposed on her.

Philomena's story clearly shows the violent intensity of a hostile environment that not only provoked a rupture in the mother–baby relationship, but also blocked the possibilities of repairing the damages caused by this rupture until Anthony had become an adult and was on the verge of dying. The key to opening the door to allowing these repairs to happen was in the hands of the nuns, especially Sister Hildegard, who denied and repressed all the duo's attempts to find each other, and systematically attacked both their perceptions; each knew, but could not know, that the other existed. The Sister upheld her cold and rigid values and truths until the end, never admitting her participation in the story. Attacks on perception, secrets, and lies normally cause serious damage to the psychic structures of children; maintaining these behaviours impedes development and fills people with guilt, leaving them impoverished.

Philomena was able to transform important aspects of herself in order to enjoy life with defences that were less rigid than those that had been imposed by the cold, inhuman place she had remained for fifty years. Almost as a devitalised piece of herself, her truth had to remain hidden. Anthony also experienced a life where his intimate truths—his relationship with his mother and his homosexuality—were kept secret until he died.

Martin helped Philomena escape her clandestine life. He helped her discover her story—not to change the unchangeable, but, rather, to join the pieces into a unit. Thus, Philomena can master her story and "close the circle", going back to the beginning in order to move forward. She accepted the journey to break internal contracts and was transformed; she wanted to stop being invisible and get to know and share her story, which reminds us of how mothers depend on someone to listen to them, especially during that period in the first three years of life that is essentially wordless.

> Having someone as a witness, an accomplice for her angst and hidden experiences, whether unknown or even forbidden . . . The mother needs this presence to release her pent up "demons", thus attributing to them some kind of meaning and purpose. (Caron, 1995)

PART III

BACK TO THE BEGINNING

CHAPTER EIGHT

The challenges and contributions of this "descent to the realm of the mothers"

In the ten years since our research began, we cannot help but mention time and the challenges of capturing the details of a life that is beginning. It is impossible, and was never our intention, to exactly reproduce the stories of the six infants (two single and two sets of twins) during their first three years of life. Like the mother with her child—and the analyst with his or her patient—we had primarily to learn to wait for/gestate feelings, thoughts, and ideas so they could be born at the right time. How could we manage something as immeasurable as this essentially female and predominantly wordless place where infants begin life? It was an arduous task to bring together all the observer reports and our own reports—random papers, recent and old—in an attempt to translate some of the experiences and challenges faced by mothers when they are thrown into the primitive world of the infant, as well as by the observer.

Perhaps the greatest challenge to writing this book has been cohesively connecting the observation material gathered in the first phase, from pregnancy to delivery, to the second phase, from birth until the third year of life, since we had only supervised the first one. Thus, we had to translate observation material that we had neither experienced nor supervised. Although having a different team for each phase brought additional difficulties to the writing, today we feel our decision was well worth it. Throughout our work we came across natural discontinuities in development that were connected to a complex interweaving of infant–environment that made us abandon previous hypotheses about continuities between the pre- and post-delivery period that had been based exclusively on foetal movements, as in Piontelli's pioneering work (1992/1995).

By extending the Bick method to the gestational period and delivery, we were able to reveal how, by the time they are born, human beings have already composed a long story. For the first time, we conducted monthly longitudinal observations during the pregnancy period, which enabled us to visualise foetal development in the intrauterine environment and the singularities of each baby, as well as of each mother in her transition into motherhood.

It was gratifying to be close to the foetal world and experience the richly illustrated coming into being of a new human in the ultrasound setting with the mother, father, and team. Being able to see the foetus in its day-to-day life in its own world showed its uncontrollable and surprising growth and revealed its sensorial perceptions (touch, smell, taste, sight, and hearing), behaviour, psychomotor skills, and singularities, and the partnership and characteristics of each pair of twins. For example, we were fascinated by the partnership between Raoni and Anahi as they faced each other and then positioned themselves so that one fit her head against the other's belly, seeming to recognise the presence of the other as different from her own; after delivery, they repeated this movement.

Before birth, the baby perceives light and sound, is able to swallow and taste, has favourite positions, sleeps, dreams, wakes up, yawns, makes faces, recognises its mother's voice, sucks its fingers, etc. It has strong reactions to, for example, an amniotic fluid test: its heart rate increases and it "runs away" to the other side of the womb when the needle is inserted to collect material. Some respond with fear, paralysis, or state of shock when the mothers suffer violent stress such as a car accident, or a natural disaster such as a cyclone or flood. In these examinations, the foetus is absolutely quiet and remains "hidden" at the bottom of the uterus. All this shows that the foetus world is neither impenetrable nor totally satisfactory, nor totally protected by the mother's abdominal walls. The foetus has psychic and sensoperceptive motor devices that become increasingly refined, and it progressively participates in both maintaining the pregnancy and initiating the delivery process. It actively participates in keeping the intrauterine environment balanced by swallowing and producing amniotic fluid, which it continues after it is born by swallowing and causing the production of maternal milk.

Babies carry their own inheritance that most characterises them. The foetal movements are the first spontaneous gestures that express the baby's nature. The observations of all the ultrasound scans demonstrated how normal foetuses present fluency and variability in their movements. The sequence of the scans permits visualising patterns and unique movements that immediately identify each foetus.

The twins, Anahi and Raoni, and the girl, Valentina, displayed fascinating spontaneous intrauterine movements that were later repeated after birth, showing impressive and surprising continuity. After delivery, the babies felt like old acquaintances to the observers.

In the case of the twins, they were described as regularly making synchronised wave movements starting at the first ultrasound. While the one on the bottom floats facing up and actively pushes its head up and down, the one on top remains quiet and still, facing down. In other scans, both make rapid diving motions in opposite positions, as if they were ballet dancing in the shape of a swing: when one is in a vertical position, the other one is upside down, both facing forward. This is repeated in other examinations.

Once the sex is confirmed—a boy and a girl—some differences are noticed. For example, the girl tries to get close to her brother; sometimes they lie face to face as if staring at each other; she lowers her head and he strokes her head; then she turns her head toward his belly and "rests". In other scans, she fits her little bottom against her brother's legs, lying "anchored" to his lap, as described by those present. The two seem always to fit. She is called a "little rascal" and is said to be the one to take the initiative when she settles herself into position for birth during the last days of pregnancy, as if she wants to get out first; her brother spends the last days with his little head up.

In the first few days after their birth, while lying on the brother's bed surrounded by cushions and separated by a long, hotdog-like pillow, the second phase observer reports her surprise at the differences between the babies. It is easy to differentiate them, with the parents adding to the discrimination—the colours of their clothes, the prams, the way their hair is combed. Each is his/her own person.

Impressed, she reports that they seem interconnected, attentive, and responsive to each other: when Raoni moves and makes noises, Anahi takes a deep breath, making a sound like a sigh; it is as if she were saying, "Calm down, I'm here". There is a strong harmonious connection between the two as they communicate through breathing, sounds, and movements. The breastfeeding pattern they develop is noticed by the observer and family members: while one nurses the other waits calmly or sleeps. When the mother finishes with one and goes to the crib, the other one is already beginning to wake up or is already waiting. When they start interacting more, there is clearly a "new" pattern in their neonatal relationship: initially, the two gaze at each other, "staring", then, in a quick movement, one lays its head on the other's lap for a while, then they alternate.

The girl, Valentina, was described at many scans by all who were observing as a delicate and beautiful baby with her own unique way of moving her tongue, lips, and mouth that gave everyone the impression she was tasting something very good and swallowing in satisfaction. Sometimes, she woke up during the scan and started swallowing in her typical fashion, "tasting", and then went back to sleep.

Immediately after delivery, the mother demanded that her baby be brought to nurse while she was still on the operating table. The observer had the strange feeling she was watching the baby on the ultrasound screen when she made the same movements of sticking out her tongue, licking her lips, and swallowing as if savouring something. Valentina pushes her face into her mother's breast, raises her head, then pushes her nose into it again, looking for the nipple while licking and swallowing. She does this many times until she is able to suck a little, smacking her lips loudly enough for everyone to hear. Then she turns her head and falls asleep.

The first phase leaves us with hypotheses and images, but it would be almost fatal to try to confirm them in the next phase. We would run the risk of creating a false continuity. Therefore, we iterate what was said earlier: that our decision to have different observers for each phase, who did not communicate with each other until the end of the observations, was correct.

It is worth remembering the natural therapeutic function of the sonographer during the scans. She gave us a very clear idea of some of the challenges faced by health professionals when they come into contact with very primitive psychic phenomenona connected to life's beginnings, which require some of the very same qualities demanded from the mother and her baby: authenticity, availability, permeability, and treating each patient individually. The same doctor conducted all the ultrasound scans for the research and was always receptive and flexible, but firm. She allowed herself to be used by those at the examination, especially the parents, sharing very powerful unconscious communication.

It is important to state that the sonographer had previous extensive research experience in ultrasound settings with the same team, which certainly inspired transformations in her work and increased her understanding, consequently making her more receptive and permeable to the unconscious communication that emerges so easily in this period of life. Her ability to interpret the images using clear and objective explanations and according to the receptivity of each individual helped to ease the tension and soften any possible traumas when viewing the images of the baby. She naturally adapted to the setting, which enabled her to meet the needs of each father and mother, including the only sibling who participated in the study.

In Valentina's case, for example, it was remarkable that the sonographer did not mention the measurements and weight of the foetus during the examinations, most probably because she noticed that the mother felt defied by the baby's growth. In Julie's case, the insecurity of the parents with regard to the mother's capacity to produce life due to a previous loss they had kept secret throughout the pregnancy caused the sonographer to explain in detail all the issues they brought up, even accepting the mother's projections on to her of being the one responsible for "giving life". At one point, she actually prolonged an examination with the parents, and another time she sent the expecting mother to the obstetrician because of the extreme oedema in her feet, which led to a premature delivery.

In the case of the Anahi and Raoni twins, which highlighted the maternal ability to contain and discriminate, the sonographer regularly distinguishes the babies in the examinations—their position, each one's measurements—and admired how the parents were able to precisely identify who was who. She played an important function in validating the parents' perceptions of their twins, and in welcoming their older son the one time he came along to the scan.

In the case of the Daniela and Renata twins, where confusion and maternal indiscrimination predominated, the sonographer occasionally identified with the mother and became confused with the data of the scan, but then soon recovered, apologised, and resumed her function.

By delivery, the mother and baby have already overcome an important developmental stage—gestation—but must continue on to the life-and-death challenge and face the mutual dependence that characterised the previous stage.

By including the delivery in the observations, we were able to witness the "cut" of birth—the first great discontinuity in human development: on the one hand, the intrauterine life that necessarily is left behind and, on the other hand, the relationship with the outside world that begins to develop. There is no doubt that birth unveils a new reality and new challenges for the mother. It is true that the intrauterine mother–baby relationship experiences small breaks in continuity that prepare the foetus for delivery and the interminable process of mother–baby separation, and that the discontinuities will remain in other phases of development, although we believe never with as much intensity as during delivery.

The distinction Winnicott (1986) makes between men and women is interesting in terms of the risks they assume in life. He believes that while men seek danger outside, such as in wars, women confront risks inside themselves by giving birth: "It is no good pretending that childbirth carries no risk . . . there is a danger inherent in the woman's natural function" (p. 193). We believe that childbirth is possibly the greatest experience of abandonment a baby and mother can undergo—the baby being totally and truly dependent, and the mother, in her state of regression, being dependent on the baby.

After the intense experience of following the mothers and babies from pregnancy to delivery, we think it is possible to understand why some mothers choose to not enter this space or to defend themselves and escape toward sanity, like some analysts. Winnicott (1987c) reminds us, "Let us also bear in mind that by the legitimate method of careful choice of case we may and usually do avoid meeting aspects of human nature that must take us beyond our technical equipment" (p. 278).

Experiencing physical and emotional regression during pregnancy and childbirth is truly an immense challenge to a woman's limits and flexibility in transitioning through different levels of her psychic structure. It requires courage. The observer's live and constant presence and her receptive capacity contributed to creating a containment setting where emotions could circulate freely. In all the cases, the mother and father used the observer intensely to alleviate the angst of the emotional impact brought on by the images of the baby. It was noted that no one missed a single scan. Therefore, we can say that the doctor and the observer—each in her own function—were fundamental in preparing for the psychic birth of each of the babies and parents in the delicate transition to parenthood by helping in the processes of development, primarily with integration.

In this project, we had the unique opportunity in all the cases to feel how the mother and baby are inseparable in the complexities and subtleties of their temporary or permanent matches–mismatches and successes–failures in this important period of building the foundations of personality, psychic health, and mental disease. It is challenging to follow the non-linear development of the pair. We were constantly surprised by reactions and incomprehensible details that caused imbalance, both for the good and the bad, in this delicate relationship, which affected the maturation of the baby and the mother. We believe the analytic process is similar in that it is delicate, subtle, challenging, and does not guarantee that it will reach its objectives.

For example, the Julie–Tânia relationship was both surprising and touching in how they matched each other in terms of growth and health after an initial mismatch that put their lives at risk and caused Julie's premature birth, facts that both mother and child contributed to. Unable to count on a caring network for Julie, Tânia came up with a creative solution: she created a workspace inside her home and, in the process, discovered her skills as an artisan. Julie's vivaciousness, spontaneity, and creativity contributed to building a custom-made relationship with her mother, which taught us a considerable amount about the mother–baby's potential for growth when there is connection and freedom, similar to that which can occur between the analyst and patient.

We confirmed that entering the state of confinement involves a struggle that is required from mothers as well as analysts and observers, and then it is necessary to leave it as the baby and the patient develop. Anyone intimately undergoing this struggle will naturally understand these challenges. It is difficult for a mother to synchronise her own time and rhythm to the time and rhythm of the baby; a mother can sometimes be ahead of the baby, or *vice versa*. She needs the baby to both enter and leave dependency, just as the analyst needs the same from the patient.

We also witnessed the deep suffering that went along with the adaptation problems that all the mothers experienced during the separation caused by going back to work. In the same way that they prepared for their anxieties about childbirth, they also prepared for their fears and concerns regarding this other important moment of separation. It was remarkable how all the mothers were similar in this, the most striking example being that of Tânia, who creatively altered her life in order to adapt herself to the changes that were brought on by this phase.

It was gratifying to see the changes that took place in the physical environment of the house, and the increasing excursions of mothers and babies outside the home space, once the mothers overcame the natural challenges of leaving the subjective world of infants. In the case of the first two months of the twins Anahi and Raoni, for example, the house became a large belly, which included the maternal grandmother and the aunt, with an exceptional capacity for meeting the needs of both mother and baby while respecting the rhythm of each one. At around two months, the babies leave the bedroom in their prams and are taken to the living room while the mother begins to go outside. The space they use gradually expands, and, at around eight months, they move to a play area that was created for them in a corner of a room in the house using safety fences. After the twins' first year of life, that play corner became a plastic toy house. The space then gradually expands to include an outside playhouse in the park next to their building.

Thus, by facilitating/adapting the environment, the child gradually leaves one enclosure and moves towards new enclosures:

> The enclosure was provided by his mother and father, by the family, by the house and the courtyard, and by the familiar sights and noises and smells. It also belongs to his own stage of immaturity and to his reliance on his parents' reliability, and to the subjective nature of the infant world. This enclosure was a natural development from the mother's arms that were put round him when he was an infant. She adapted in an intimate way to her infant's needs, and then she gradually deadapted, according to the rate at which he became able to enjoy meeting the unexpected and the new. And so, since children are not really very like each other, the mother finds that she has made an

> enclosure in which each child lives; and it is out of this enclosure that her son and daughter now emerges – ready for a different kind of group, a new kind of enclosure, at least for a few hours a day. In other words, the child will go to school. (Winnicott, 1999b, p. 35).

The "coupling–de-coupling" is an unnatural process that remains a lifelong challenge. The mother, like the analyst, is fundamental in this process; there are many matches and mismatches in this coming and going. We must remember, as Winnicott (1971b) warned towards the end of his life and after extensive experience as an analyst, that "psychoanalysis is no way of life. We all hope our patients will finish with us and forget us, and that they will find living itself to be the therapy that makes sense" (p. 116).

Winnicott understands and welcomes regression, while always respecting the unique needs of each patient at a given moment and always keeping growth in mind. When a child is "on the outside, it is not easy for him to come back inside again or feel he is inside [the enclosure], except if he is tired or ill, when you reassemble this enclosure for his benefit" (Winnicott, 1999b, p. 35). The mother who enters a regressive state, at some point has to leave it. Otherwise, what he calls "normal madness" becomes "pathological madness". Besides, we should not idealise regression, remembering that the "idea of a wonderful time in the womb (the oceanic feeling, etc.) is a complex organization of denial of dependence" (Winnicott, 1990, p. 159) and all its implications.

We can say that being able to follow pregnancy, delivery, and the first three years of life was an experience that particularly demonstrated the potential of the Bick method as a tool for clinical work with infants and their mothers, where the inner setting—the consistency, predictability, attitude, reliability, permeability, and concern of the analyst—is more important than his or her theoretical knowledge or ability to interpret.

In re-reading all the collected research material, we were able to see clearly how numerous aspects of the observer's function helped to unveil the extraordinary life of parents–babies–relatives as they interacted with the family. The observer is in a position of extreme receptivity and tolerance, thus being able to listen to everything that is communicated without concern about selecting or feeling pressure to treat the family. The observer is like a "sponge for anxieties", absorbing all the disconcerting content and then emptying it out at the weekly supervision meetings, thus functioning as an emotional drain. The observer and the supervisors together try to understand, and make sense out of, the raw, concrete experiences that are brought in from the observation situations. This processing allows the observer more easily to resume her function when she returns to the family. It is an excellent training opportunity for an observer to learn to support the stability of the setting and internal flexibility, both being essential environmental qualities during this period of development.

We believe it is important that the observer does not know the family before the observations, and to be different from any of the relatives. The observer does not give opinions, educate, or treat, but, rather, is a trained person with different outside perspectives that the family often anxiously awaits. The observers participate by "silently" digesting the facts. Their movements of coming in–going out brings circulation and "opens the windows" to air out and detoxify the environment in order to lessen the confinement of this stage and absorb the impact of the sudden mutations brought on by the baby's presence. The observer enables a live encounter that helps develop a relationship of trust, sharing, and friendship with the family, which, in turn, contributes to the growth of the parents–infant relationship. Thus, the observer has an important pre-emptive role that can promote psychic health. As the observer's role develops, she becomes an intermediary space that can be used to ease the mother–baby separation and discrimination process and help their departure from the exhausting loneliness caused by the confinement of that initial period of dependence.

Based on our extensive twenty-year experience with the standard Bick method of infant observation, on the group supervisions we conducted, and on the applications we implemented, we can affirm that the common thread that connects classic observation to application is the observers' training and the continuous transformations they experience for two years, all of which fine-tunes their ability to listen to primitive psychic phenomena. The observer carries a highly developed internal setting which functions as a tool for adapting to external settings, such as an obstetrics ultrasound examination room, or an obstetrics centre, allowing her to exercise a very welcome therapeutic function during this stage of life.

The opportunity to observe these situations is always remarkable and challenges what we already know, our experience, and our techniques, despite the fact that we have an entire arsenal of basic theory. Our work with these pairs—tiny patients and their parents—allows us to observe history in the making because we are present at the time and place of the events occurring. We can, thus, confirm that parents and infants make unique contributions to the established research problems and their respective treatments.

Each case is unique. Both Winnicott and Bick left an important legacy of theory based on making detailed observations and elaborating ideas related to initial life experiences during neonatal and infancy periods, but abstained from developing techniques for treating infants between zero and three years of age. Consequently, the babies and their mothers did not benefit from their contributions to analytical theory and technique, possibly in part because of Winnicott's and Bick's deep concern for not interfering in the initial mother–baby relationship.

None the less, we believe that training in the Bick method opens up a new field for reflecting on therapeutic approaches that could benefit infants and their mothers in that stage of life, while still respecting the pair's needs and conditions for mutual dependence. Bick (1964) stated that finding mothers willing to accept observations in their homes was easier than expected, and that they were explicitly clear about how much they appreciated the observer's systematic visits and benefited from them.

Winnicott often iterated the basic principles of therapeutic work in the female place that is so important for the birth of a new being:

> In our *therapeutic* work over and over again we become involved with a patient; we pass through a phase in which were are vulnerable (as the mother is) because of our involvement; we are identified with the child who is temporarily dependent on us to an alarming degree; we watch the shedding of the child's false selves; we see the new beginning of a true self, a true self with an ego that is strong because, like the mother with her infant, we have been able to give ego support. If all goes well, we may find the child has emerged, a child whose ego can organize its own defences against anxieties that belong to id impulse and experience. A "new" being is born because of what we do, a real human being capable of having an independent life. My thesis is that what we do in therapy is to attempt to imitate the natural process that characterizes the behavior of any mother of her own

> infant. If I am right, it is the mother–infant couple that can teach us the basic principles on which we may base our therapeutic work, when we ate treating children whose early mothering was "not good enough", or was interrupted. (Winnicott, 1999a, p. 20)

On numerous different occasions, we found ourselves transitioning between infant observations and the clinic. Although the methods and objectives are different, many natural connections emerged that carried implications for clinical work with babies and mothers, since, in this context, the analyst deals with primitive transference–countertransference phenomena in which the setting becomes more important than interpretation. We thought of shifting between the two methods in a way that would allow an exchange or cross-fertilisation. It was in this spirit that we began applying the Bick method to primitive stages such as pregnancy and delivery.

We confirm that working through powerful experiences using the Bick standard infant observation method and its applications to pregnancy and delivery changes the participants. Numerous observer accounts described greater sensitivity towards aspects of non-verbal communication, increased intuition, stimulated emotions and imagination, greater contact with their own psychic reality and that of their patients, changes to how they worked in the clinic, and more reflection before formulating interpretations. The greatest modification was how their psychoanalytic listening skills became more finely tuned after diving into the depths of their own experiences and anxieties. The Bick method proved especially effective in helping the observers overcome their own resistance to this process in order to use their emotions and lived experiences as technique instruments (countertransference). It has also had a catalyst effect that stimulated new research and new theoretical–technical questions.

In conclusion, we would like to say that maternity—like analysis—is a risky journey that has an unpredictable end. In fact, it is interminable and has infinite possibilities of mutual enrichment and maturation for the mother–infant, analyst–patient pairs. We went in and out of the place where mothers live with their babies many times during pregnancy and in the first three years of life. We learnt from the singularities and differences of each pair. There are no rules. We were faced with the paradox of putting into words what is experienced predominantly without words. Finding the right words for each unique experience and taking them to that place where they do not normally reach required the same patience and self-giving that a mother has with her baby and the analyst has with a patient, and helped us better understand and discriminate between the observed facts.

Our years of work were a growing spiral of movements that went from raw observation data to our writing and *vice versa*, and caused each mother's experience to echo in our own lives. We hope that our reflections can echo in the lives of the analysts and all the professionals who are dedicated to caring for children between the ages of zero and three. We are deeply grateful to the mothers and infants who continue teaching us so much about human nature and analytic technique, and to all our colleagues who helped us in different stages of this research.

The authenticity of the mothers helped us change our moral prejudices that labelled mothers as good or bad. The subconscious interactions we experienced are too complex and complicated to express in quick, superficial statements. A mother's true self, when present, is a very important guide because, when she is true, she is reliable and predictable. The false mother, on the other hand, attacks perception and leaves the child defenceless and confused. In the words of Winnicott:

> In order to be consistent, and so to be predictable for our children, we must be *ourselves*. If we are ourselves our children can get to know us. Certainly if we are acting a part we shall be found out when we get caught without our make-up. (1999d, p. 123)

We leave here a live witness account of four years of observation work and many others spent developing the material for these unforgettable—and ordinarily inaccessible—first three years of life. This work was made possible through being carried out by a truly motivated team of observers, the doctor, and supervisors, as well as the mothers and babies.

As we conclude this observation work, we ask ourselves what unconscious marks/memories from this period remained with the babies that we followed. The last case, Philomena's story, as taken from a film, helps us understand the fact that we go through periods that leave indelible marks on all human beings. Her story is an example of a relationship that remained alive despite having been severed when the baby was adopted at age three, which kept them searching for each other until death.

We can say that we have come full circle. Our work has led us to the "unacknowledged mother of the first stages" and we feel complete in being able to give her recognition and remove her from the darkness, solitude, and isolation that she experiences in the beginning of the life of each man and woman.

> In practical sense the little child needs to break away from the mother's arms and lap, but not to go into space; the breaking away has to be to a wider area of control; something which is symbolical of the lap from which the child has broken away. A slightly older child runs away from home, but at the bottom of the garden has finished running away. The garden fence is now symbolical of the narrower aspect of holding which has just been broken up, shall we say, the house. Later, the child works out all these things in going to school and in relation to other groups that are outside the home. In each case these outside groups represent a getting away from the home, and yet at the same time they are symbolical of the home that has been broken away from and in fantasy broken up. (Winnicott, 1999c, p. 91)

NOTES

1. Donald Woods Winnicott, British analyst, was born on 7 April 1896 in Plymouth, where he lived up to the end of his life, in 1971. He was analysed by Strachey and later by Joan Riviere. He married in 1923, divorced, and married again. He did not have children.
2. British analyst, born on 4 July 1902, in Przemys'l, Poland. She died on 20 July 1983, in London, where she had lived since the Second World War. She was analysed by Balint and later by Klein. She worked for several years at the Tavistock Clinic in London. Divorced, she had no children.
3. Like Winnicott, Bick gave a lot of importance to the early environment. In her final paper (Bick, 1986), she mentioned that infant observation is a misnomer because what the observer sees is a family into which a baby was born. All family members are affected by the baby's presence (Caron et al., 2008).
4. One can see her extreme coherence and consistency as an analyst, reaffirming Borgogno's (2004) proposition, presented earlier, that psychoanalytic knowledge is born from the analyst's "intense personal participation" (p. 18).
5. The stages of the method and their main challenges in the observer's journey were previously discussed and published in Caron and colleagues, 2012.

6. Equivalent to Winnicott's unthinkable anxieties.
7. Equivalent to Winnicott's concept of "false self".
8. Even though she has not developed as profoundly as Winnicott her ideas on the baby's condition of dependence, Bick also considers that this is a human being's primary state.
9. Winnicott borrowed the term "nursing couple" from Middlemore, a British analyst who published, in 1941, a book with this title on the observation of breastfeeding.
10. We did not use the film footage in producing the clinical reports that will be presented in the following chapters, only the written reports.
11. Prior to the publication of the article, we had presented a paper on this topic at the Annual Symposium of APdeBA—Clinical reports—in 2011.
12. Translator's note: Grêmio is a Brazilian professional football team from Porto Alegre, in the state of Rio Grande do Sul.
13. Translator's note: a *Colorada* is a person who supports Internacional, a Brazilian football team based in Porto Alegre in the state of Rio Grande do Sul.
14. Reminiscent of the two caves the observer described in the first ultrasound.
15. We might think that she had been chosen to be this repository, not because of being fragile, as was believed by the mother, but, on the contrary, because of being strong and tenacious, especially as Renata becomes more fragile and dependent.
16. Translator's note: *Fantástico* is a popular television news magazine programme shown every Sunday night in Brazil.
17. Translator's note: Monica is a popular Brazilian children's comic book character developed by Maurício de Sousa.
18. It is worth noting here that this behaviour of reprimanding and then invalidating by asking for a smile or to blow kisses will be frequently seen in the mother's relationship with her daughter after birth.
19. She says she is sure this pregnancy will be successful because she constantly stroked her belly with her hands, something she had not done in the previous, unsuccessful pregnancy.
20. She decided the baby was a girl and interpreted her movements and characteristics.
21. Alice needed what she projected to be contained.
22. As we saw in the post-birth observations, Mário's perplexity continued until the end of Valentina's first year. He did not quite understand who that being was walking around the house.

23. The baby's weight was an issue that pervaded Valentina's first three years.
24. Philomena is a retired nurse who today is over eighty years old.
25. An adaptation of the book *The Lost Child of Philomena Lee*, by Martin Sixsmith.
26. The first scene introduces the man who becomes her "partner in the journey" (Martin Sixsmith, played by Steve Coogan).
27. It was a breech birth and the nuns did not provide painkillers. The girls were forced to deliver their babies in pain as penance for their "sins".
28. The photo had been taken by Anunciata, the same nun who had saved her and her baby's life during childbirth. It had been given to her in secret.
29. In fact, this is Sister Hildegard, though we do not know it yet.
30. This kind of non-verbal connection is not uncommon in infant observations. On many occasions, the observer thinks something that is, soon after, verbalised or acted out.
31. Now it is her turn to say she wants quiet time.

REFERENCES

Bick, E. (1964). Notes on infant observation in psychoanalytic training. *International Journal of Psychoanalysis, 45*: 558–566.

Bick, E. (1968). The experience of the skin in early object relations. *International Journal of Psychoanalysis, 49*: 484–486.

Bick, E. (1986). Further considerations of the function of the skin in early object relations – findings from infant observation integrated into child and adult analysis. *British Journal of Psychotherapy, 2*: 292–299.

Borgogno, F. (2004). *Psicanálise como percurso*, M. Rossi (Trans.). Rio de Janeiro: Imago.

Caron, N. A. (1995). Fundamentos teóricos para a aplicação do método E. Bick. *Revista Brasileira de Psicanálise, 29*(2): 283–291.

Caron, N. A. (2000a). O ambiente intrauterino e a relação materno fetal. In: N. A. Caron (Ed.), *A relação pais bebê: da observação à clínica* (pp. 11–134). São Paulo: Casa do Psicólogo.

Caron, N. A. (2000b). Terapias breves das relações pais-bebês. In: N. A. Caron (Ed.), *A relação pais bebê: da observação à clínica* (pp. 311–328). São Paulo: Casa do Psicólogo.

Caron, N. A., & Fonseca, M. (2011). A presença de irmãos no exame de ultrassonografia pré-natal. *Revista de Psicanálise da SPPA, XVIII*(2): 417–442.

Caron, N. A. & Lopes, R. C. S. (2015). When the internal setting becomes more important than the therapist/analyst's interpretative capacity: extending the infant observation method to the prenatal and perinatal period. *International Journal of Infant Observation and Its Applications, 18*(1): 83–95.

Caron, N. A., & Maltz, R. S. (1994). Intervenções em grávidas com anomalias congênitas. *Revista de psiquiatria do Rio Grande do Sul, 16*(3): 202–207.

Caron, N. A., Fonseca, M. M., & Kompinsky, E. (2000). Aplicação da observação na ultrassonografia obstétrica. In: N. A. Caron (Ed.), *A relação pais bebê: da observação à clínica* (pp. 178–206). São Paulo: Casa do Psicólogo.

Caron, N. A., Fonseca, M., & Lopes, R. C. S. (2008). The baby and his majesties: some considerations on human helplessness. *International Journal of Infant Observation and Its Applications, 11*(1): 67–75.

Caron, N. A., Lopes, R. C. S., & Donelli, T. S. (2013). A place where verbalization has no meaning. *International Journal of Infant Observation and its Applications, 16*(2): 170–182.

Caron, N. A., Lopes, R. C. S., Steibel, D., & Donelli, T. S. (2012). Writing as a challenge in the observer's journey through the Bick method of infant observation. *International Journal of Infant Observation and Its Applications, 15*(3): 221–230.

Coogan, S., & Pope, J. (2013). Philomena adapted screenplay. http://1e36a764da2f6b46c156-0fa6f106d654e15326ee14d2a07c02d0.r64.cf1.rackcdn.com/2014/02/Philomena.pdf

Donelli, T. S. (2008). *Descortinando a vivência emocional de mulheres em um centro obstétrico: uma investigação sobre o parto através do método Bick.* Porto Alegre: RS. Tese de doutorado não publicada.

Freud, S. (1892–1893). A case of successful treatment by hypnotism. *S. E., 1*: 115–128. London: Hogarth.

Freud, S. (1900a). *The Interpretation of Dreams. S. E., 4–5*. London: Hogarth.

Freud, S. (1905e). *Fragment of an Analysis of a Case of Hysteria. S. E., 7*: 1–122. London: Hogarth.

Freud, S. (1912e). Recommendations to physicians practising psycho-analysis. *S. E., 12*: pp. 109–120. London: Hogarth.

Freud, S. (1914d). On the history of the psycho-analytic movement. *S. E., 14*: 1–66. London: Hogarth.

Freud, S. (1919h). The 'uncanny'. *S. E., 17*: 217–256. London: Hogarth.

Freud, S. (1920g). *Beyond the Pleasure Principle. S. E., 18*: 12–19. London: Hogarth.

Freud, S. (1923a). Two encyclopaedia articles. *S. E., 18*: 233–259. London: Hogarth.

Freud, S. (1925d). An autobiographical study. *S. E., 20*: 1–74. London: Hogarth.

Freud, S. (1926d). *Inhibitions, Symptoms and Anxiety. S. E., 20*: 75–175. London: Hogarth.

Goethe, J. M. V. (2007). *Faust*, J. K. Segall (Trans.). São Paulo: Ed. 34.

Haag, M., & Haag, G. (1997). De Colóquio em Colóquio, por que esse sucesso? In: M. B. Lacroix & M. Monmayrant (Eds.), *Os laços de encantamento: a observação de bebês, segundo Esther Bick, e suas aplicações*, F. F. Settineri (Trans.) (pp. 3–11). Porto Alegre: Artes Médicas.

King, P., & Steiner, R. (1991). *The Freud–Klein Controversies 1941–45*. London: Routledge.

Lino, C. F. (2001). *Cavernas*. São Paulo: Editora Gaia.

Middlemore, M. (1941). *The Nursing Couple*. London: Hamish Hamilton.

Ogden, T. H. (2002). Lendo Winnicott. *Revista Brasileira de Psicanálise, 36*(4): 737–756.

Piontelli, A. (1995). *De feto a criança*, J. Wilheim, N. L. Gomes, & S. M. Godoy (Trans.). Rio de Janeiro: Imago.

Spitz, R. (1964). The derailment of dialogue: stimulus overload, action cycles, and the completion gradient. *Journal of the American Psychoanalytic Association, 12*: 752–774.

Winnicott, D. W. (1971a). Mirror-role of mother and family in child development. In: *Playing and Reality* (pp. 149–159). London: Routledge (originally published in 1967).

Winnicott, D. W. (1971b). The use of an object and relating through identifications. In: *Playing and Reality* (pp. 115–127). London: Routledge (originally published in 1969).

Winnicott, D. W. (1971c). Creativity and its origins. In: *Playing and Reality* (pp. 87–114). London: Routledge (originally published in 1969).

Winnicott, D. W. (1986). This feminism. In: *Home Is Where We Start From* (pp. 183–194). London: Penguin (originally published in 1964).

Winnicott, D. W. (1987a). Primary maternal preoccupation. In: *Through Paediatrics to Psycho-analysis* (pp. 330–305). London: Tavistock (originally published in 1956).

Winnicott, D. W. (1987b). Anxiety associated with insecurity. In: *Through Paediatrics to Psycho-analysis* (pp. 97–100). London: Tavistock (originally published in 1952).

Winnicott, D. W. (1987c). Metapsychological and clinical aspects of regression within the psychoanalytical set-up. In: *Through Paediatrics to Psycho-analysis* (pp. 278–294). London: Tavistock (originally published in 1954).

Winnicott, D. W. (1987d). Birth memories, birth trauma, and anxiety. In: *Through Paediatrics to Psycho-analysis* (pp. 174–193). London: Hogarth (originally published in 1949).

Winnicott, D. W. (1987e). Primitive emotional development. In: *Through Paediatrics to Psycho-analysis* (pp. 145–156). London: Hogarth (originally published in 1945).

Winnicott, D. W. (1988a). Communication between infant and mother and mother and infant: compared and contrasted. In: *Babies and Their Mothers* (pp. 89–103). London: Free Association Books (originally published in 1968).

Winnicott, D.W. (1988b). Communicating and not communicating leading to a study of certain opposites. In: *The Maturational Processes and The Facilitating Environment* (pp. 179–202). New York: International Universities Press (originally published in 1963).

Winnicott, D. W. (1988c). The ordinary devoted mother. In: *Babies and Their Mothers* (pp. 1–14). London: Free Association Books (originally published in 1966).

Winnicott, D. W. (1988d). Dependence in child care. In: *Babies and Their Mothers* (pp. 83–88). London: Free Association Books (originally published in 1970).

Winnicott, D. W. (1988e). Environmental health in infancy. In: *Babies and Their Mothers* (pp. 59–68). London: Free Association Books (originally published in 1968).

Winnicott, D. W. (1988f). Breast-feeding as communication. In: *Babies and Their Mothers* (pp. 23–34). London: Free Association Books (originally published in 1968).

Winnicott, D. W. (1989a). The mother–infant experience of mutuality. In: *Psycho-analytic Explorations* (pp. 251–260). London: Karnac (originally published in 1969).

Winnicott D. W. (1989b). Physiotherapy and human relations. In: *Psycho-analytic Explorations* (pp. 561–568). London: Karnac (originally published in 1969).

Winnicott, D. W. (1990). Environment. In: *Human Nature* (pp. 152–159) (originally published in 1988).

Winnicott, D. W. (1999a). The relationship of a mother to her baby at the beginning. In: *The Family and Individual Development* (pp. 15–20). London: Routledge (originally published in 1960).

Winnicott, D. W. (1999b). The five-year-old. In: *The Family and Individual Development* (pp. 34–39). London: Routledge (originally published in 1962).

Winnicott, D. W. (1999c). The family and emotional maturity. In: *The Family and Individual Development* (pp. 88–96). London: Routledge (originally published in 1960).

Winnicott, D. W. (1999d). The building up of trust. In: *Talking to Parents* (pp. 121–134). Cambridge: Perseus (originally published in 1969).

INDEX